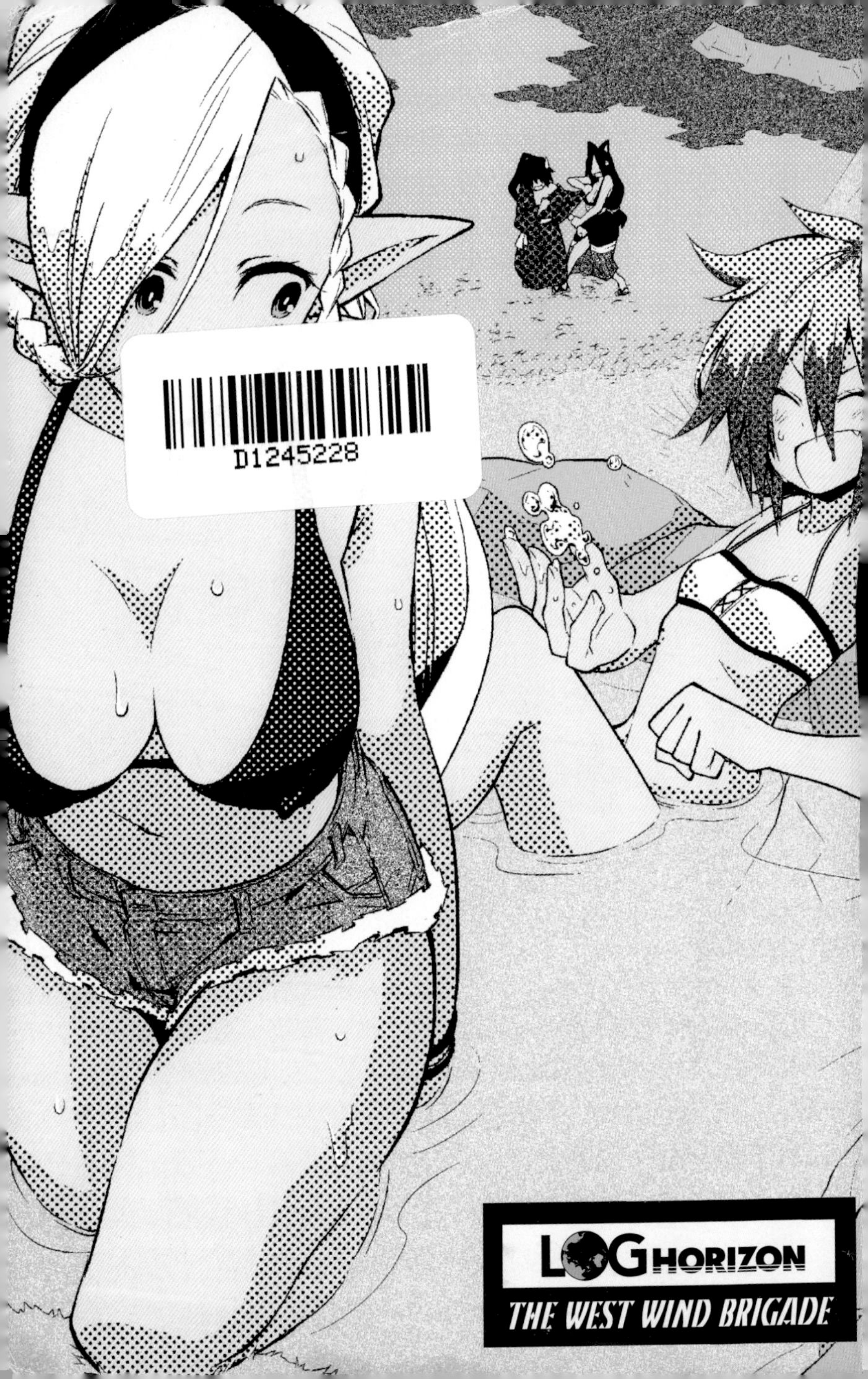
LOG HORIZON
THE WEST WIND BRIGADE

## [CONTENTS]

LOG HORIZON **THE WEST WIND BRIGADE**

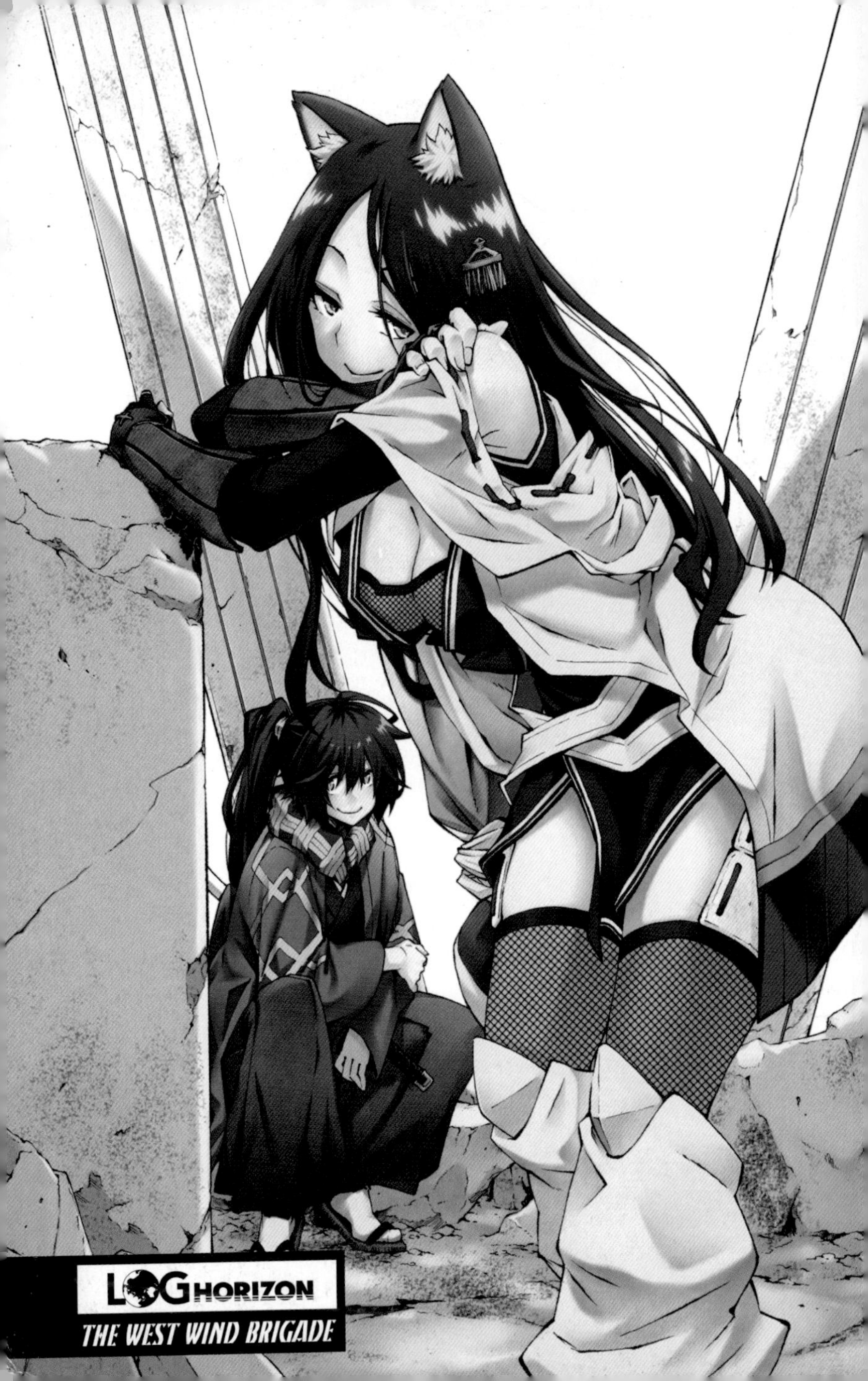
LOG HORIZON
THE WEST WIND BRIGADE

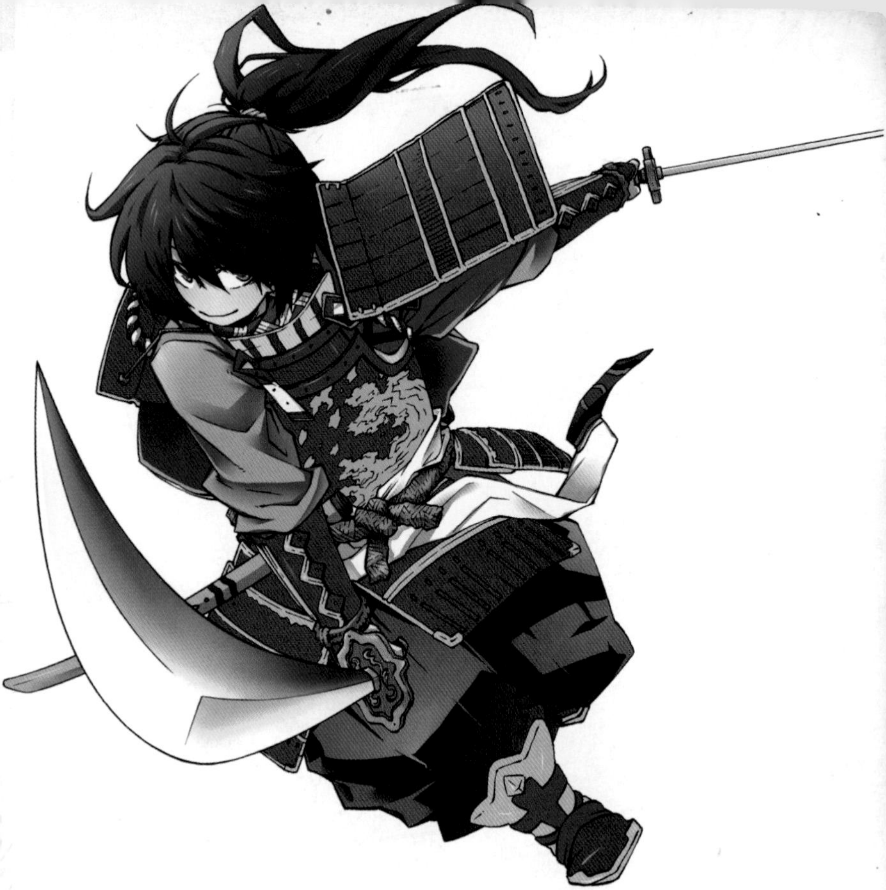

LOG HORIZON
THE WEST WIND BRIGADE

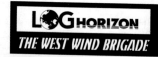

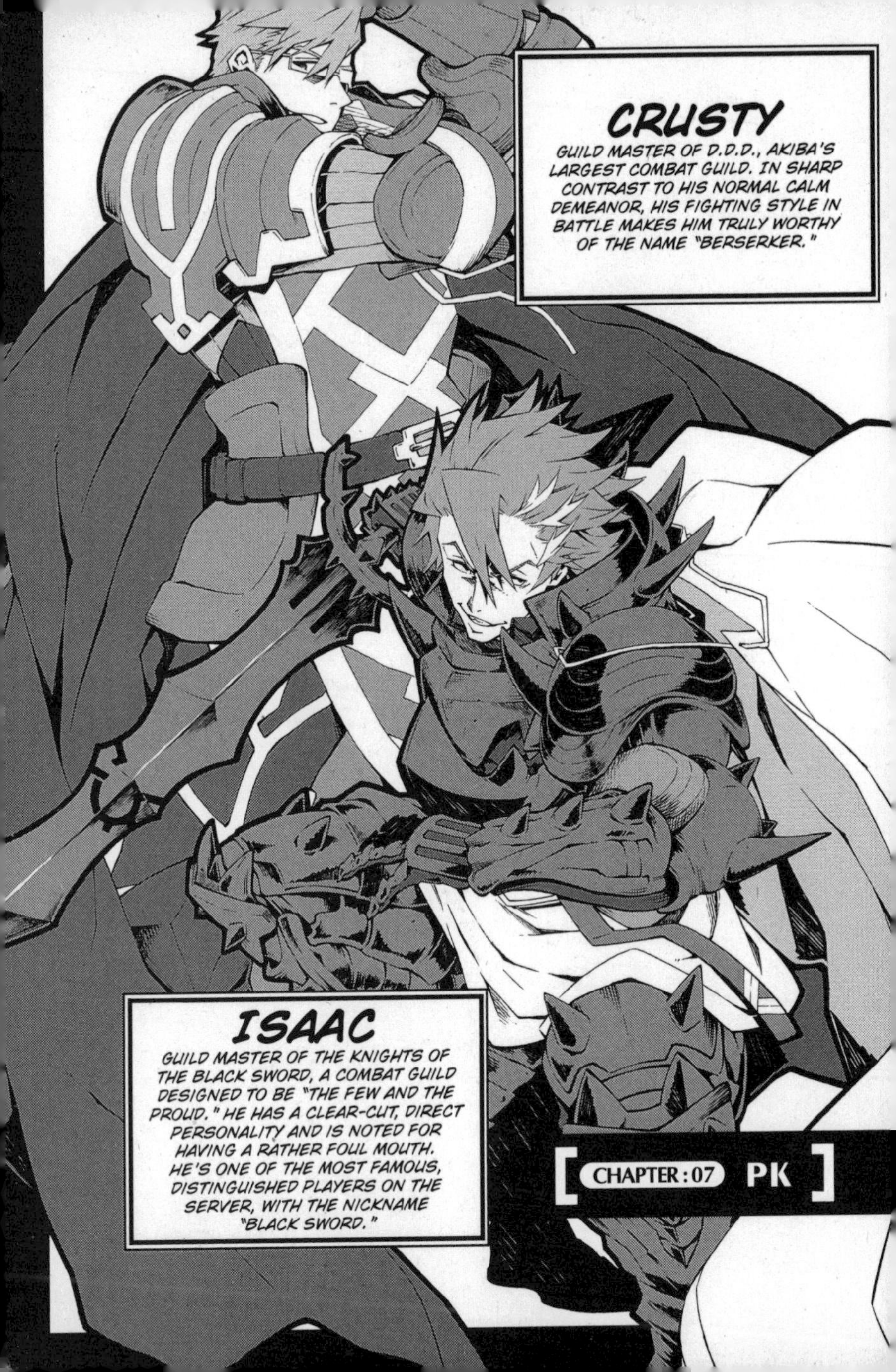
CRUSTY
GUILD MASTER OF D.D.D., AKIBA'S LARGEST COMBAT GUILD. IN SHARP CONTRAST TO HIS NORMAL CALM DEMEANOR, HIS FIGHTING STYLE IN BATTLE MAKES HIM TRULY WORTHY OF THE NAME "BERSERKER."
ISAAC
GUILD MASTER OF THE KNIGHTS OF THE BLACK SWORD, A COMBAT GUILD DESIGNED TO BE "THE FEW AND THE PROUD." HE HAS A CLEAR-CUT, DIRECT PERSONALITY AND IS NOTED FOR HAVING A RATHER FOUL MOUTH. HE'S ONE OF THE MOST FAMOUS, DISTINGUISHED PLAYERS ON THE SERVER, WITH THE NICKNAME "BLACK SWORD."
[ CHAPTER : 07 PK ]

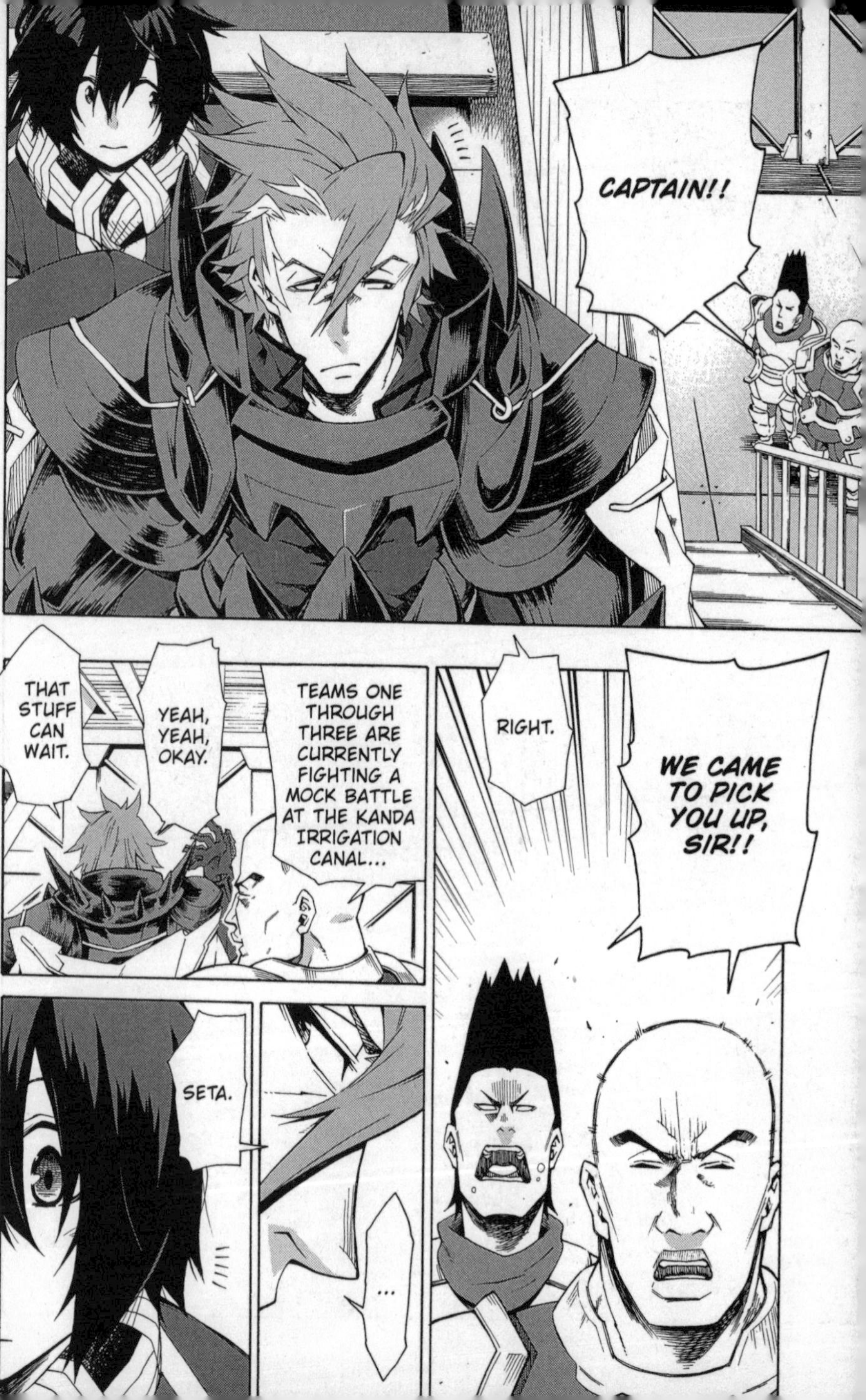
CAPTAIN!!
WE CAME TO PICK YOU UP, SIR!!
RIGHT.
TEAMS ONE THROUGH THREE ARE CURRENTLY FIGHTING A MOCK BATTLE AT THE KANDA IRRIGATION CANAL...
YEAH, YEAH, OKAY.
THAT STUFF CAN WAIT.
...
SETA.

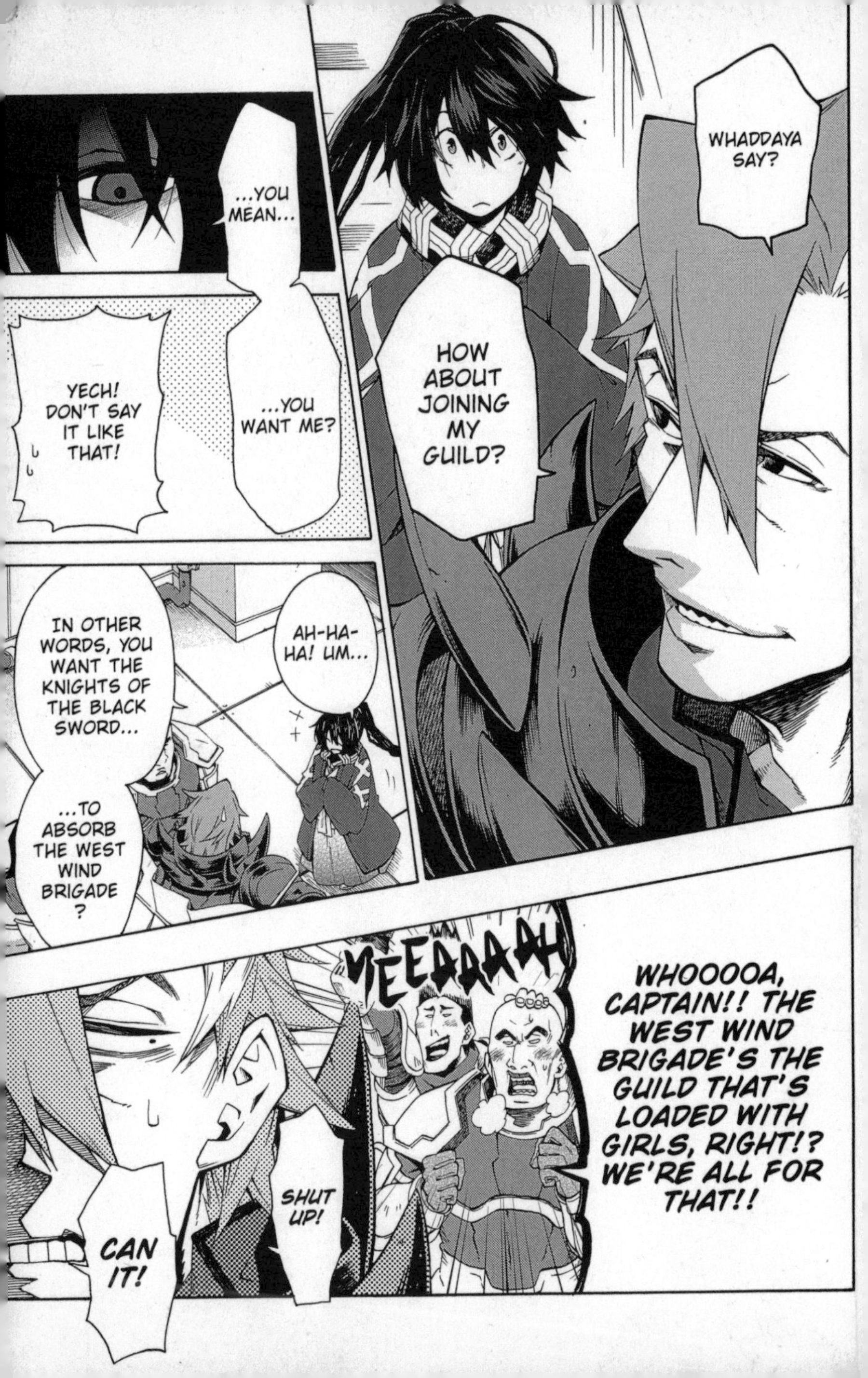
WHADDAYA SAY?
HOW ABOUT JOINING MY GUILD?
...YOU MEAN...
...YOU WANT ME?
YECH! DON'T SAY IT LIKE THAT!
AH-HA-HA! UM...
IN OTHER WORDS, YOU WANT THE KNIGHTS OF THE BLACK SWORD...
...TO ABSORB THE WEST WIND BRIGADE?
WHOOOOA, CAPTAIN!! THE WEST WIND BRIGADE'S THE GUILD THAT'S LOADED WITH GIRLS, RIGHT!? WE'RE ALL FOR THAT!!
YEEAAAAH
SHUT UP!
CAN IT!

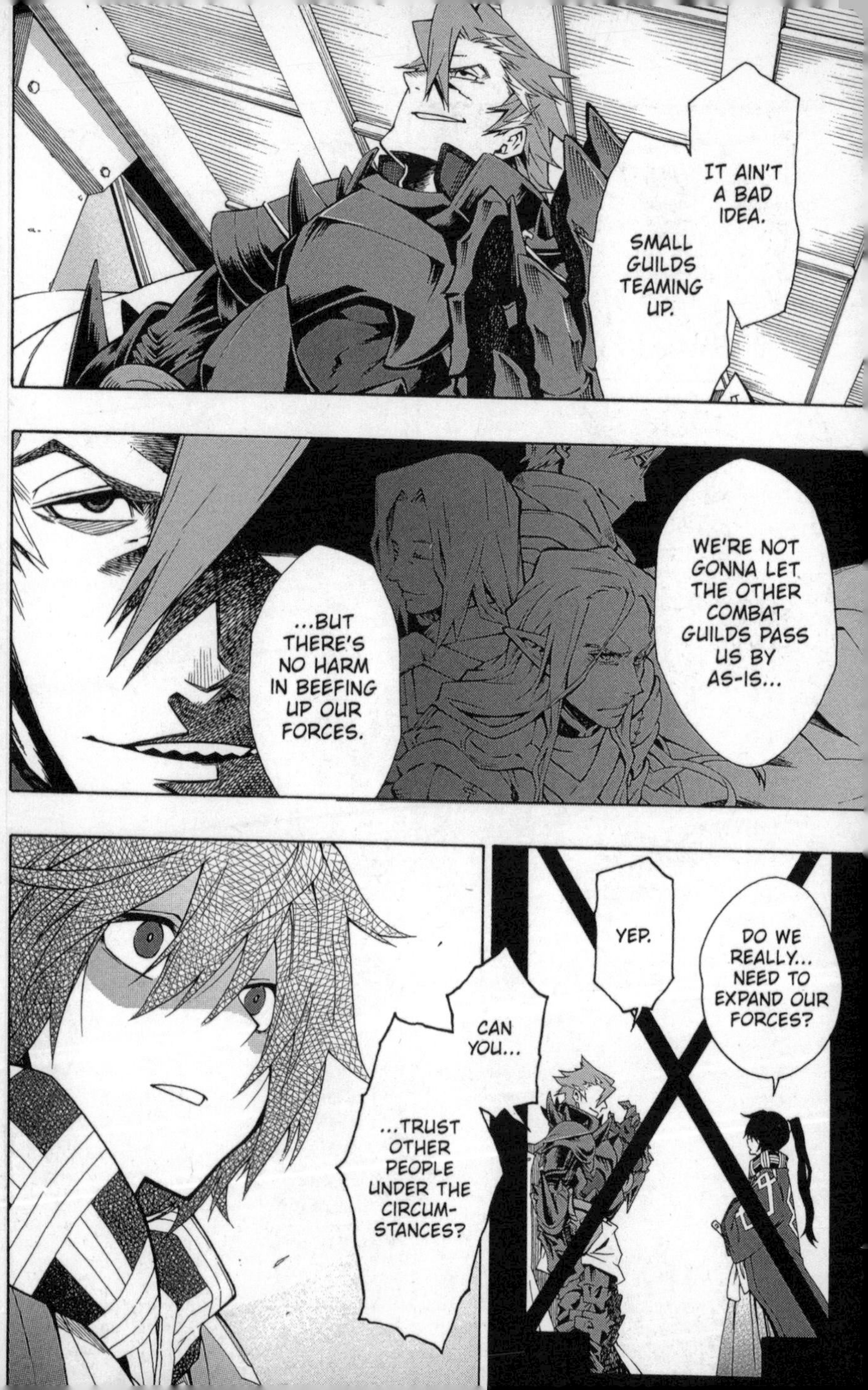
IT AIN'T A BAD IDEA.
SMALL GUILDS TEAMING UP.
WE'RE NOT GONNA LET THE OTHER COMBAT GUILDS PASS US BY AS-IS...
...BUT THERE'S NO HARM IN BEEFING UP OUR FORCES.
DO WE REALLY... NEED TO EXPAND OUR FORCES?
YEP.
CAN YOU...
...TRUST OTHER PEOPLE UNDER THE CIRCUM-STANCES?

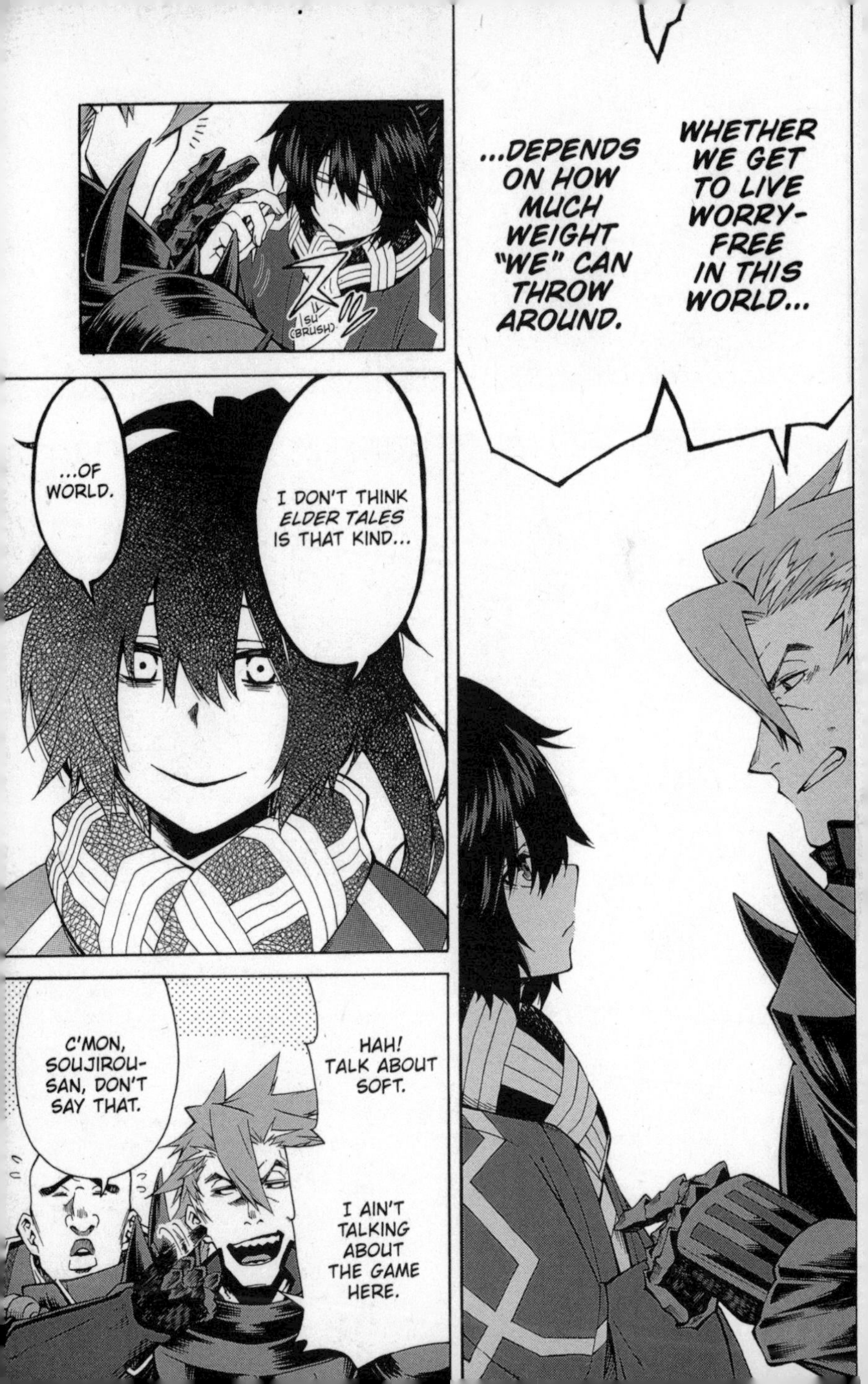
WHETHER WE GET TO LIVE WORRY-FREE IN THIS WORLD...
...DEPENDS ON HOW MUCH WEIGHT "WE" CAN THROW AROUND.
SU (BRUSH)
I DON'T THINK *ELDER TALES* IS THAT KIND...
...OF WORLD.
HAH! TALK ABOUT SOFT.
I AIN'T TALKING ABOUT THE GAME HERE.
C'MON, SOUJIROU-SAN, DON'T SAY THAT.

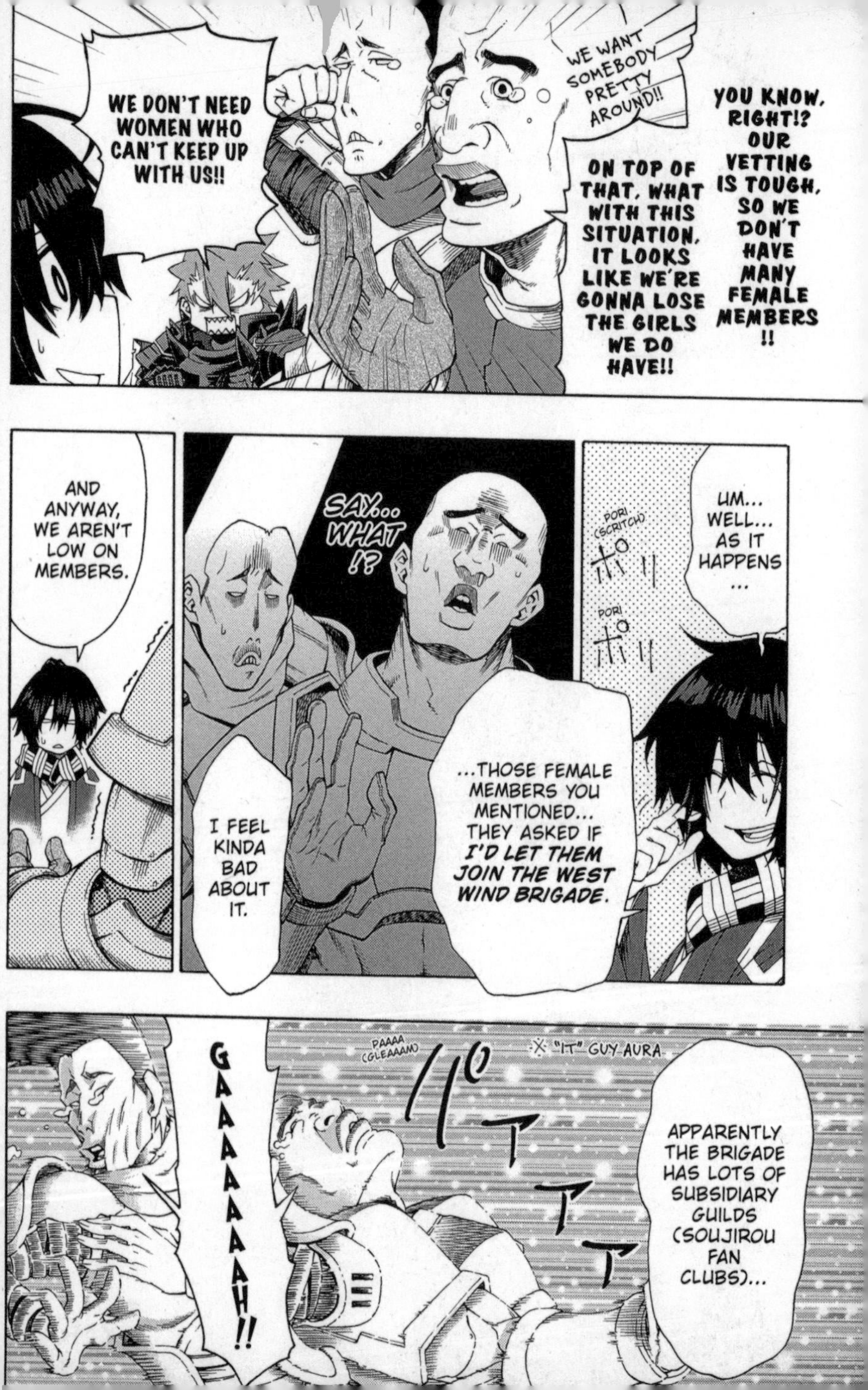
YOU KNOW, RIGHT!? OUR VETTING IS TOUGH, SO WE DON'T HAVE MANY FEMALE MEMBERS!!
WE WANT SOMEBODY PRETTY AROUND!!
ON TOP OF THAT, WHAT WITH THIS SITUATION, IT LOOKS LIKE WE'RE GONNA LOSE THE GIRLS WE DO HAVE!!
WE DON'T NEED WOMEN WHO CAN'T KEEP UP WITH US!!
UM... WELL... AS IT HAPPENS...
PORI (SCRITCH)
PORI
...THOSE FEMALE MEMBERS YOU MENTIONED... THEY ASKED IF *I'D LET THEM JOIN THE WEST WIND BRIGADE*.
SAY... WHAT!?
I FEEL KINDA BAD ABOUT IT.
AND ANYWAY, WE AREN'T LOW ON MEMBERS.
※ "IT" GUY AURA
APPARENTLY THE BRIGADE HAS LOTS OF SUBSIDIARY GUILDS (SOUJIROU FAN CLUBS)...
PAAAA (GLEAAAM)
GAAAAAAAAH!!

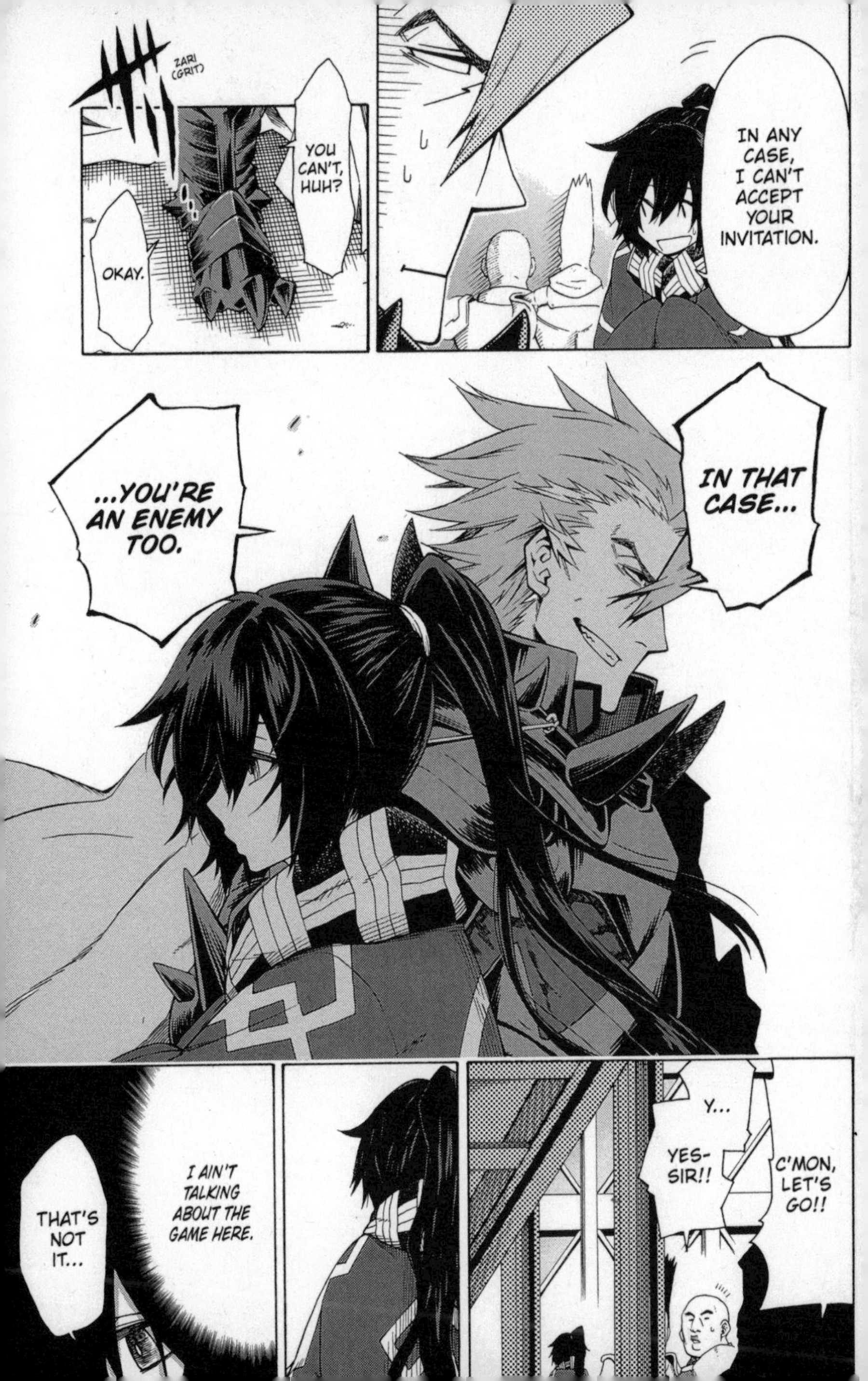
IN ANY CASE, I CAN'T ACCEPT YOUR INVITATION.
YOU CAN'T, HUH?
ZARI (GRIT)
OKAY.
IN THAT CASE...
...YOU'RE AN ENEMY TOO.
C'MON, LET'S GO!!
Y...
YES-SIR!!
I AIN'T TALKING ABOUT THE GAME HERE.
THAT'S NOT IT...

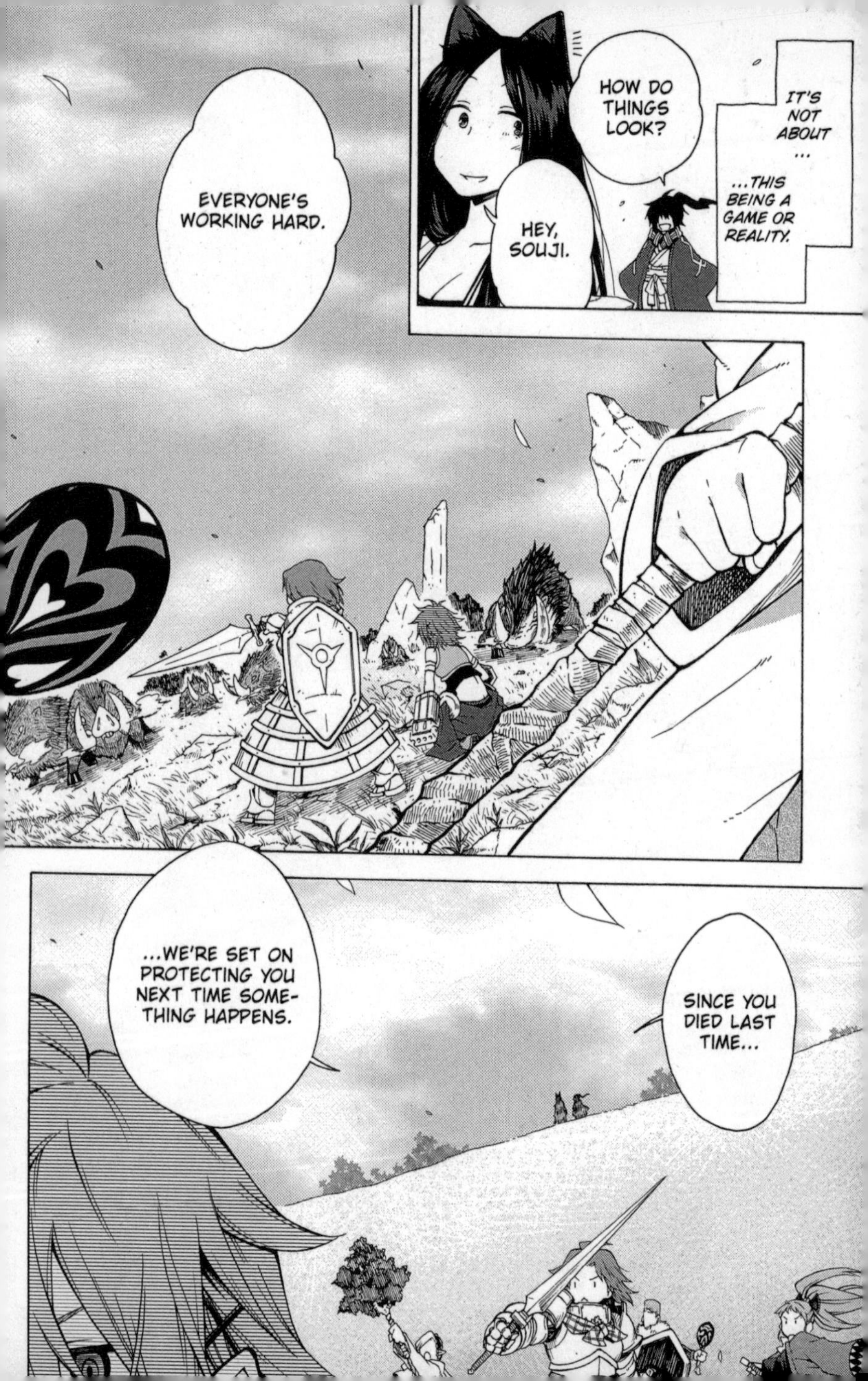
IT'S NOT ABOUT ...
...THIS BEING A GAME OR REALITY.
HOW DO THINGS LOOK?
HEY, SOUJI.
EVERYONE'S WORKING HARD.
SINCE YOU DIED LAST TIME...
...WE'RE SET ON PROTECTING YOU NEXT TIME SOME-THING HAPPENS.

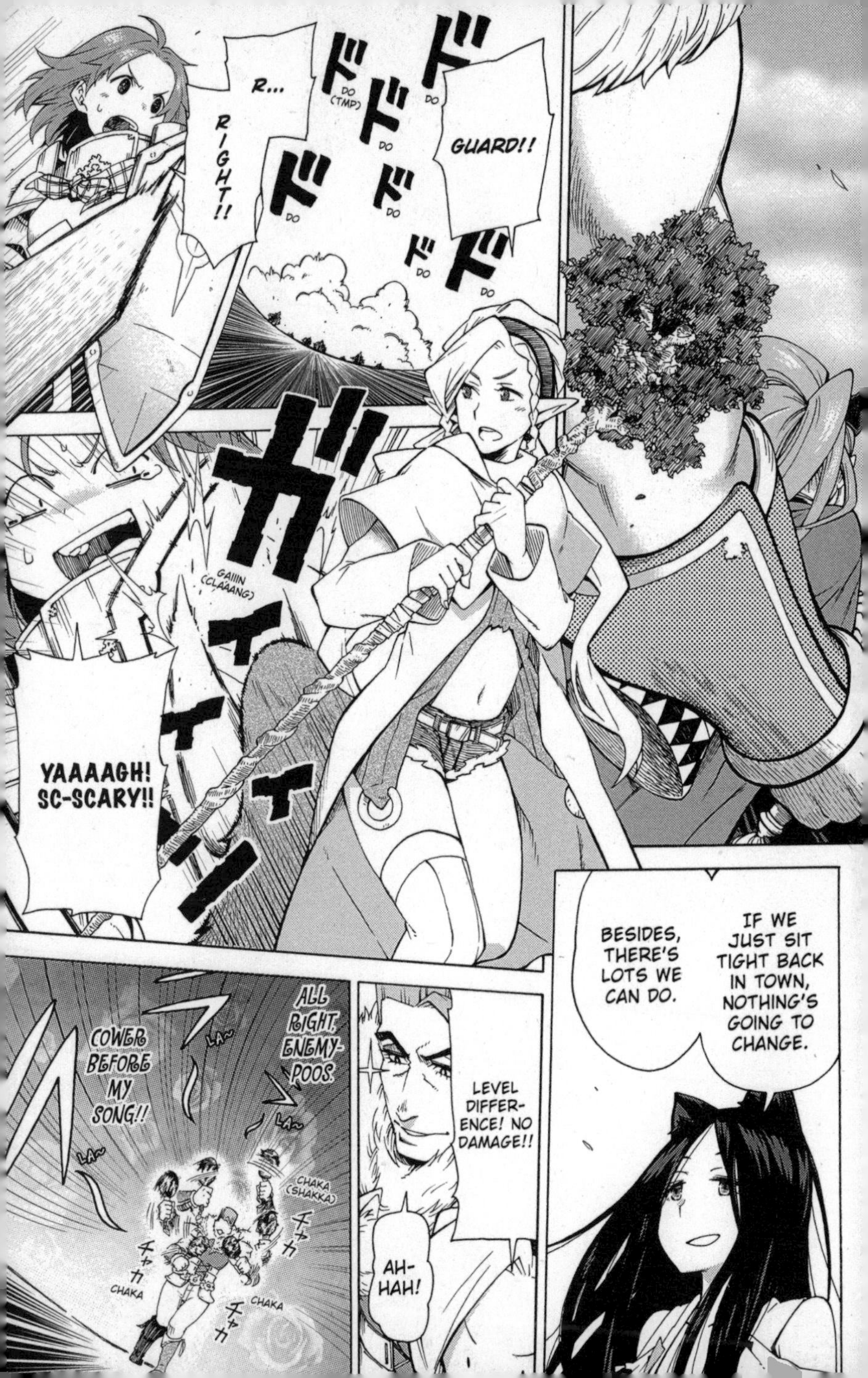
GUARD!!
DO
DO
DO
DO
DO (TMP)
DO
DO
DO
R...
RIGHT!!
GAIIIN (CLAAANG)
YAAAAGH! SC-SCARY!!
IF WE JUST SIT TIGHT BACK IN TOWN, NOTHING'S GOING TO CHANGE.
BESIDES, THERE'S LOTS WE CAN DO.
LEVEL DIFFERENCE! NO DAMAGE!!
AH-HAH!
ALL RIGHT, ENEMY-POOS.
COWER BEFORE MY SONG!!
LA~
LA~
LA~
CHAKA (SHAKKA)
CHAKA
CHAKA

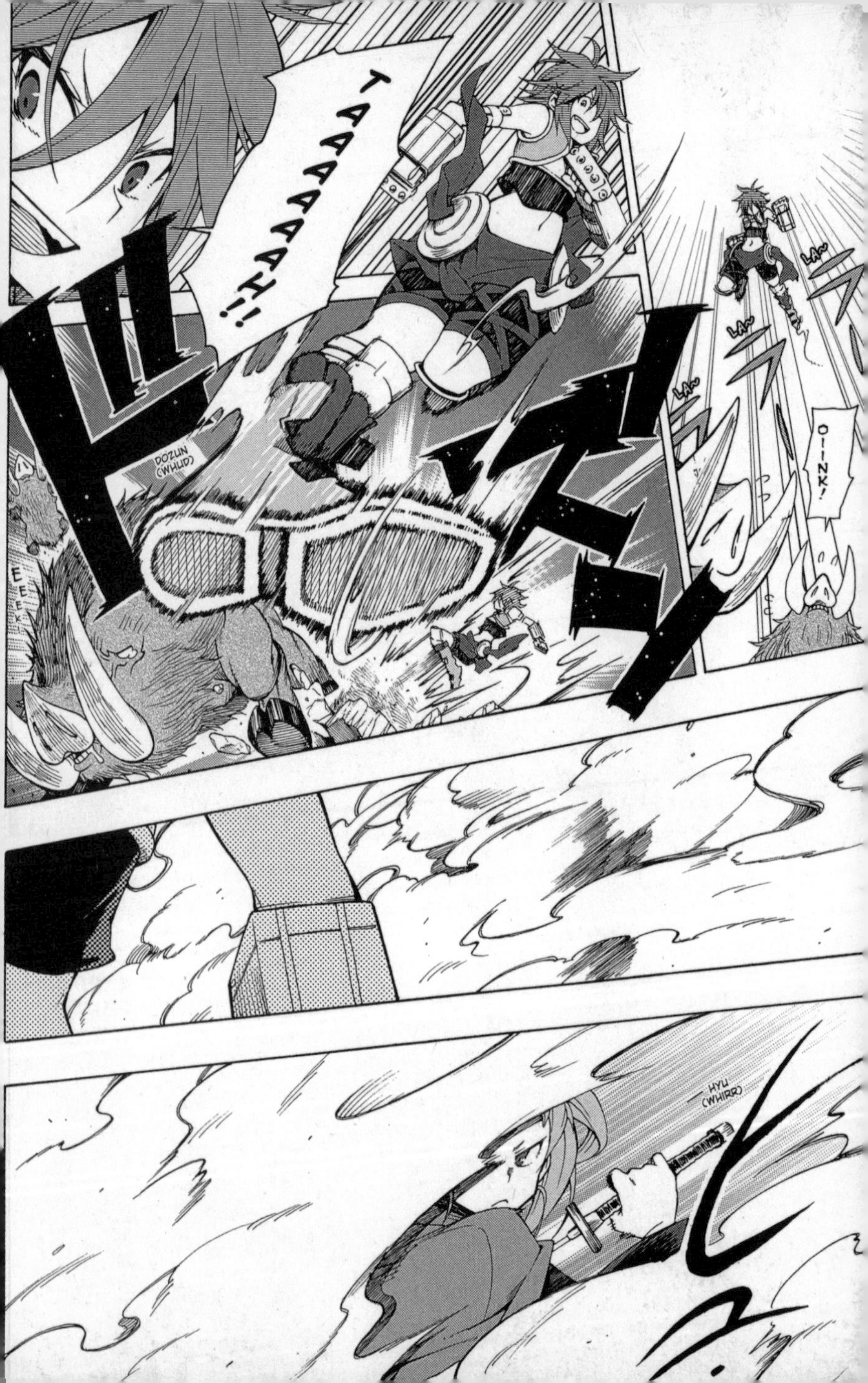
LA~
LA~
LA~
OIIINK!
TAAAAAAAAAH!!
DOZUN (WHUD)
EEEK!
HYU (WHIRR)

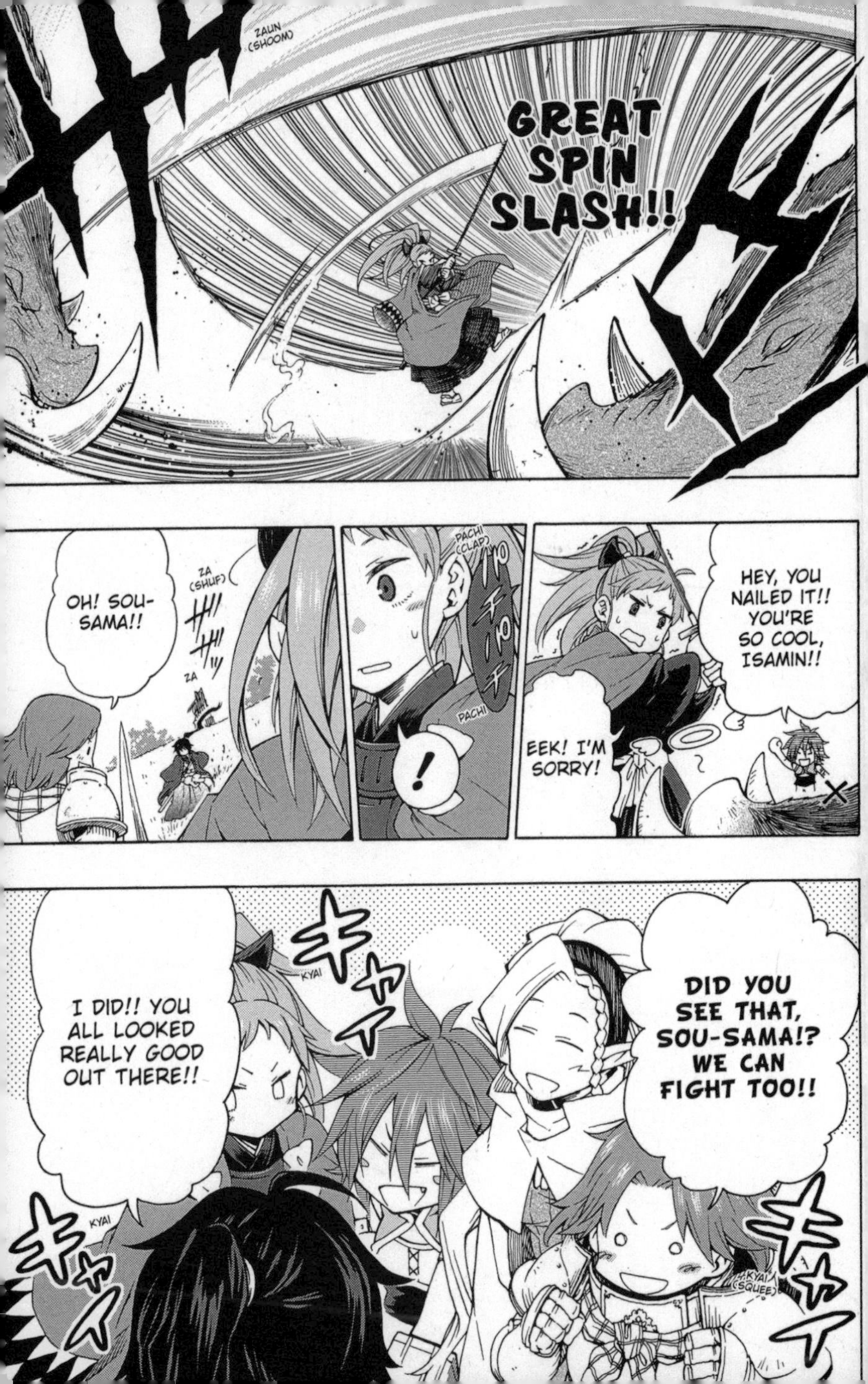
ZAUN (SHOOM)
GREAT SPIN SLASH!!
HEY, YOU NAILED IT!! YOU'RE SO COOL, ISAMIN!!
EEK! I'M SORRY!
PACHI (CLAP)
PACHI
!
OH! SOU-SAMA!!
ZA (SHUF)
ZA
DID YOU SEE THAT, SOU-SAMA!? WE CAN FIGHT TOO!!
KYAI (SQUEE)
KYAI
I DID!! YOU ALL LOOKED REALLY GOOD OUT THERE!!
KYAI

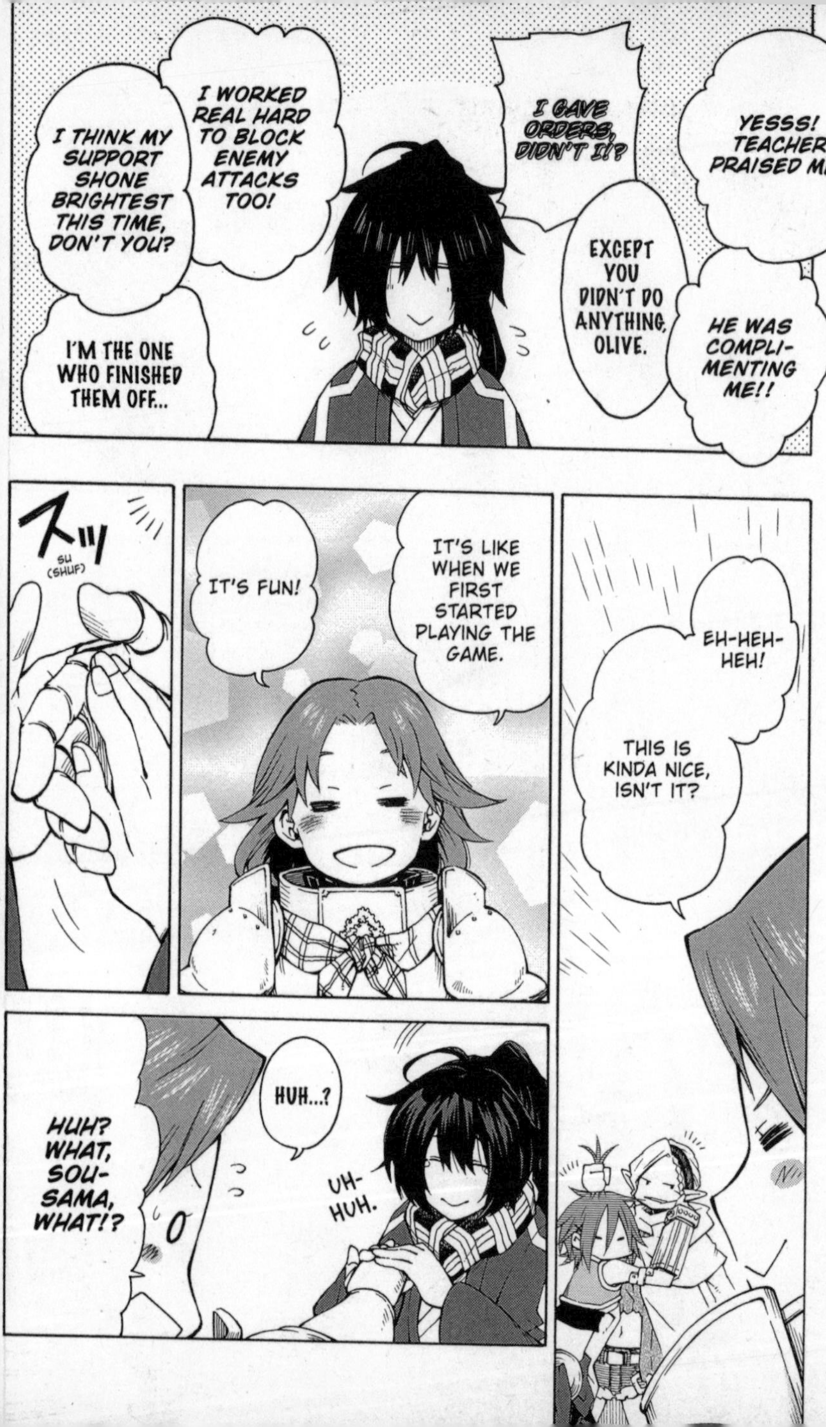
YESSS! TEACHER PRAISED ME!
I GAVE ORDERS, DIDN'T I!?
I WORKED REAL HARD TO BLOCK ENEMY ATTACKS TOO!
I THINK MY SUPPORT SHONE BRIGHTEST THIS TIME, DON'T YOU?
HE WAS COMPLIMENTING ME!!
EXCEPT YOU DIDN'T DO ANYTHING, OLIVE.
I'M THE ONE WHO FINISHED THEM OFF...
EH-HEH-HEH!
THIS IS KINDA NICE, ISN'T IT?
IT'S LIKE WHEN WE FIRST STARTED PLAYING THE GAME.
IT'S FUN!
スッ
SU (SHUF)
HUH...?
UH-HUH.
HUH? WHAT, SOU-SAMA, WHAT!?

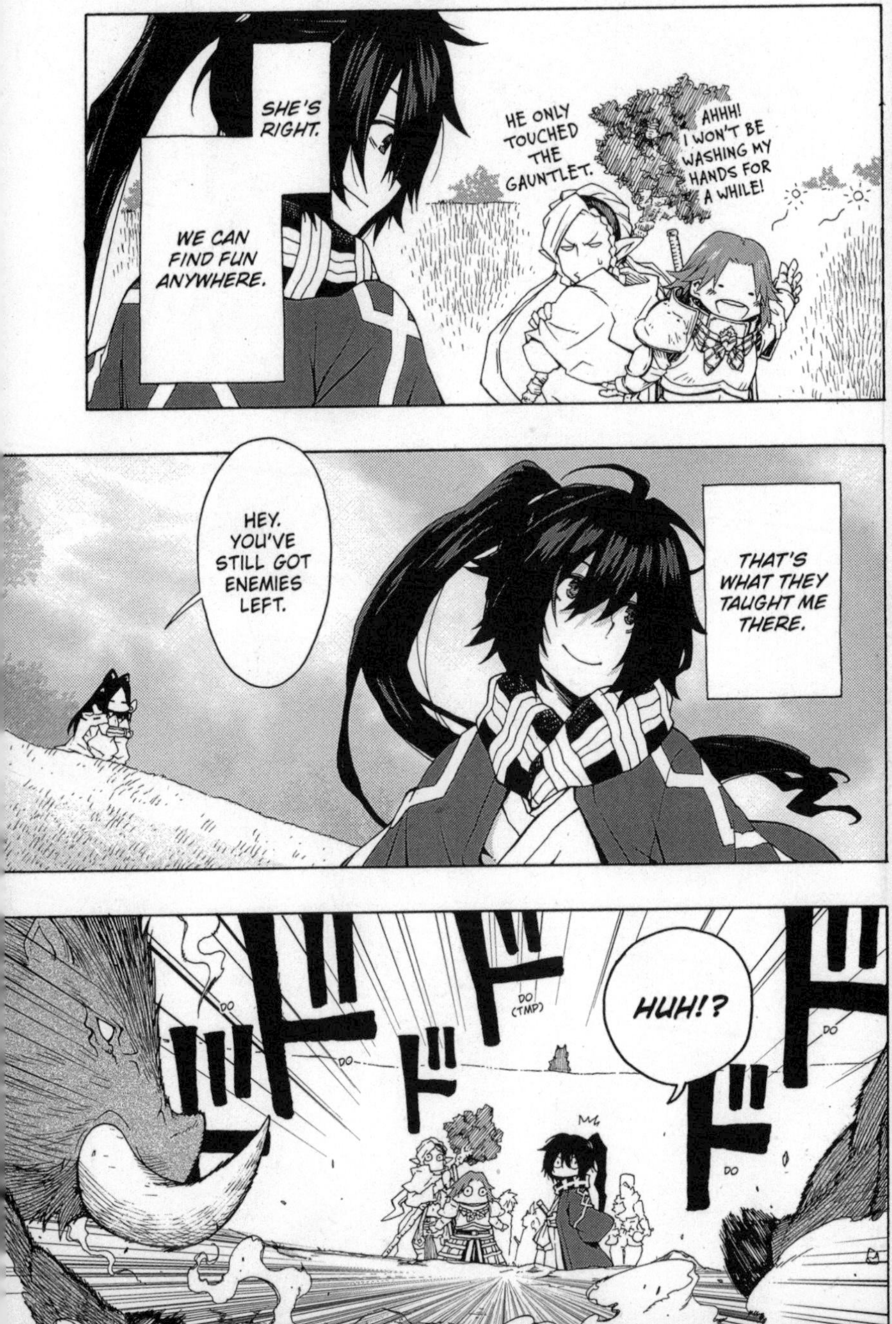
AHHH! I WON'T BE WASHING MY HANDS FOR A WHILE!
HE ONLY TOUCHED THE GAUNTLET.
SHE'S RIGHT.
WE CAN FIND FUN ANYWHERE.
THAT'S WHAT THEY TAUGHT ME THERE.
HEY. YOU'VE STILL GOT ENEMIES LEFT.
DO
HUH!?
DO
DO (TMP)
DO
DO
DO

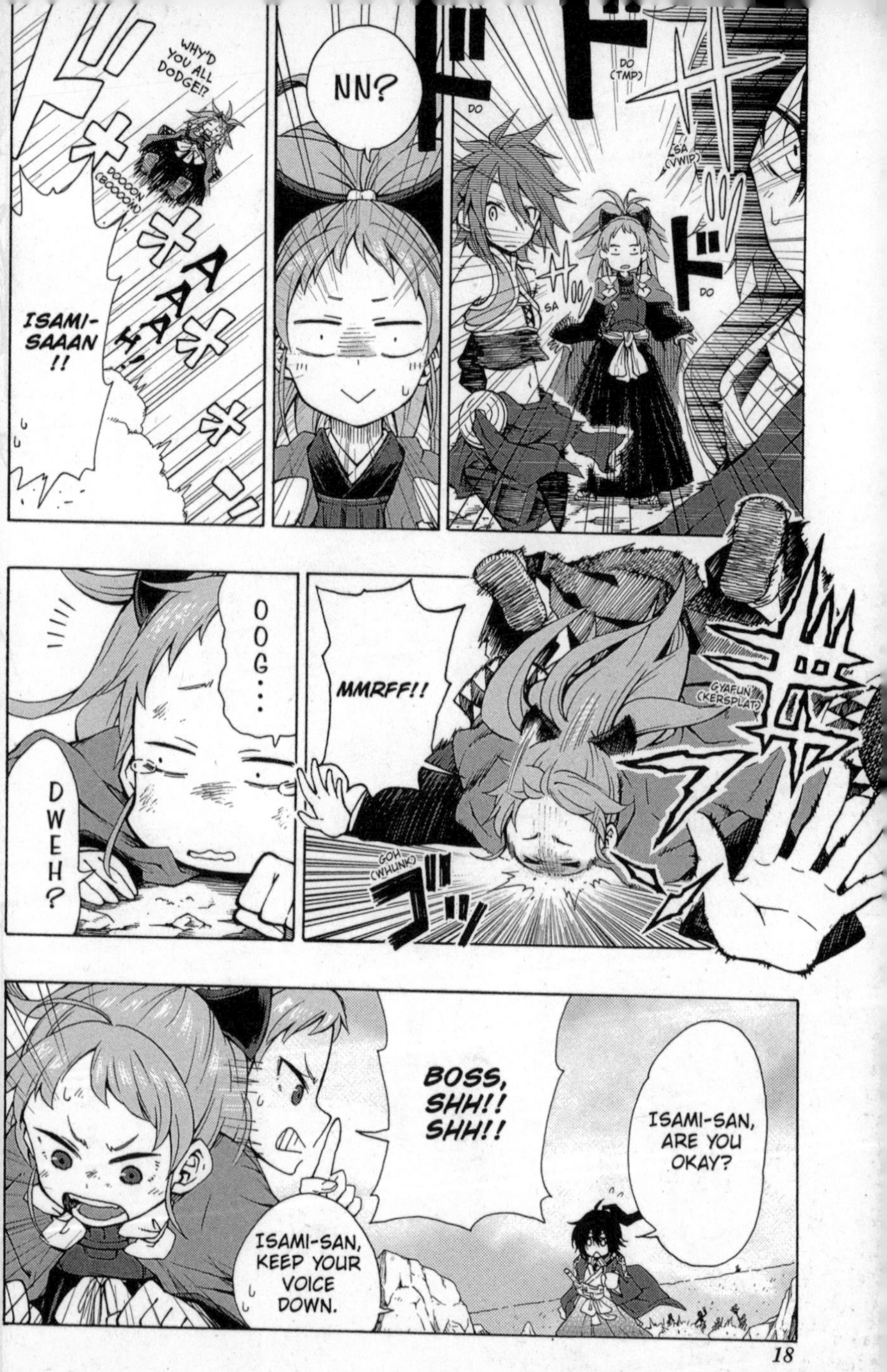
DO (TMP)
DO
SA (VWIP)
SA
DO
NN?
WHY'D YOU ALL DODGE!?
DOOOON (BOOOOM)
AAAAH!
ISAMI-SAAAN!!
GYAFUN (KERSPLAT)
MMRFF!!
GOH (WHUNK)
OOG...
DWEH?
ISAMI-SAN, ARE YOU OKAY?
BOSS, SHH!! SHH!!
ISAMI-SAN, KEEP YOUR VOICE DOWN.

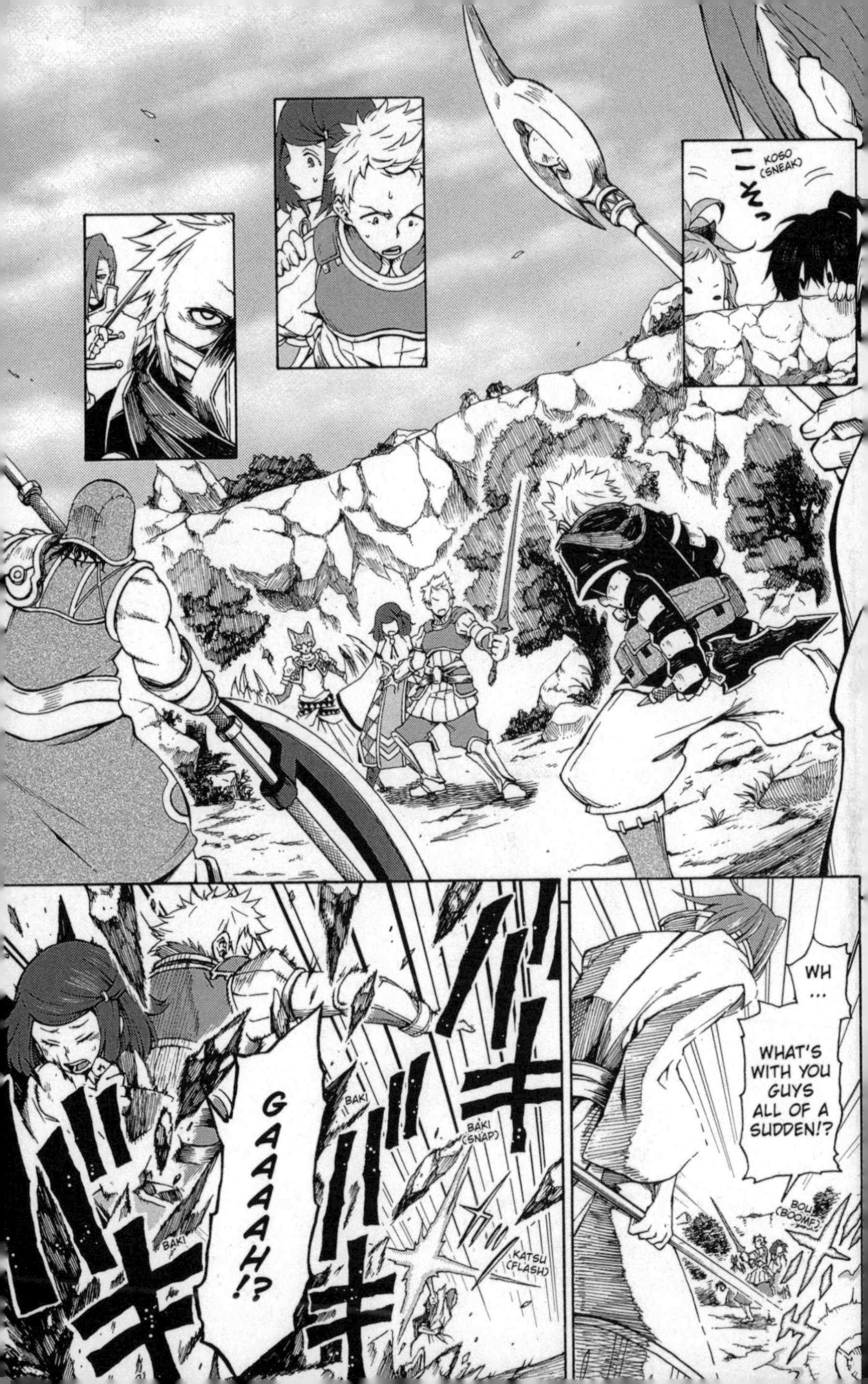
KOSO (SNEAK)
WH ...
WHAT'S WITH YOU GUYS ALL OF A SUDDEN!?
BOU (BOOMP)
BAKI
BAKI (SNAP)
GAAAAAH!?
KATSU (FLASH)
BAKI

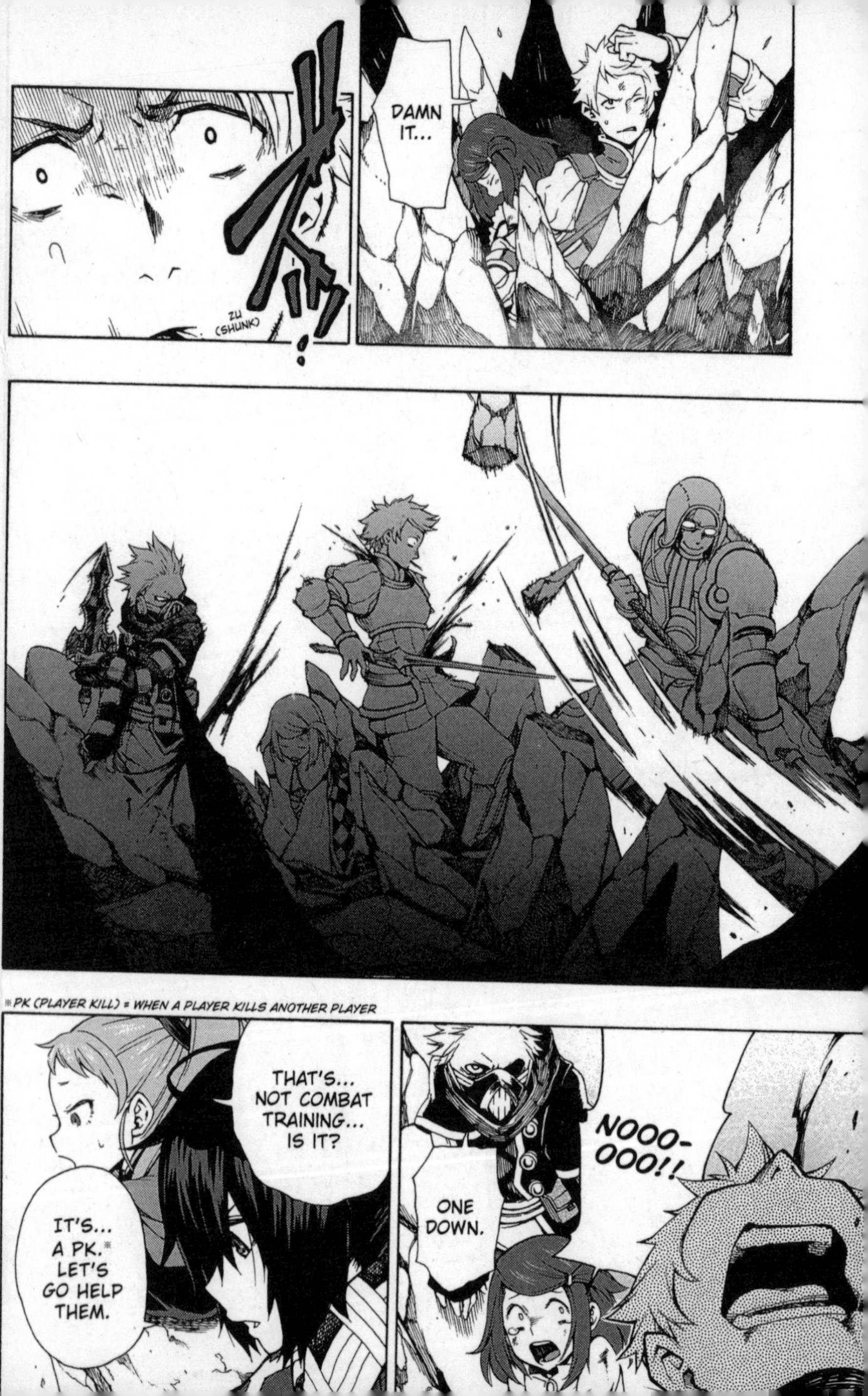
DAMN IT...
ZU (SHUNK)
NOOO-OOO!!
ONE DOWN.
THAT'S... NOT COMBAT TRAINING... IS IT?
IT'S... A PK.※ LET'S GO HELP THEM.

※PK (PLAYER KILL) = WHEN A PLAYER KILLS ANOTHER PLAYER

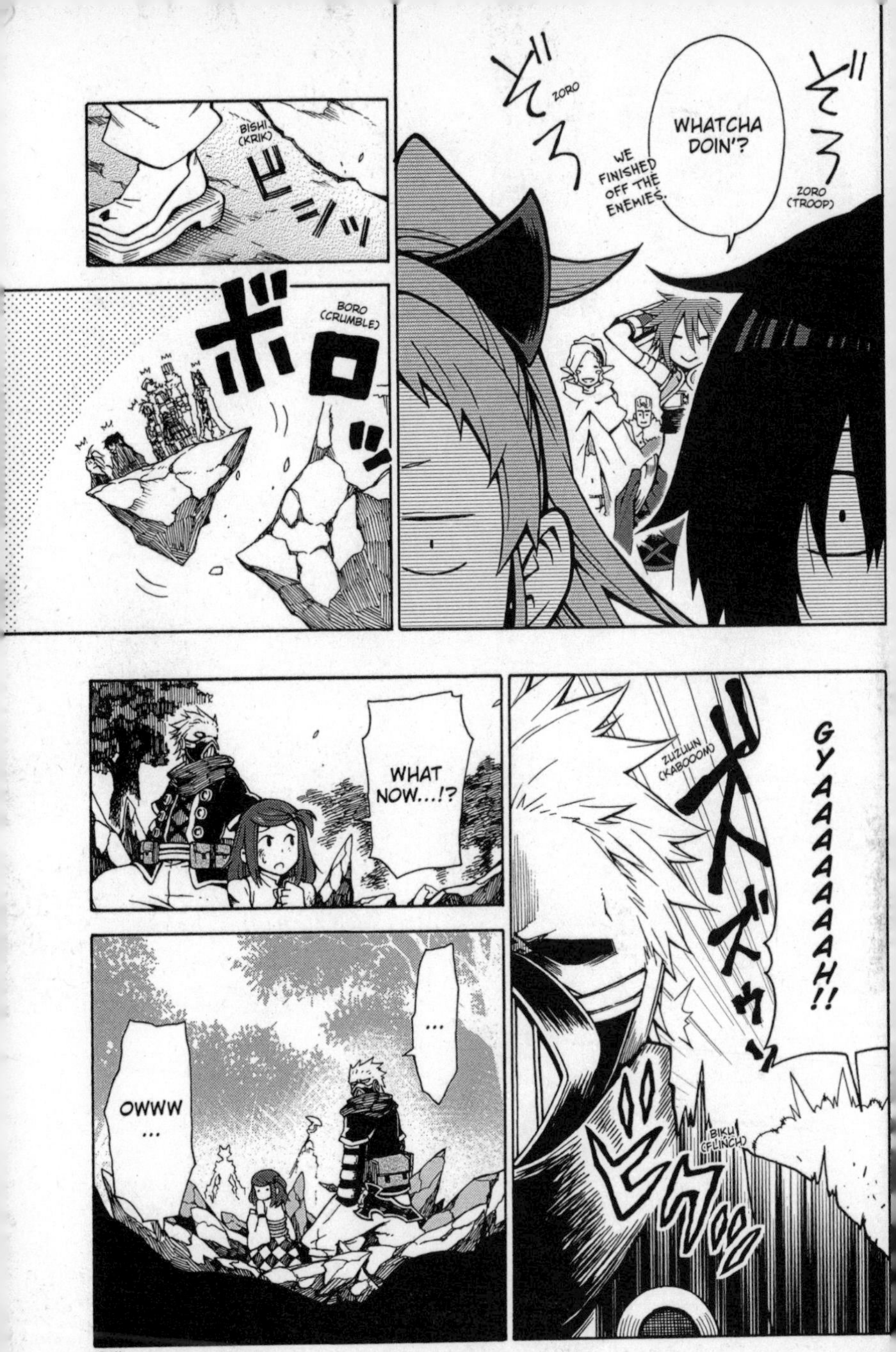
ZORO (TROOP)
WHATCHA DOIN'?
ZORO
WE FINISHED OFF THE ENEMIES.
BISHI (KRIK)
BORO (CRUMBLE)
GYAAAAAAAAH!!
ZUZUUN (KABOOOM)
BIKU (FLINCH)
WHAT NOW...!?
...
OWWW ...

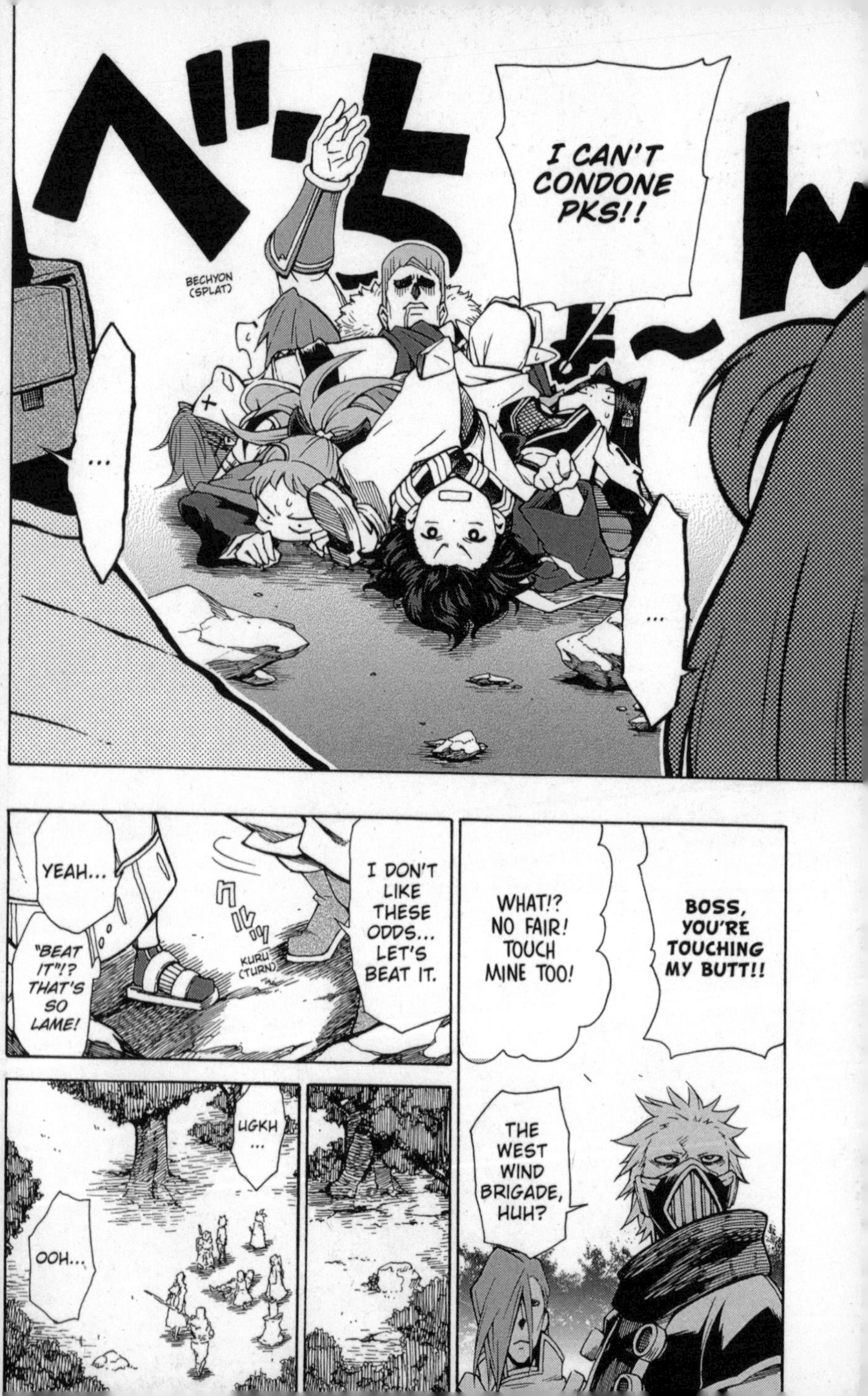
I CAN'T CONDONE PKS!!
BECHYON (SPLAT)
...
...
BOSS, YOU'RE TOUCHING MY BUTT!!
WHAT!? NO FAIR! TOUCH MINE TOO!
I DON'T LIKE THESE ODDS... LET'S BEAT IT.
KURU (TURN)
YEAH...
"BEAT IT"!? THAT'S SO LAME!
THE WEST WIND BRIGADE, HUH?
UGKH ...
OOH...

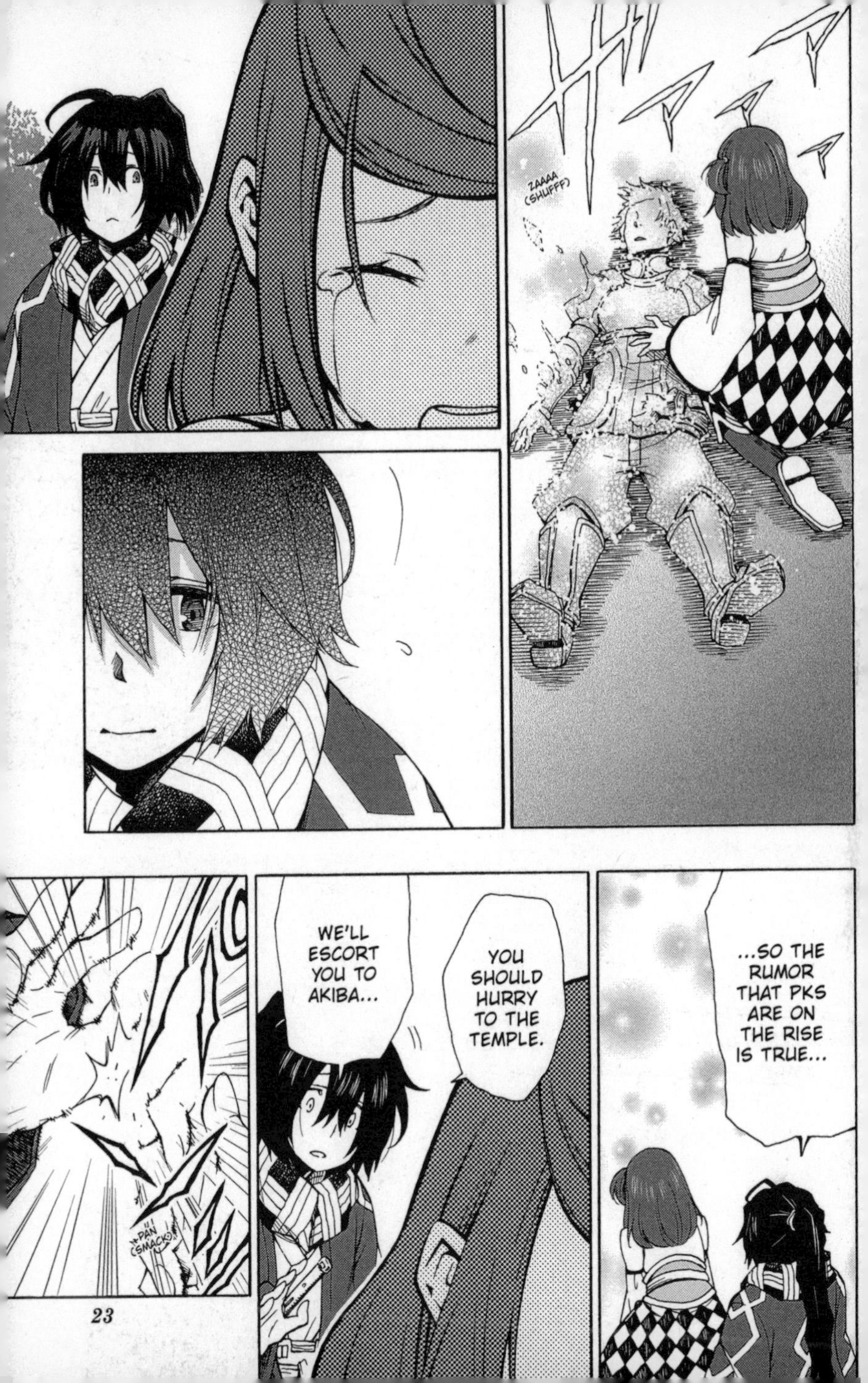
ZAAAA
(SHUFFF)
...SO THE RUMOR THAT PKS ARE ON THE RISE IS TRUE...
YOU SHOULD HURRY TO THE TEMPLE.
WE'LL ESCORT YOU TO AKIBA...
PAN
(SMACK)

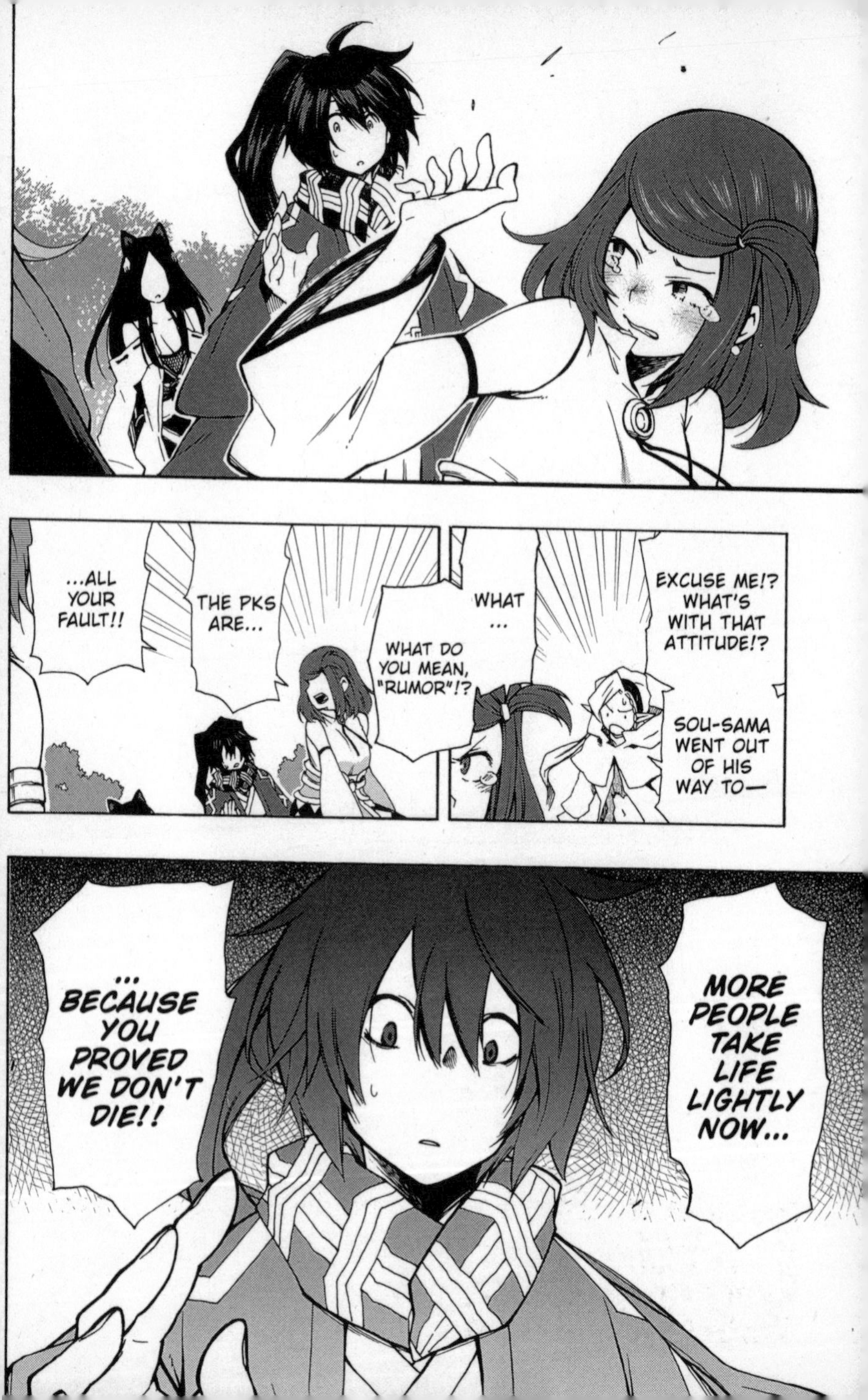
EXCUSE ME!? WHAT'S WITH THAT ATTITUDE!?
SOU-SAMA WENT OUT OF HIS WAY TO—
WHAT ...
WHAT DO YOU MEAN, "RUMOR"!?
THE PKS ARE...
...ALL YOUR FAULT!!
MORE PEOPLE TAKE LIFE LIGHTLY NOW...
... BECAUSE YOU PROVED WE DON'T DIE!!

LOG HORIZON

THE WEST WIND BRIGADE

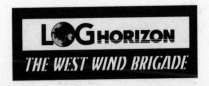

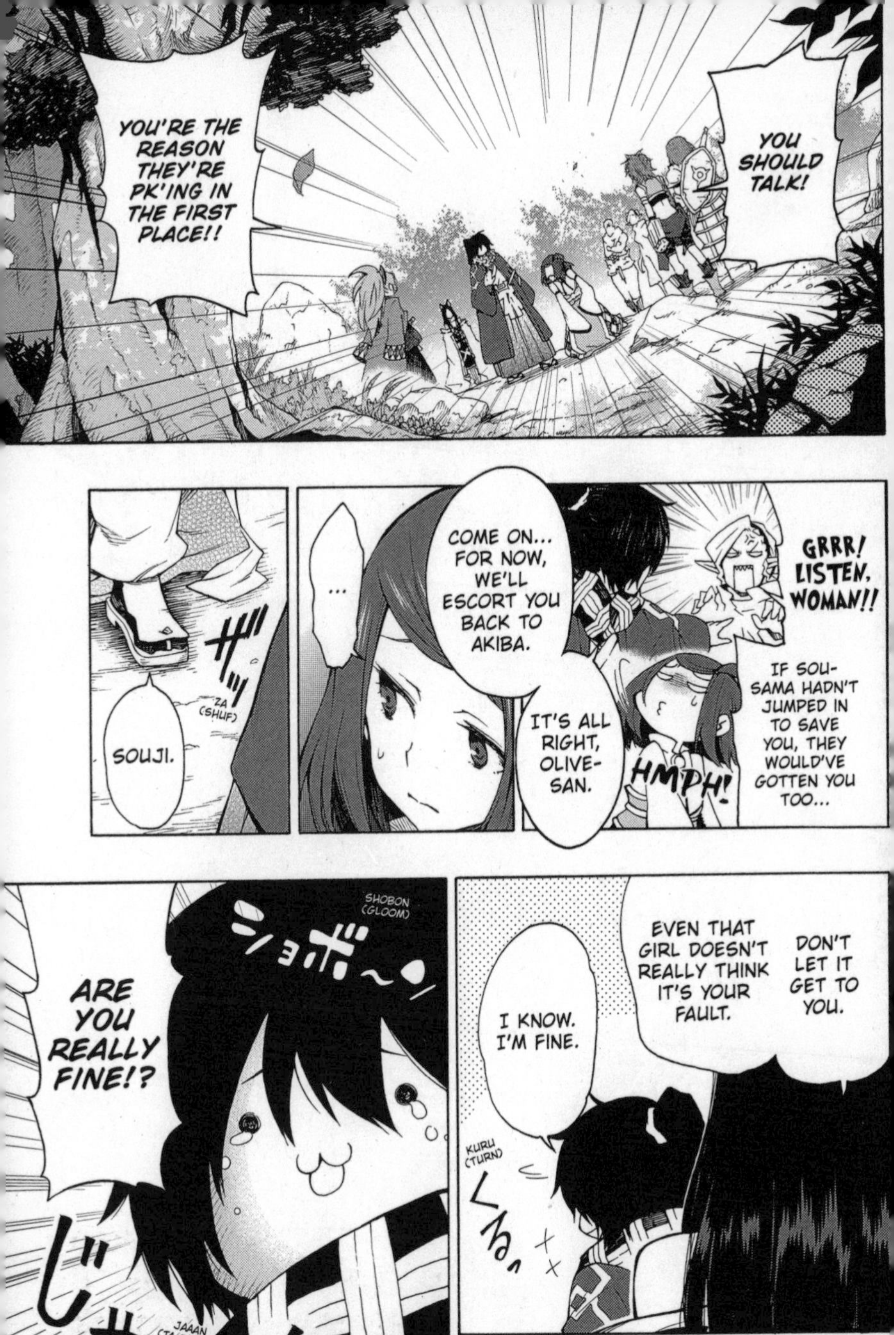
YOU SHOULD TALK!
YOU'RE THE REASON THEY'RE PK'ING IN THE FIRST PLACE!!
GRRR! LISTEN, WOMAN!!
IF SOU-SAMA HADN'T JUMPED IN TO SAVE YOU, THEY WOULD'VE GOTTEN YOU TOO...
HMPH!
IT'S ALL RIGHT, OLIVE-SAN.
COME ON... FOR NOW, WE'LL ESCORT YOU BACK TO AKIBA.
...
ザッ
ZA (SHUF)
SOUJI.
DON'T LET IT GET TO YOU.
EVEN THAT GIRL DOESN'T REALLY THINK IT'S YOUR FAULT.
I KNOW. I'M FINE.
くるっ
KURU (TURN)
ショボ～ん
SHOBON (GLOOM)
ARE YOU REALLY FINE!?
じゃ～ん
JAAAN (TA-DAAAH)

**[CHAPTER : 08 HAMELIN]**

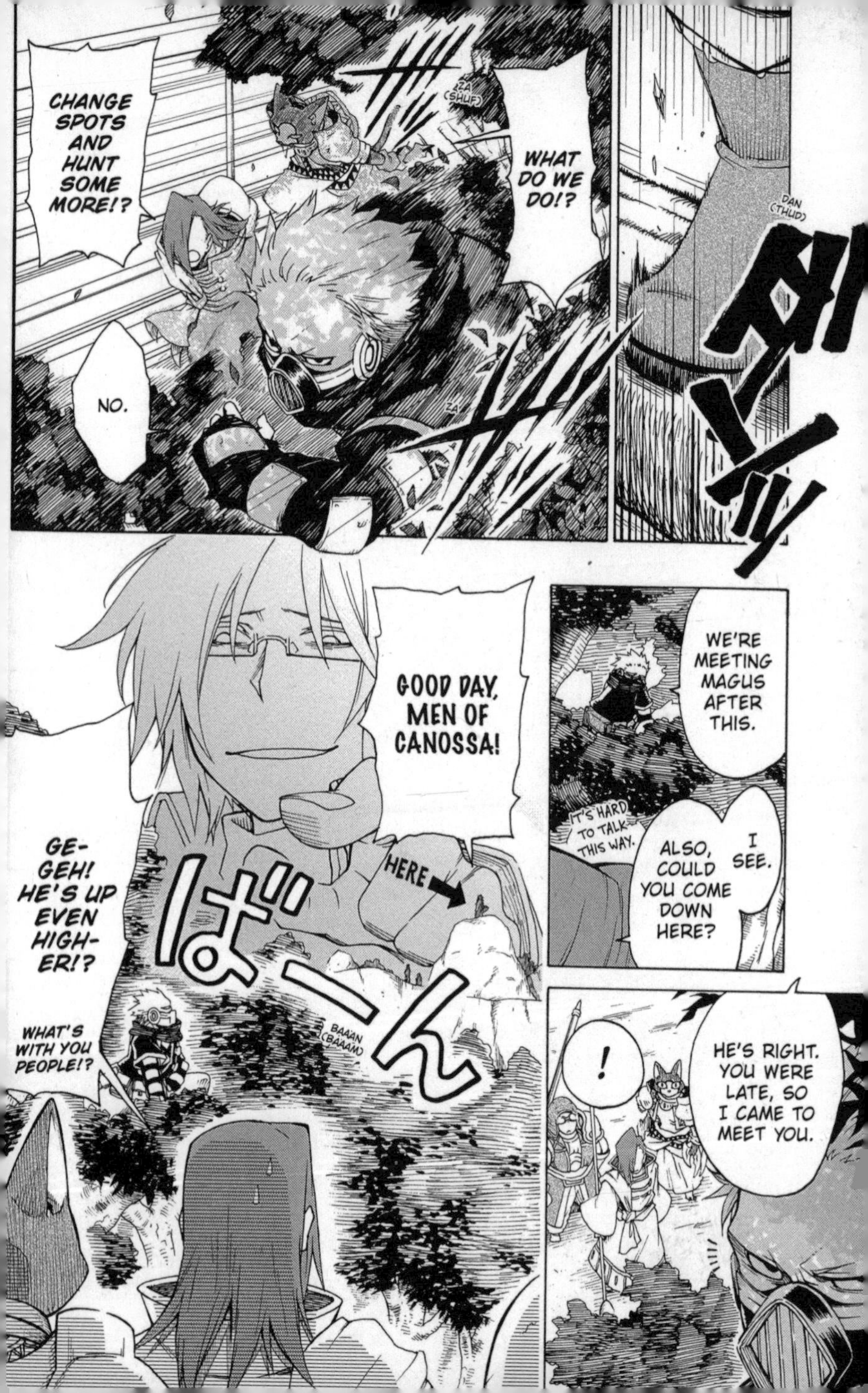
DAN (THUD)
ZA (SHUF)
WHAT DO WE DO!?
CHANGE SPOTS AND HUNT SOME MORE!?
ZA
NO.
WE'RE MEETING MAGUS AFTER THIS.
I SEE.
ALSO, COULD YOU COME DOWN HERE?
IT'S HARD TO TALK THIS WAY.
HE'S RIGHT. YOU WERE LATE, SO I CAME TO MEET YOU.
!
GOOD DAY, MEN OF CANOSSA!
HERE
BAAAN (BAAAM)
GE-GEH! HE'S UP EVEN HIGHER!?
WHAT'S WITH YOU PEOPLE!?

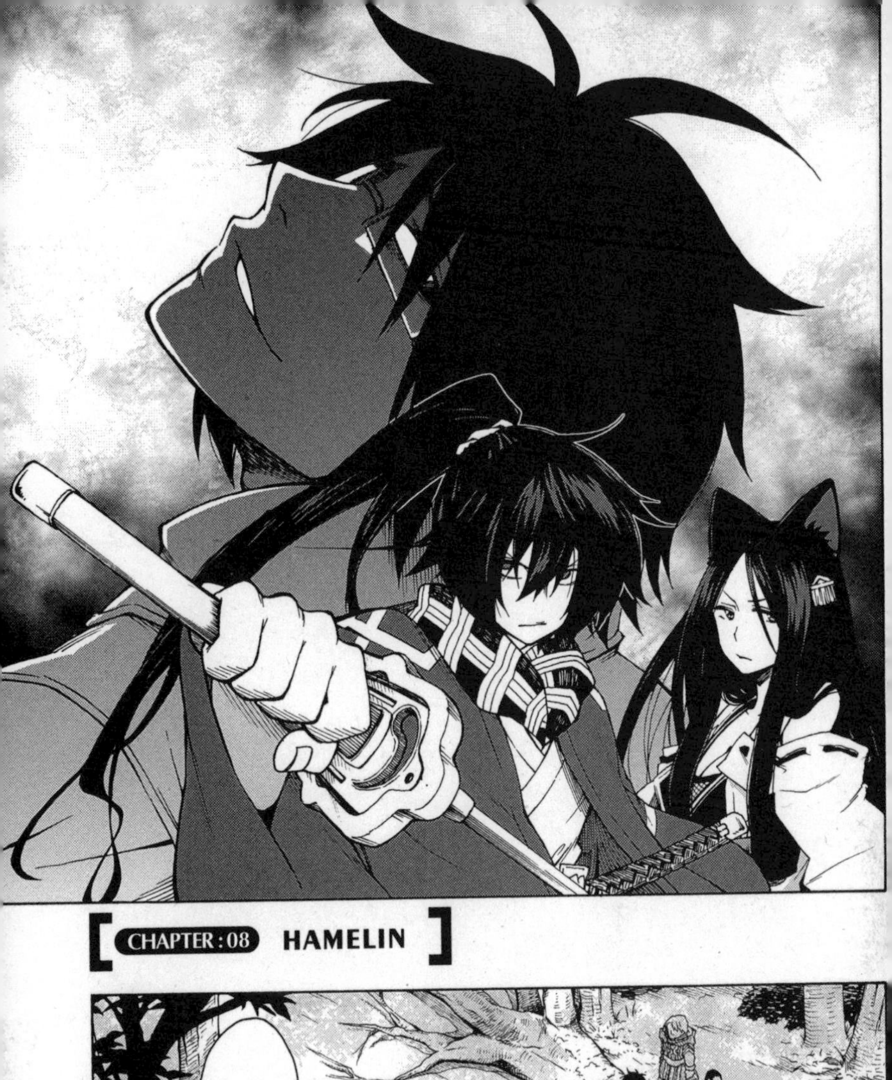

CHAPTER : 08 **HAMELIN**

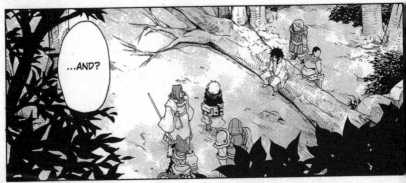

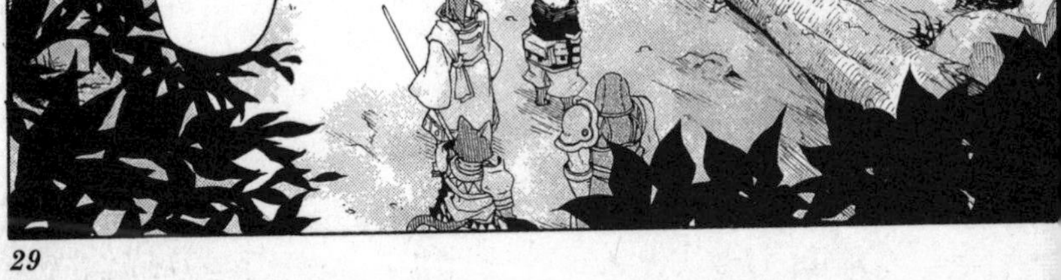
...AND?

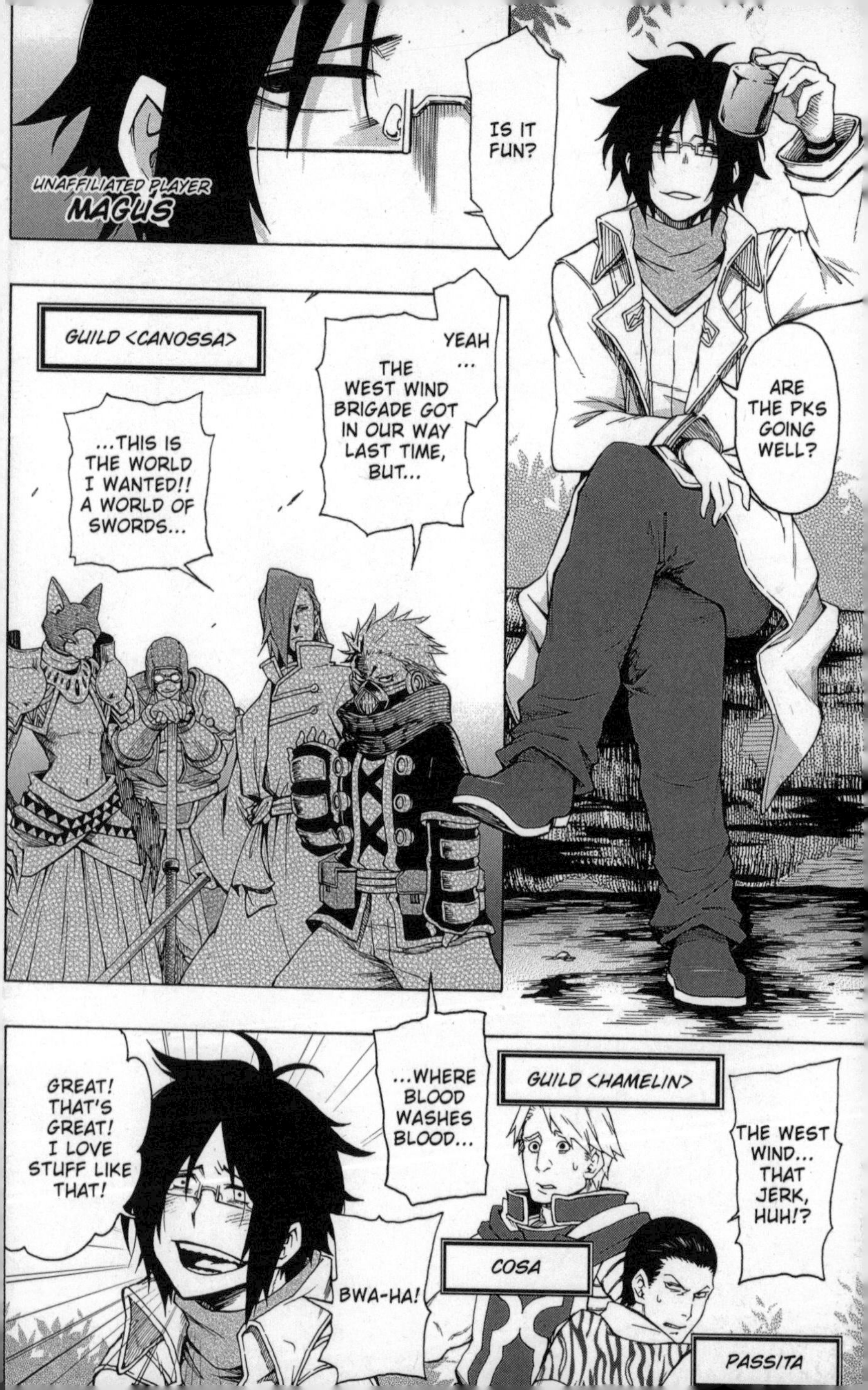
IS IT FUN?
ARE THE PKS GOING WELL?
UNAFFILIATED PLAYER MAGUS
GUILD <CANOSSA>
YEAH... THE WEST WIND BRIGADE GOT IN OUR WAY LAST TIME, BUT...
...THIS IS THE WORLD I WANTED!! A WORLD OF SWORDS...
GUILD <HAMELIN>
THE WEST WIND... THAT JERK, HUH!?
COSA
PASSITA
...WHERE BLOOD WASHES BLOOD...
BWA-HA!
GREAT! THAT'S GREAT! I LOVE STUFF LIKE THAT!

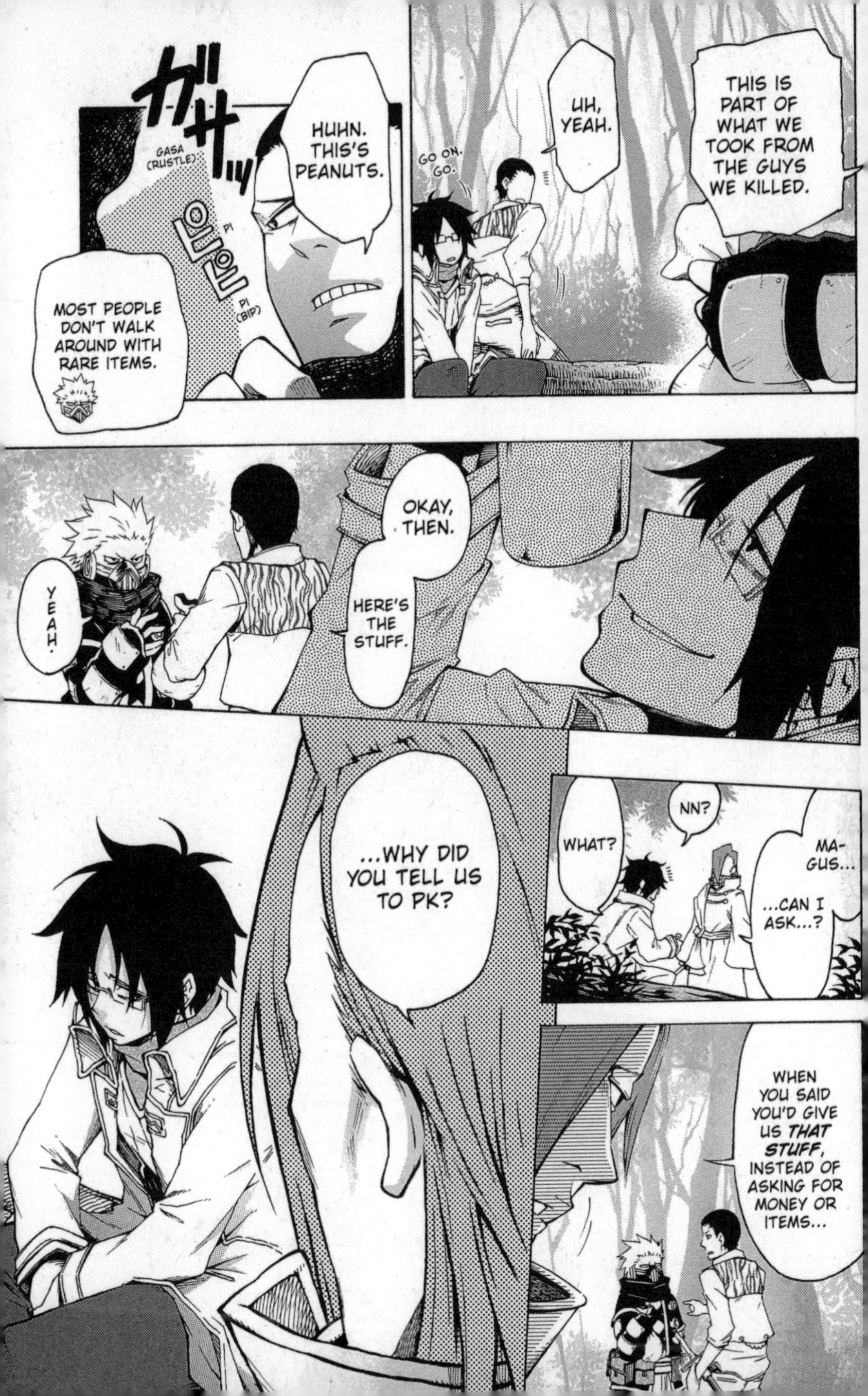
THIS IS PART OF WHAT WE TOOK FROM THE GUYS WE KILLED.
UH, YEAH.
GO ON. GO.
ガサッ
GASA (RUSTLE)
HUHN. THIS'S PEANUTS.
ピピ
PI PI (BIP)
MOST PEOPLE DON'T WALK AROUND WITH RARE ITEMS.
OKAY, THEN.
HERE'S THE STUFF.
YEAH.
MA-GUS...
...CAN I ASK...?
NN?
WHAT?
WHEN YOU SAID YOU'D GIVE US *THAT STUFF*, INSTEAD OF ASKING FOR MONEY OR ITEMS...
...WHY DID YOU TELL US TO PK?

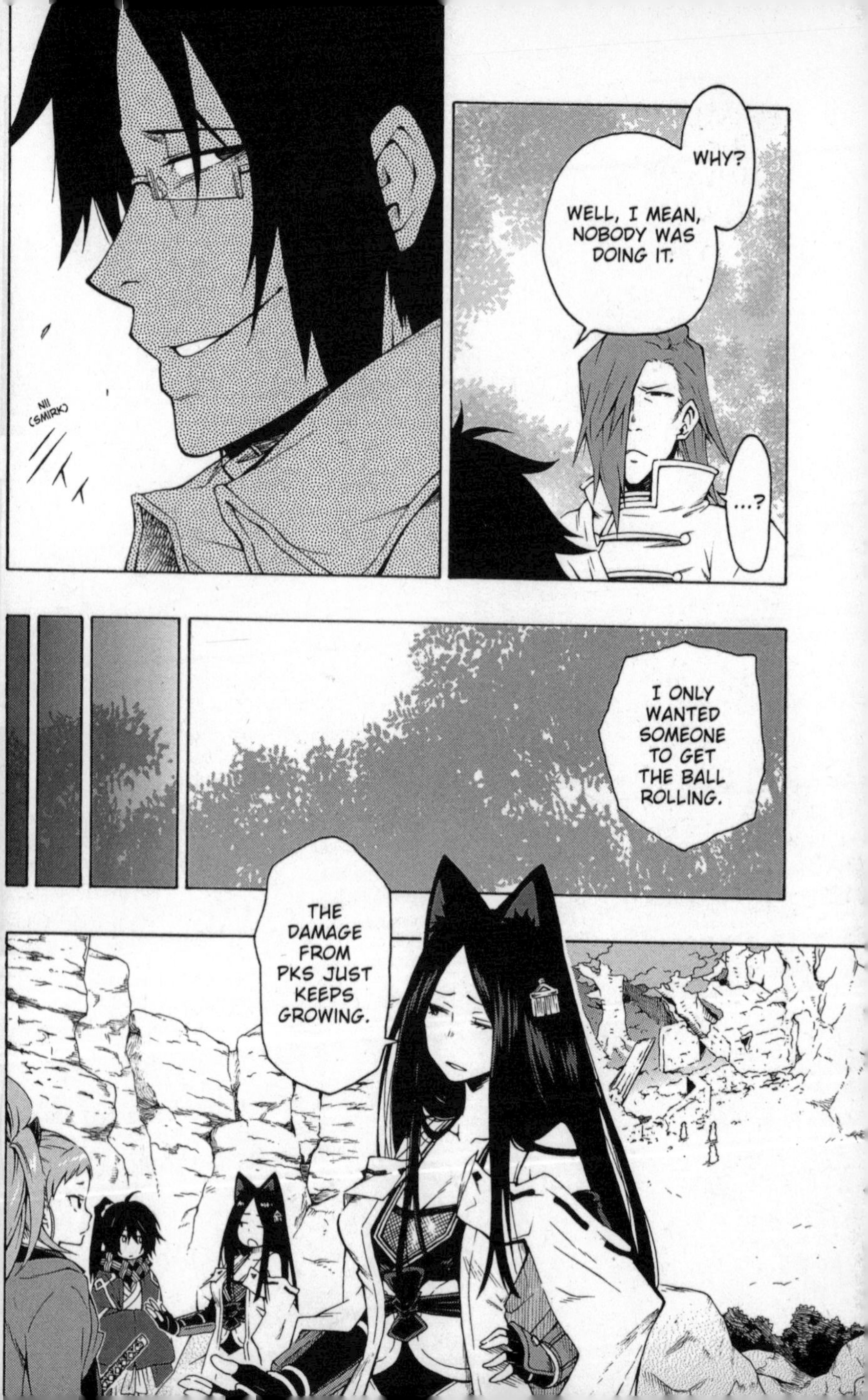
WHY?
WELL, I MEAN, NOBODY WAS DOING IT.
...?
NII (SMIRK)
I ONLY WANTED SOMEONE TO GET THE BALL ROLLING.
THE DAMAGE FROM PKS JUST KEEPS GROWING.

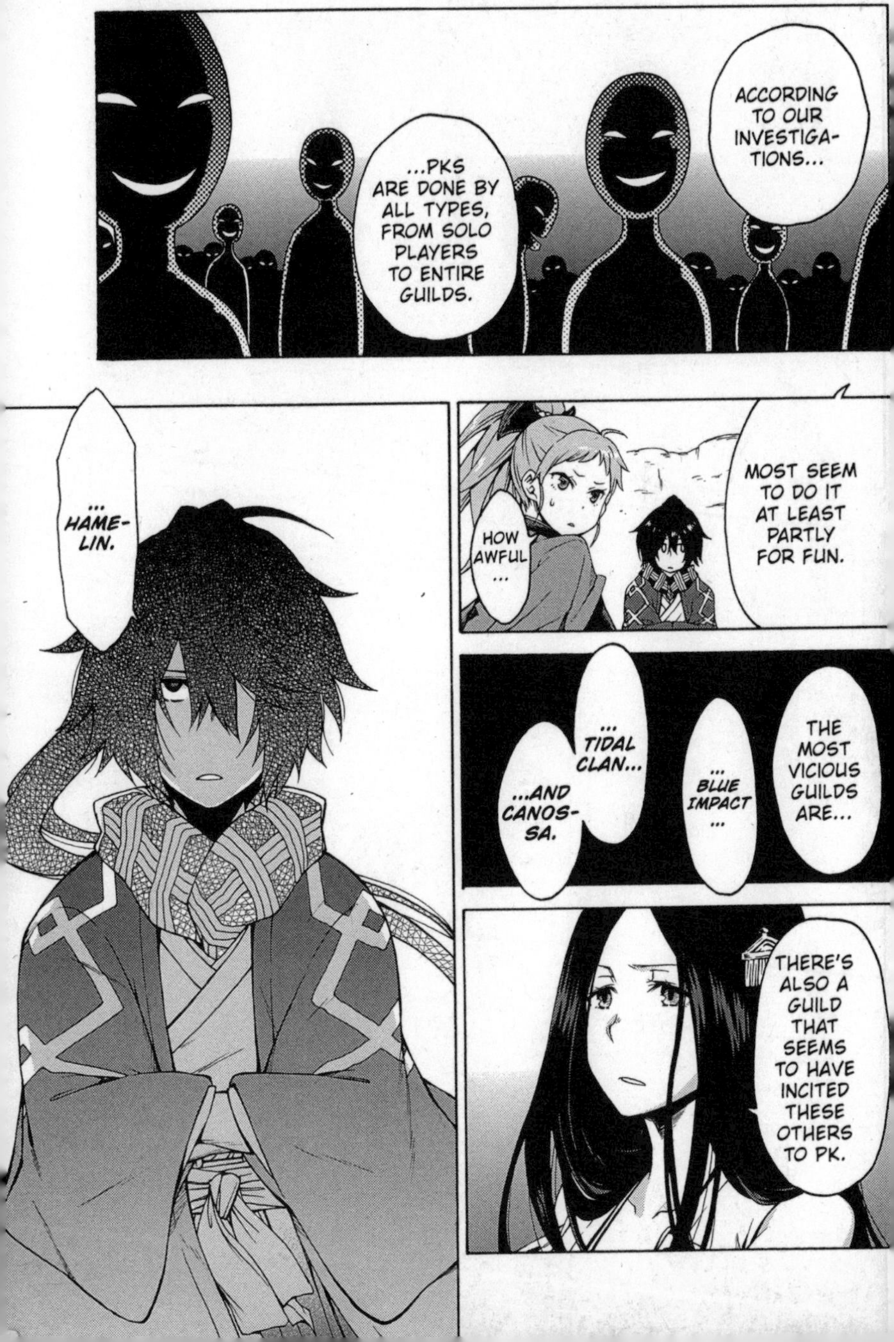
ACCORDING TO OUR INVESTIGATIONS...
...PKS ARE DONE BY ALL TYPES, FROM SOLO PLAYERS TO ENTIRE GUILDS.
MOST SEEM TO DO IT AT LEAST PARTLY FOR FUN.
HOW AWFUL...
THE MOST VICIOUS GUILDS ARE...
...BLUE IMPACT...
...TIDAL CLAN...
...AND CANOSSA.
THERE'S ALSO A GUILD THAT SEEMS TO HAVE INCITED THESE OTHERS TO PK.
...HÄMELIN.

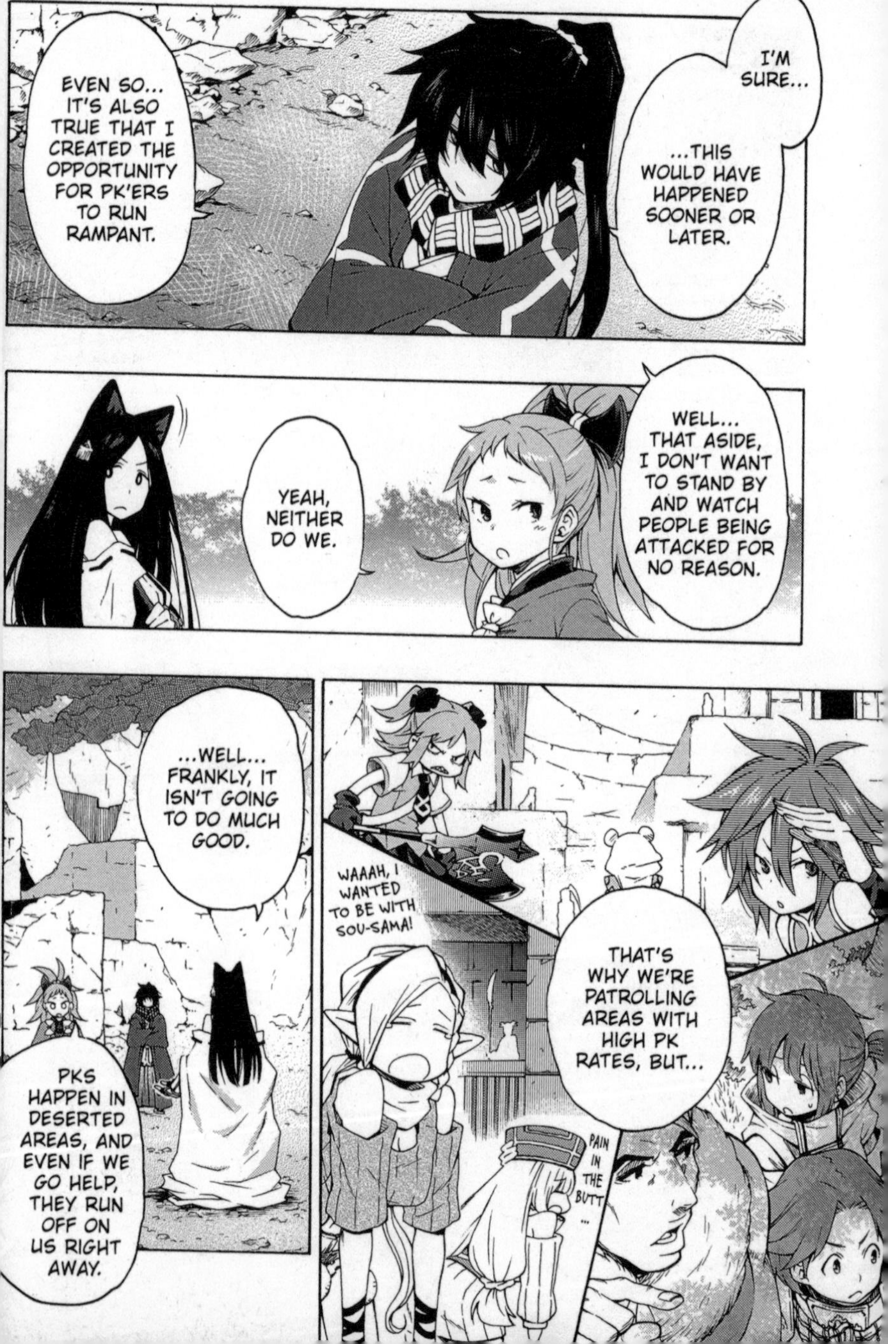
I'M SURE...
...THIS WOULD HAVE HAPPENED SOONER OR LATER.
EVEN SO... IT'S ALSO TRUE THAT I CREATED THE OPPORTUNITY FOR PK'ERS TO RUN RAMPANT.
WELL... THAT ASIDE, I DON'T WANT TO STAND BY AND WATCH PEOPLE BEING ATTACKED FOR NO REASON.
YEAH, NEITHER DO WE.
THAT'S WHY WE'RE PATROLLING AREAS WITH HIGH PK RATES, BUT...
WAAAH, I WANTED TO BE WITH SOU-SAMA!
PAIN IN THE BUTT...
...WELL... FRANKLY, IT ISN'T GOING TO DO MUCH GOOD.
PKS HAPPEN IN DESERTED AREAS, AND EVEN IF WE GO HELP, THEY RUN OFF ON US RIGHT AWAY.

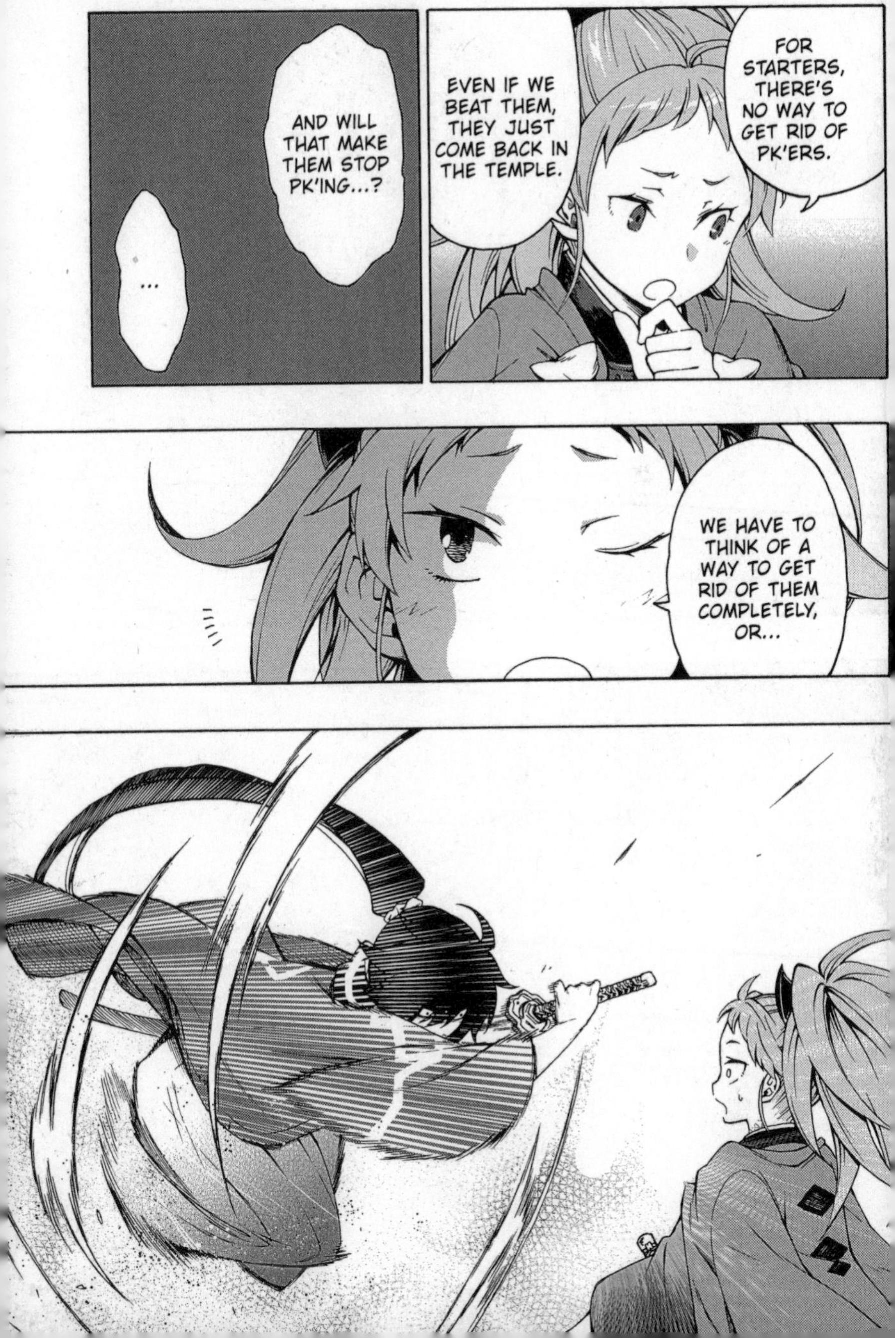
FOR STARTERS, THERE'S NO WAY TO GET RID OF PK'ERS.
EVEN IF WE BEAT THEM, THEY JUST COME BACK IN THE TEMPLE.
AND WILL THAT MAKE THEM STOP PK'ING...?
...
WE HAVE TO THINK OF A WAY TO GET RID OF THEM COMPLETELY, OR...

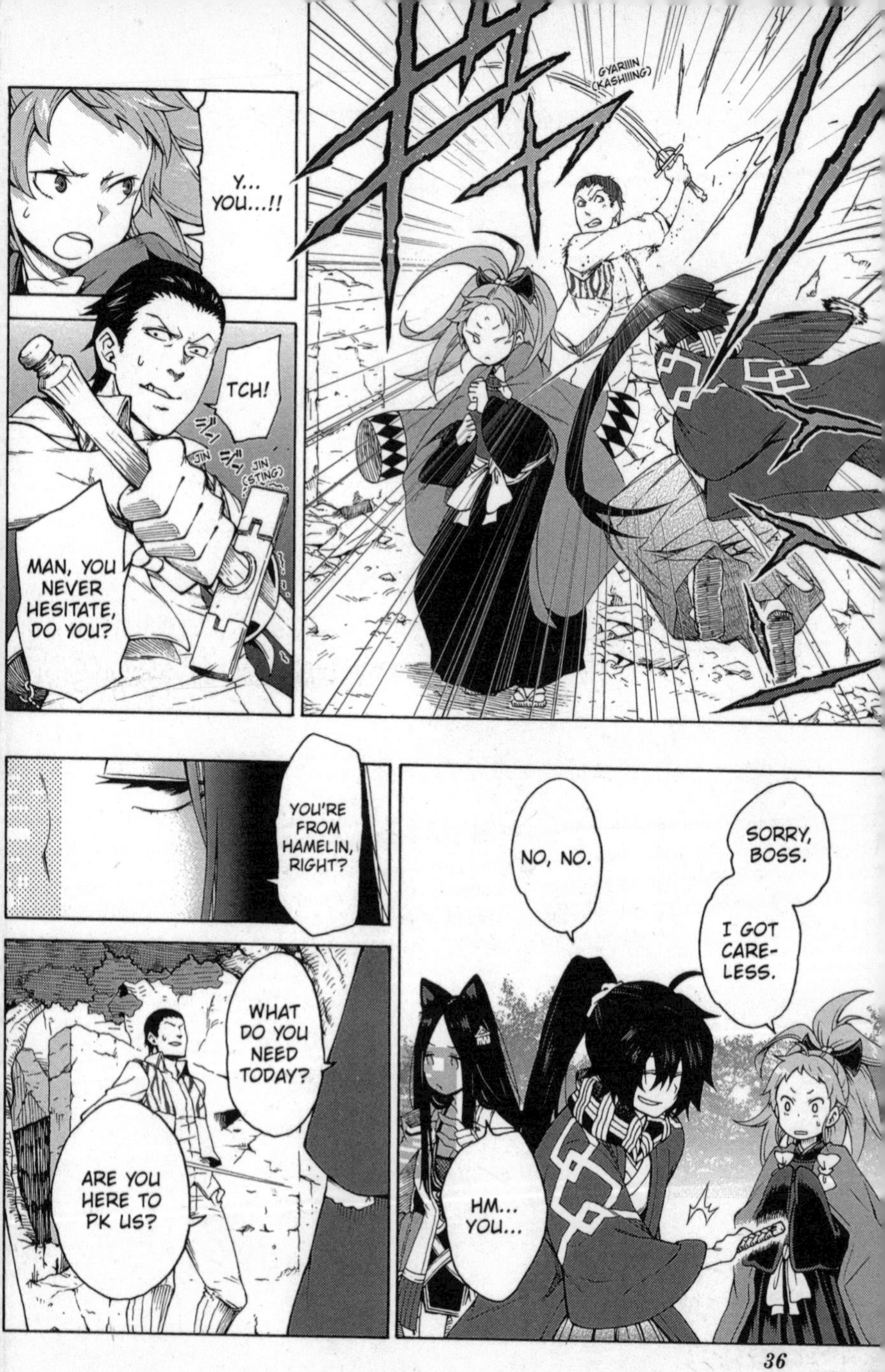
GYARIIIN (KASHIIING)
Y... YOU...!!
TCH!
JIN JIN (STING)
MAN, YOU NEVER HESITATE, DO YOU?
SORRY, BOSS.
I GOT CARE-LESS.
NO, NO.
HM... YOU...
YOU'RE FROM HAMELIN, RIGHT?
WHAT DO YOU NEED TODAY?
ARE YOU HERE TO PK US?

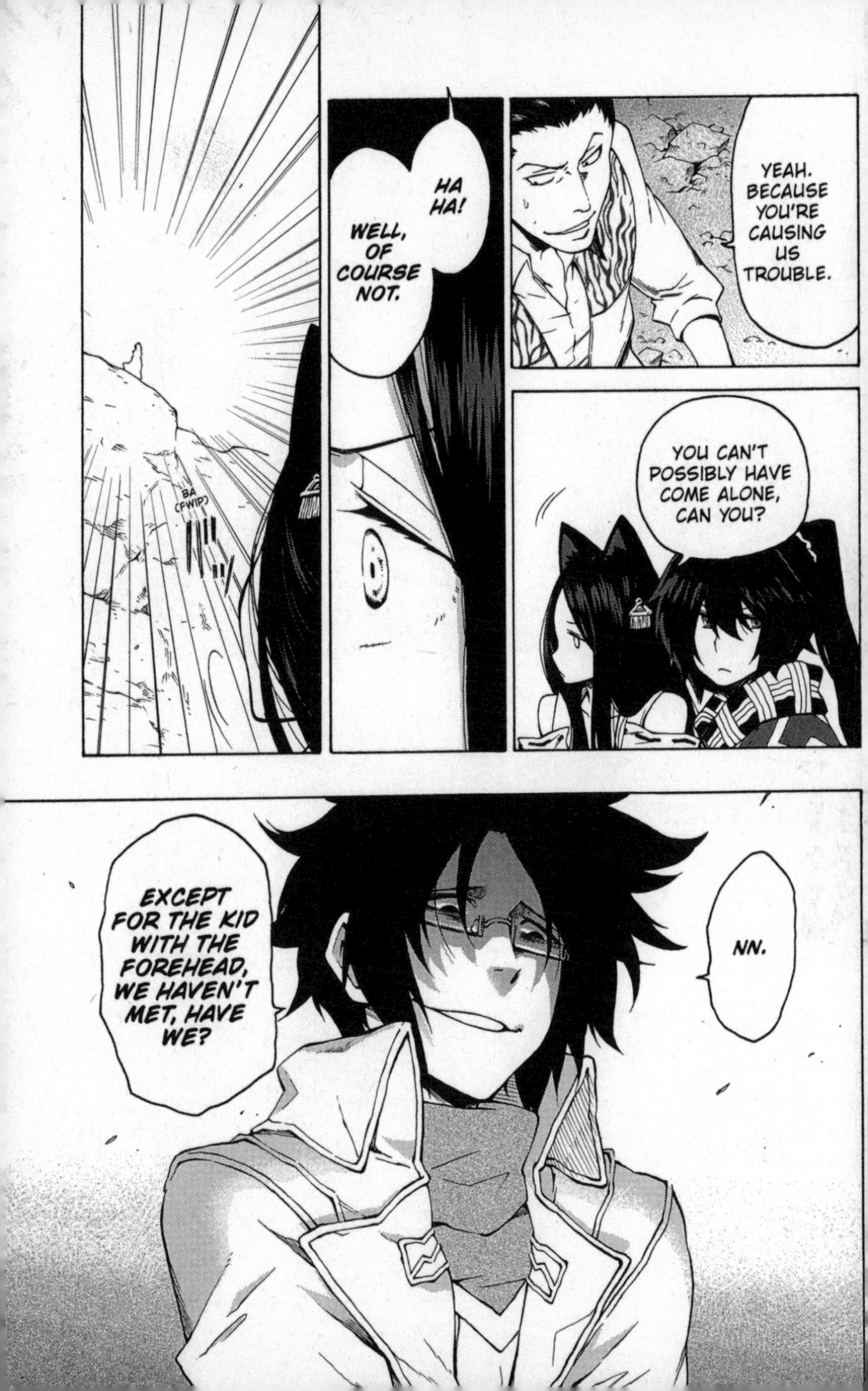

YEAH. BECAUSE YOU'RE CAUSING US TROUBLE.
YOU CAN'T POSSIBLY HAVE COME ALONE, CAN YOU?
HA HA! WELL, OF COURSE NOT.
BA (FWIP)
NN.
EXCEPT FOR THE KID WITH THE FOREHEAD, WE HAVEN'T MET, HAVE WE?

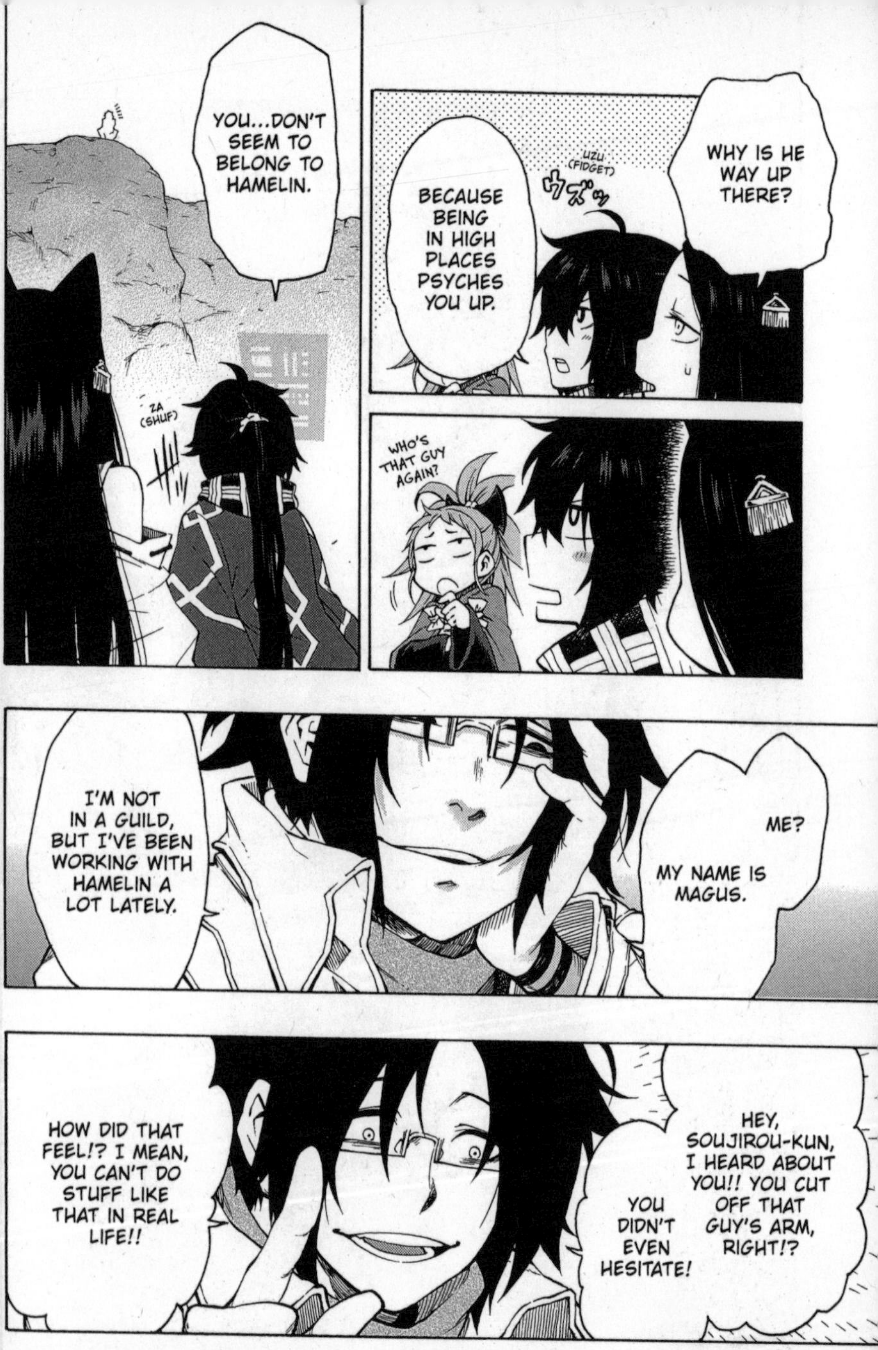
WHY IS HE WAY UP THERE?
UZU (FIDGET)
BECAUSE BEING IN HIGH PLACES PSYCHES YOU UP.
WHO'S THAT GUY AGAIN?
YOU...DON'T SEEM TO BELONG TO HAMELIN.
ZA (SHUF)
ME?
MY NAME IS MAGUS.
I'M NOT IN A GUILD, BUT I'VE BEEN WORKING WITH HAMELIN A LOT LATELY.
HEY, SOUJIROU-KUN, I HEARD ABOUT YOU!! YOU CUT OFF THAT GUY'S ARM, RIGHT!?
YOU DIDN'T EVEN HESITATE!
HOW DID THAT FEEL!? I MEAN, YOU CAN'T DO STUFF LIKE THAT IN REAL LIFE!!

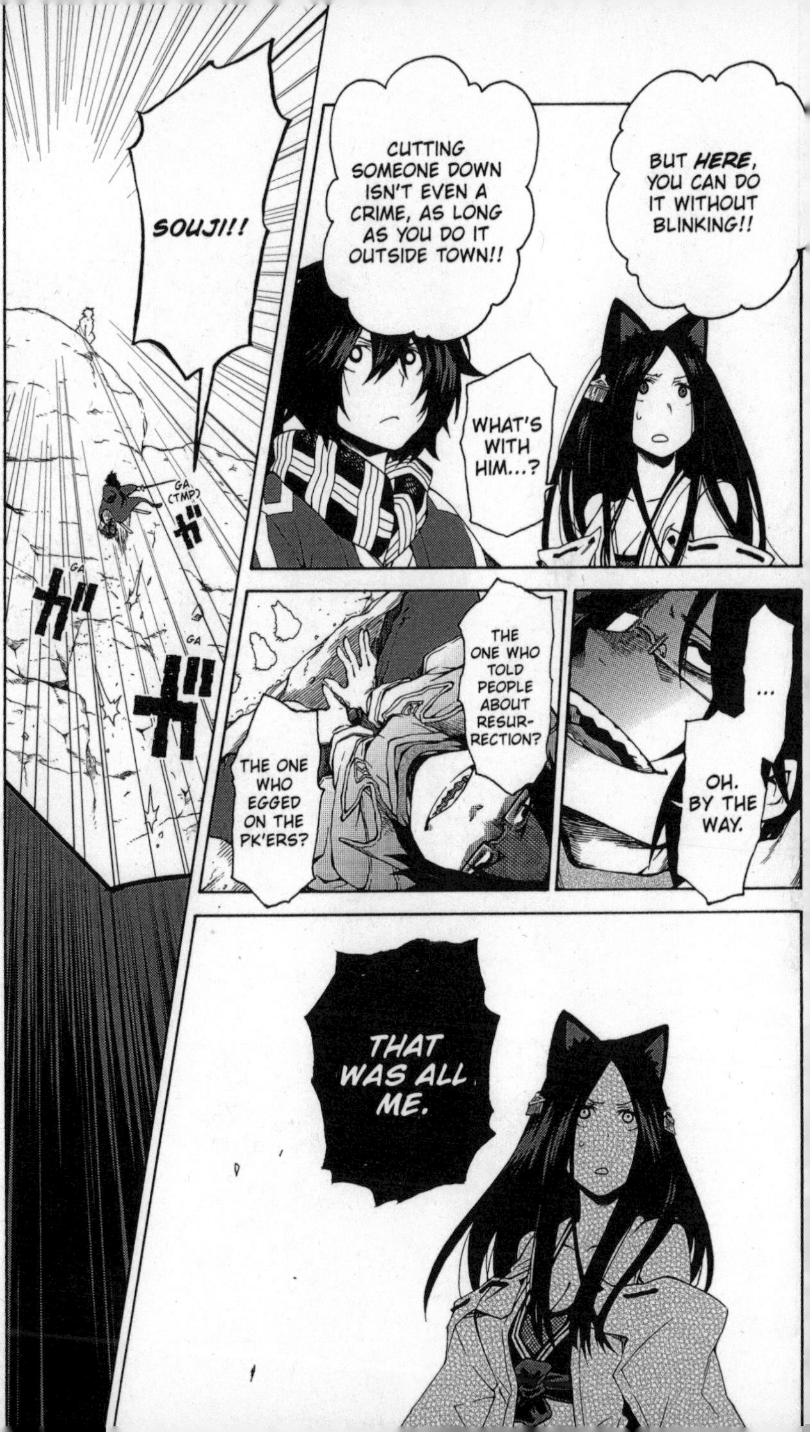
BUT *HERE*, YOU CAN DO IT WITHOUT BLINKING!!
CUTTING SOMEONE DOWN ISN'T EVEN A CRIME, AS LONG AS YOU DO IT OUTSIDE TOWN!!
WHAT'S WITH HIM...?
...
OH. BY THE WAY.
THE ONE WHO TOLD PEOPLE ABOUT RESUR-RECTION?
THE ONE WHO EGGED ON THE PK'ERS?
THAT WAS ALL ME.
SOUJI!!
GA (TMP)
ガ
GA
ガ"
GA
ガ"

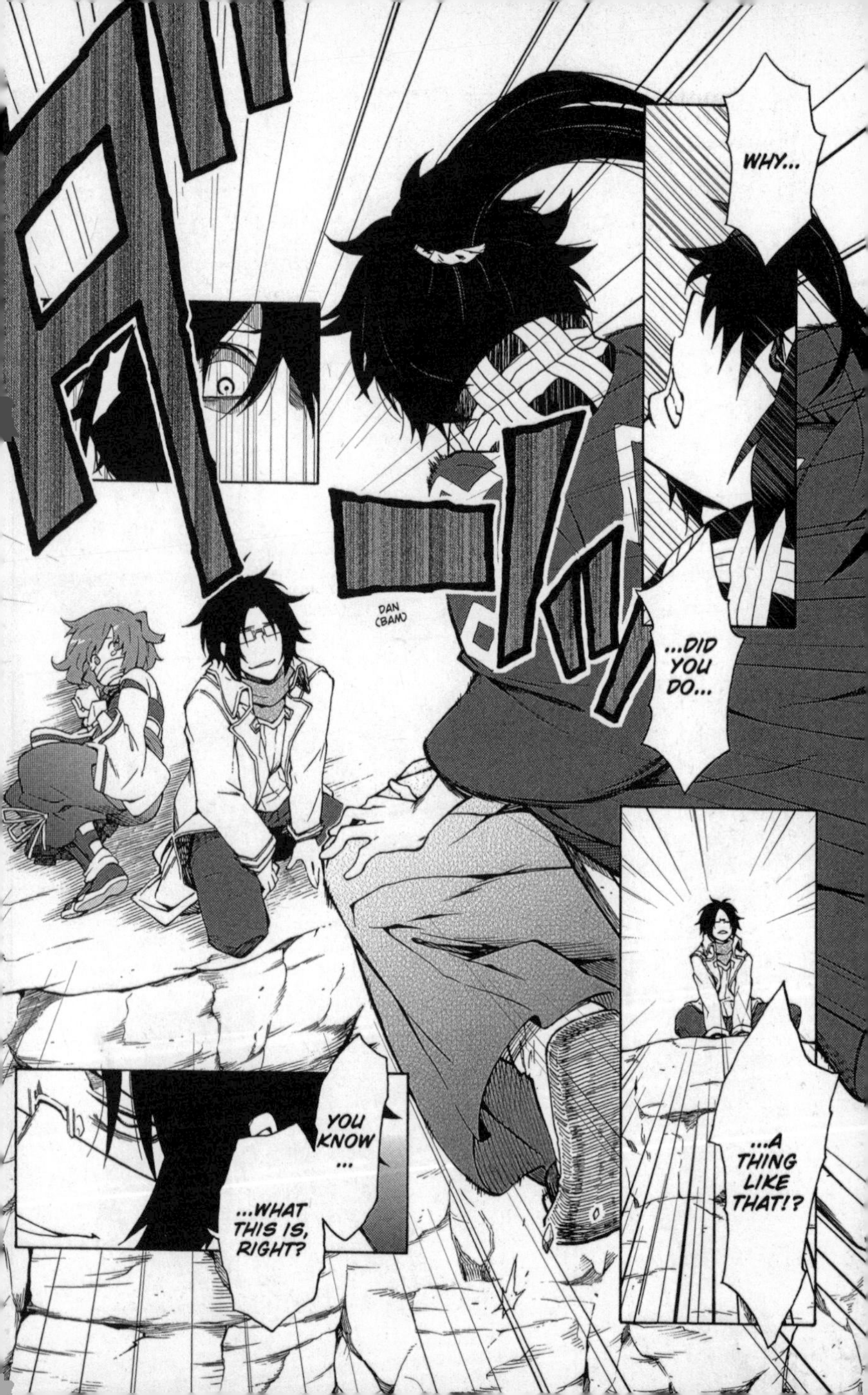
WHY...
...DID YOU DO...
DAN (BAM)
...A THING LIKE THAT!?
YOU KNOW...
...WHAT THIS IS, RIGHT?

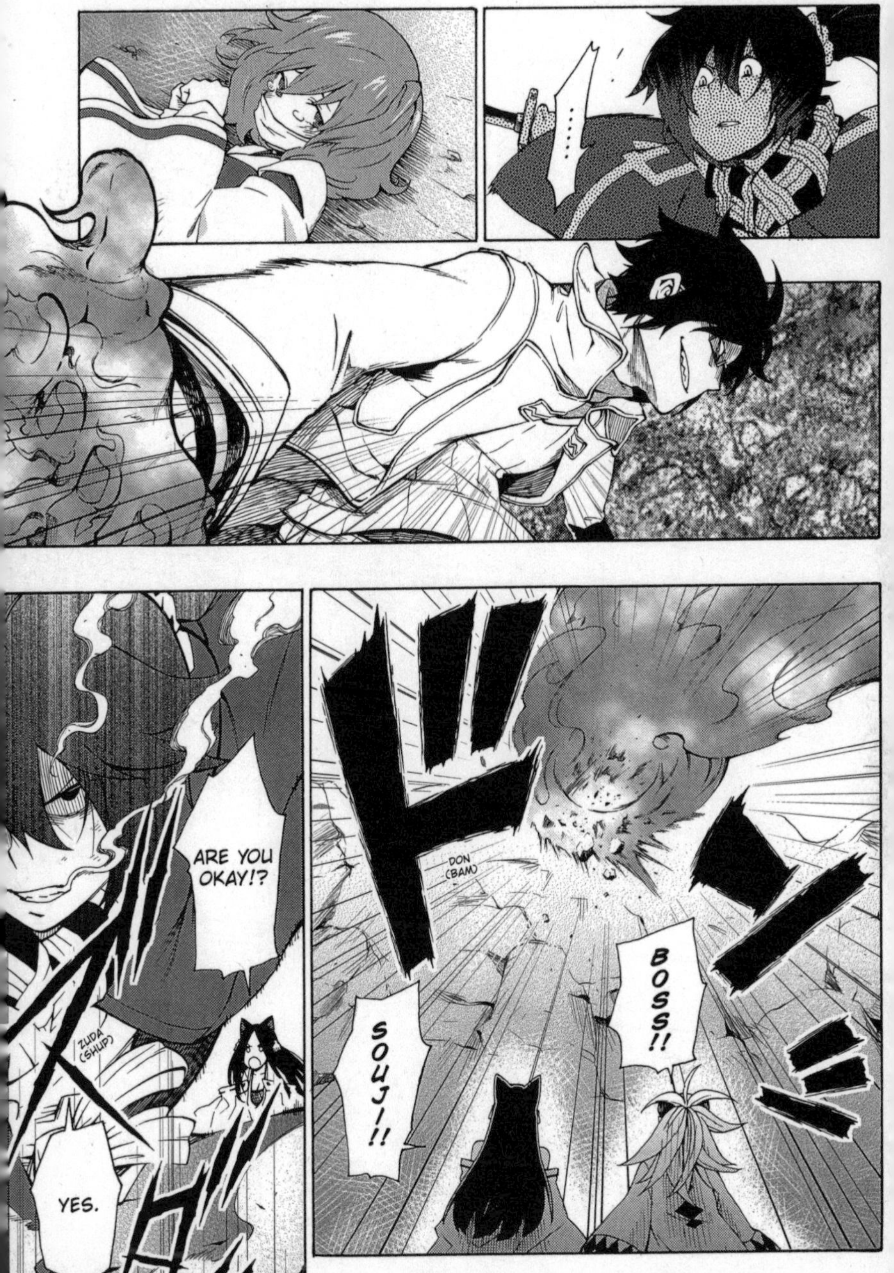
......
!
DON (BAM)
BOSS!!
SOUJI!!
ARE YOU OKAY!?
ZUDA (SHUP)
YES.

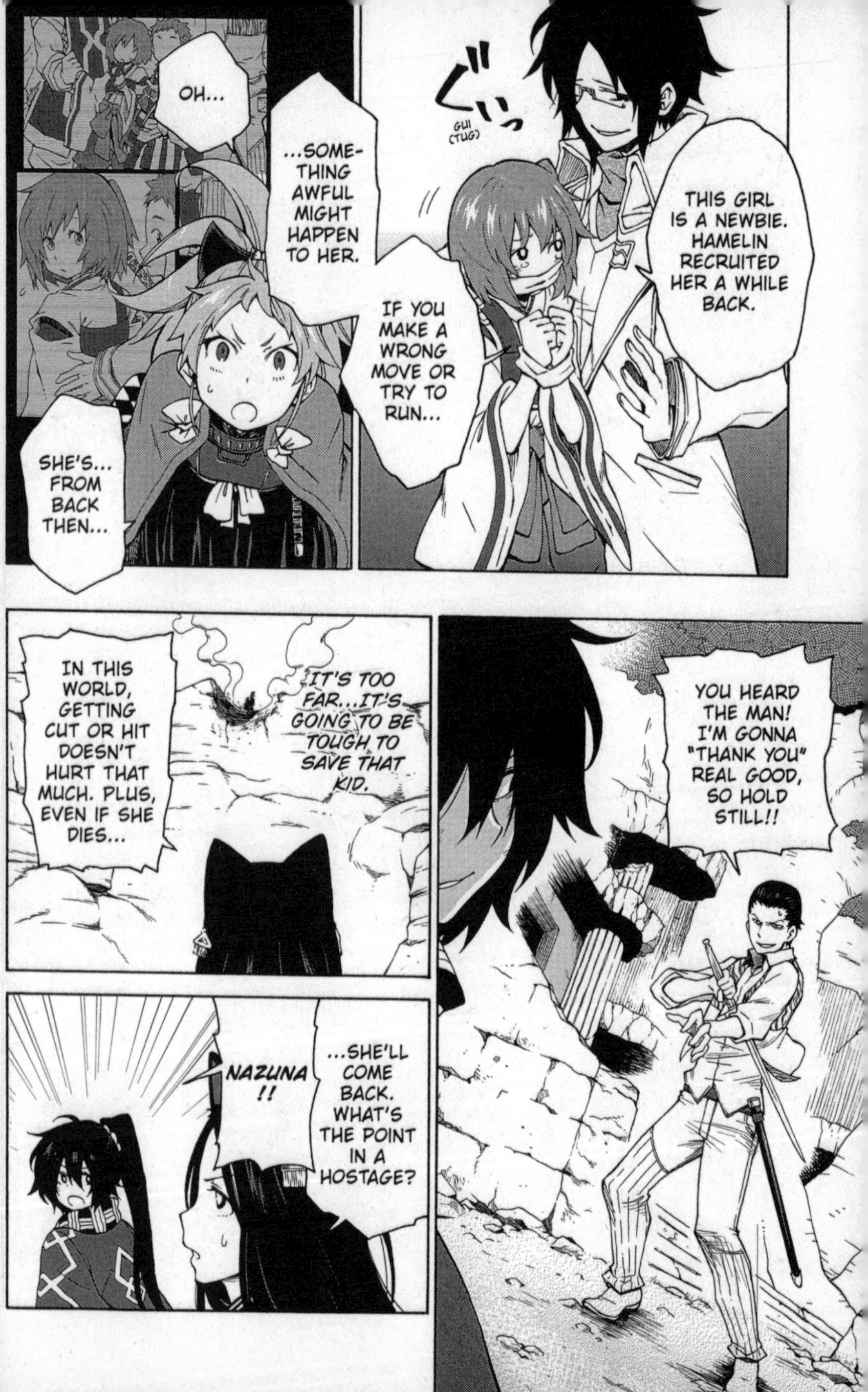
ぐいっ
GUI (TUG)
THIS GIRL IS A NEWBIE. HAMELIN RECRUITED HER A WHILE BACK.
IF YOU MAKE A WRONG MOVE OR TRY TO RUN...
...SOME-THING AWFUL MIGHT HAPPEN TO HER.
OH...
SHE'S... FROM BACK THEN...
YOU HEARD THE MAN! I'M GONNA "THANK YOU" REAL GOOD, SO HOLD STILL!!
IT'S TOO FAR...IT'S GOING TO BE TOUGH TO SAVE THAT KID.
IN THIS WORLD, GETTING CUT OR HIT DOESN'T HURT THAT MUCH. PLUS, EVEN IF SHE DIES...
...SHE'LL COME BACK. WHAT'S THE POINT IN A HOSTAGE?
NAZUNA!!

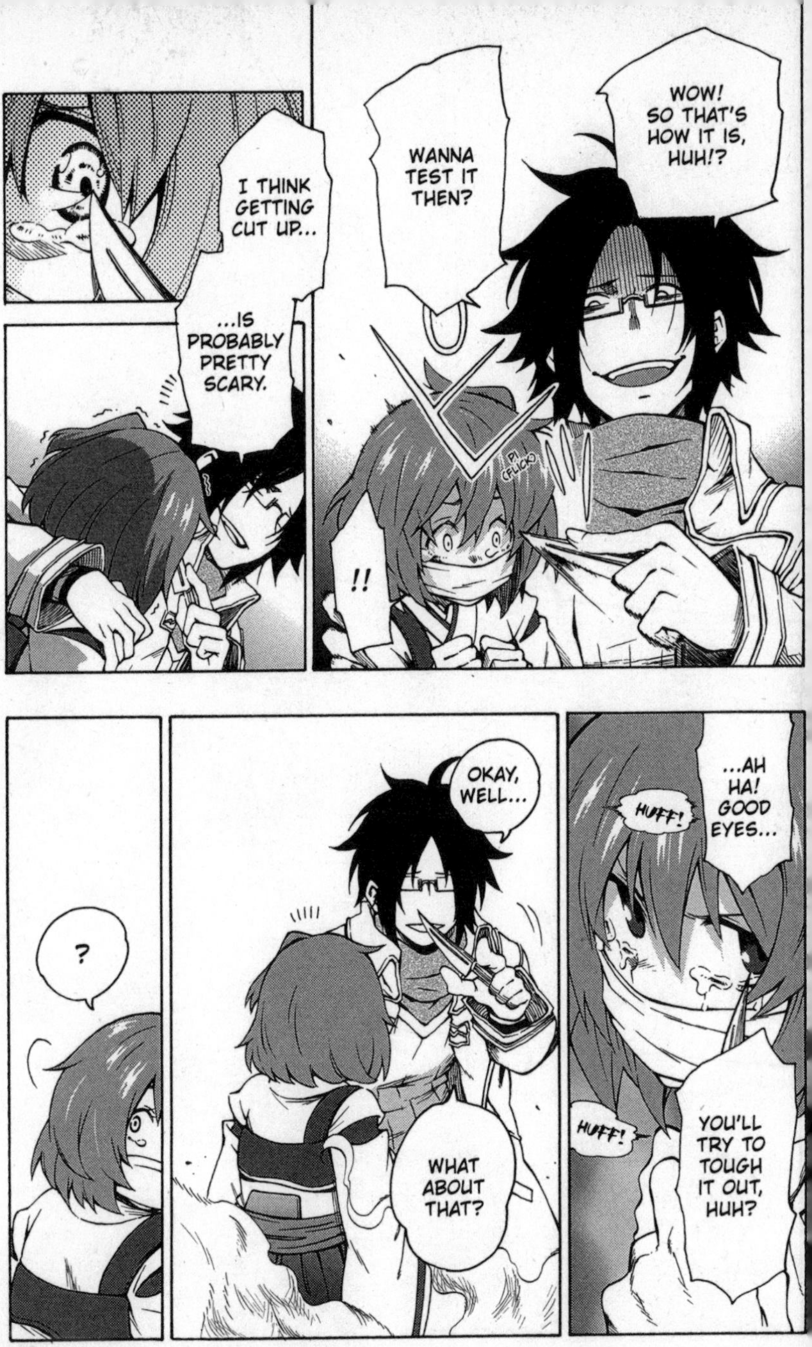
WOW! SO THAT'S HOW IT IS, HUH!?
WANNA TEST IT THEN?
PI (FLICK)
!!
I THINK GETTING CUT UP...
...IS PROBABLY PRETTY SCARY.
...AH HA! GOOD EYES...
HUFF!
HUFF!
YOU'LL TRY TO TOUGH IT OUT, HUH?
OKAY, WELL...
WHAT ABOUT THAT?
?

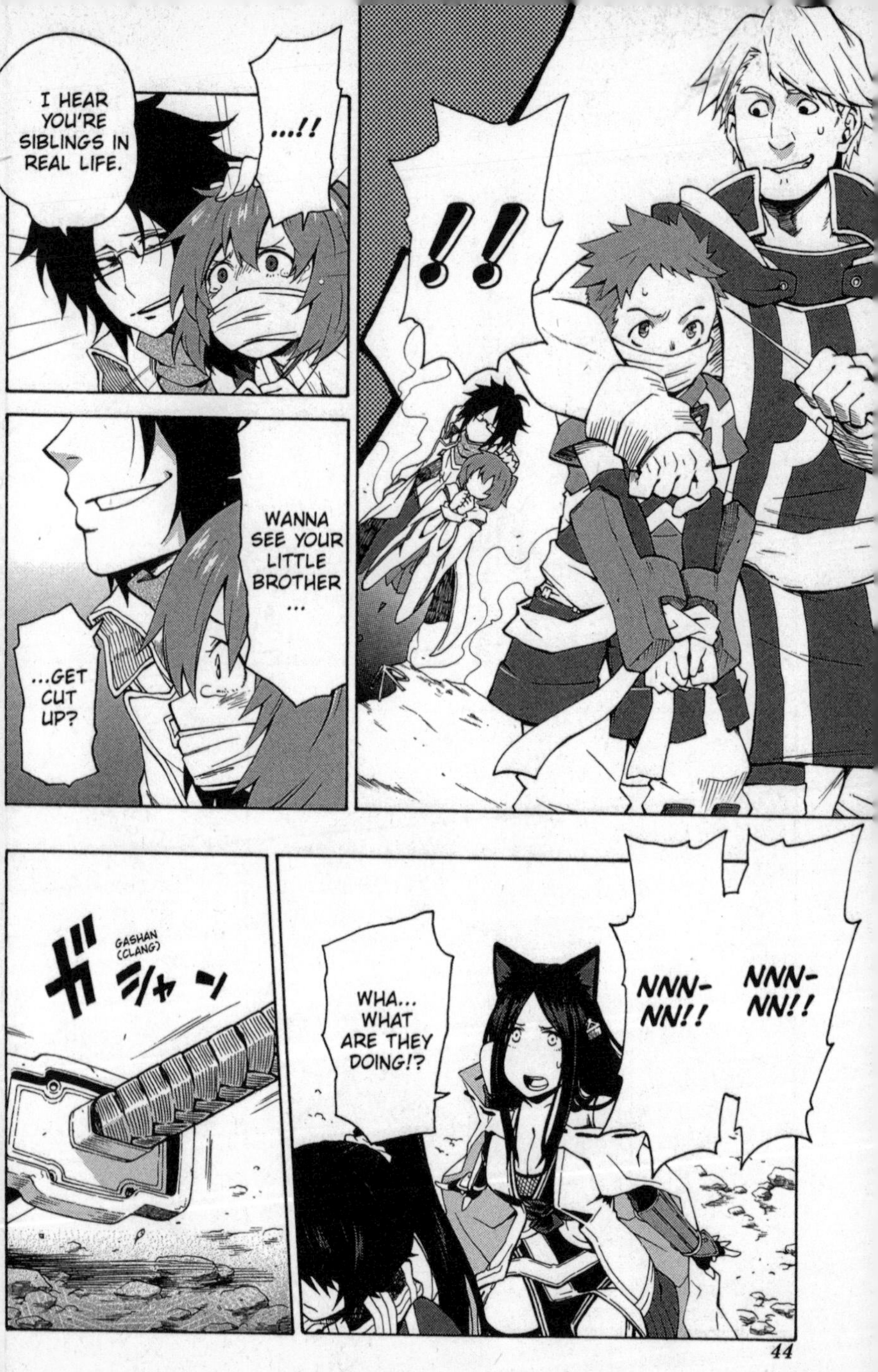
!!
...!!
I HEAR YOU'RE SIBLINGS IN REAL LIFE.
WANNA SEE YOUR LITTLE BROTHER ...
...GET CUT UP?
NNN-NN!!
NNN-NN!!
WHA... WHAT ARE THEY DOING!?
GASHAN (CLANG)

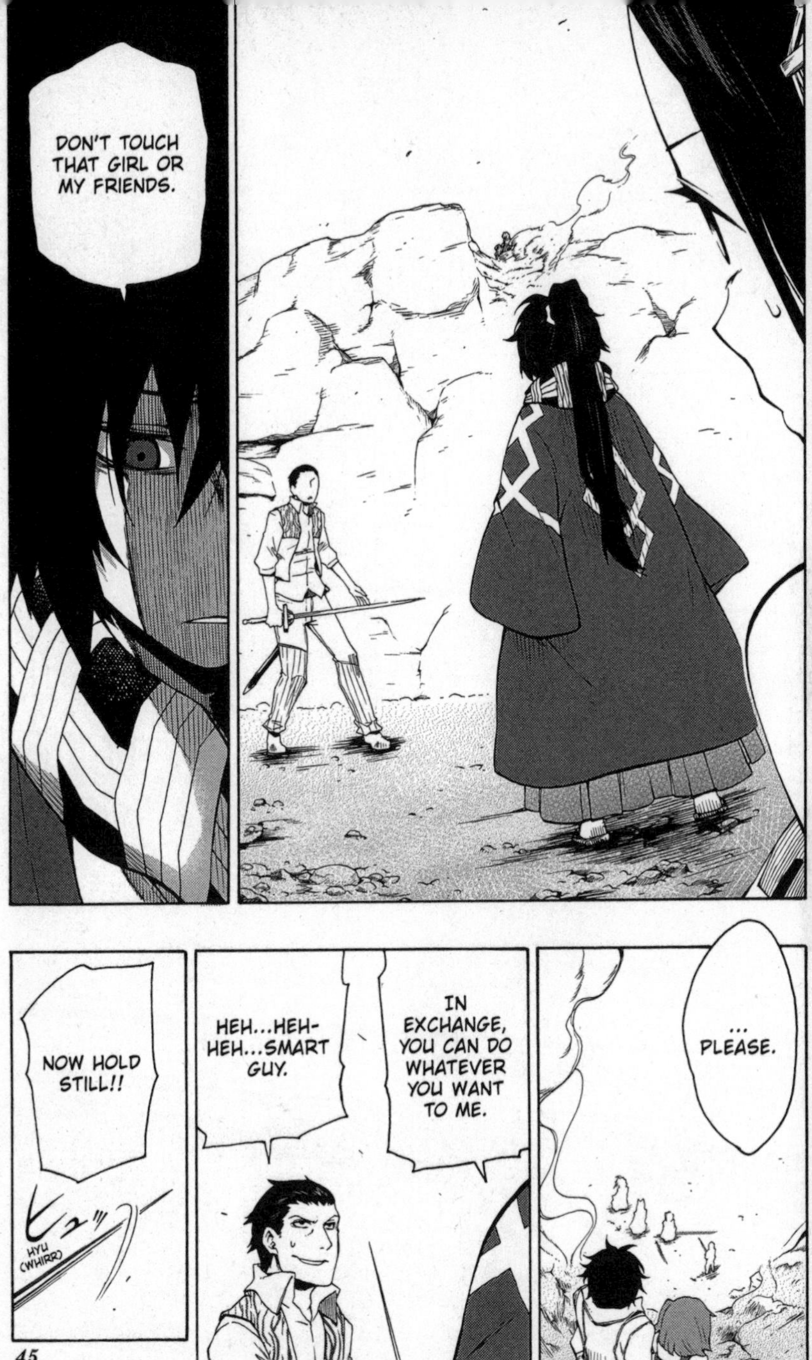
DON'T TOUCH THAT GIRL OR MY FRIENDS.
...PLEASE.
IN EXCHANGE, YOU CAN DO WHATEVER YOU WANT TO ME.
HEH...HEH-HEH...SMART GUY.
NOW HOLD STILL!!
HYU (WHIRR)

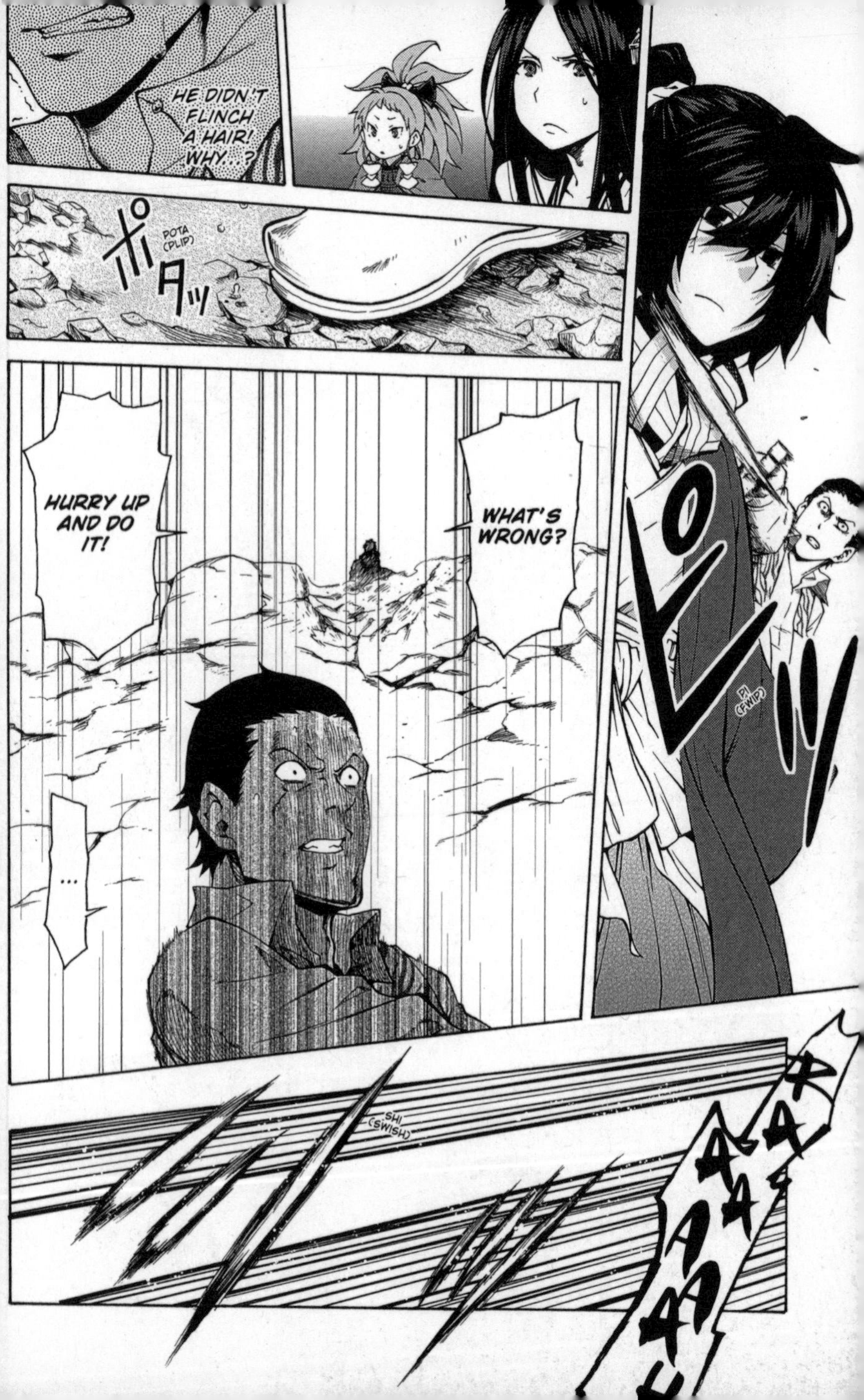
PI (FWIP)
HE DIDN'T FLINCH A HAIR! WHY...?
POTA (PLIP)
WHAT'S WRONG?
HURRY UP AND DO IT!
...
RAAAAAAA
SHI (SWISH)

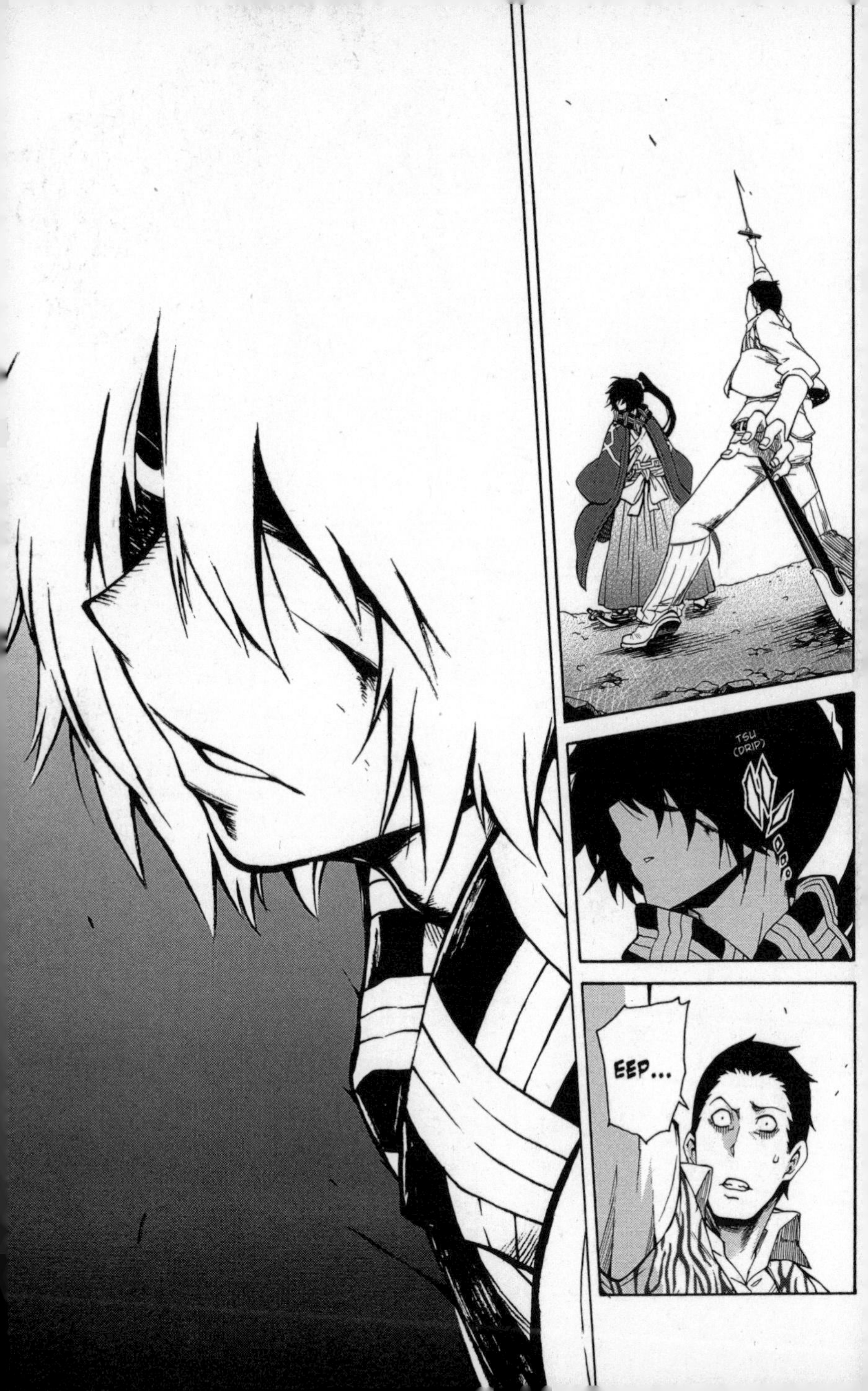
TSU
(DRIP)
EEP...

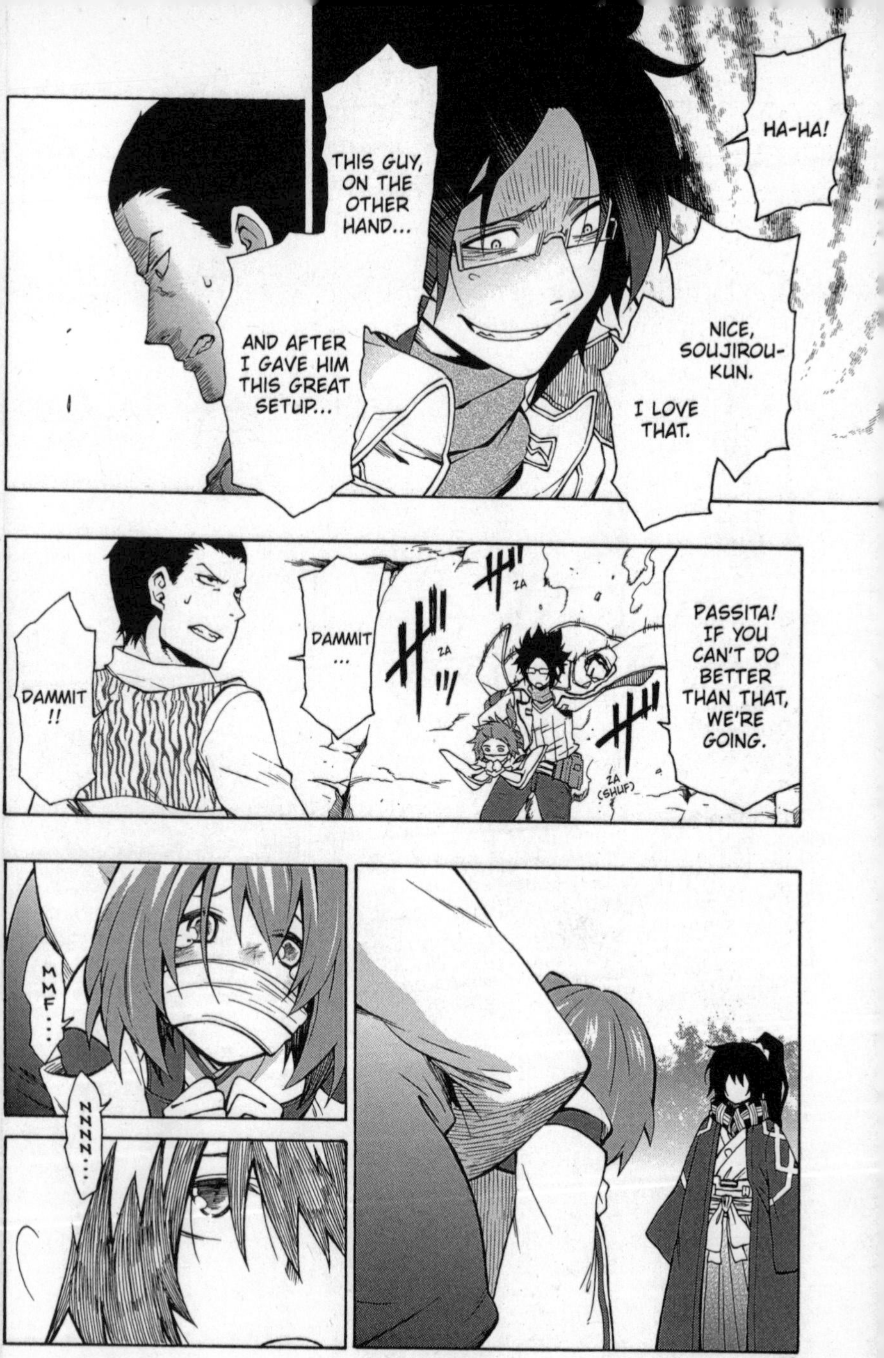
HA-HA!
NICE, SOUJIROU-KUN.
I LOVE THAT.
THIS GUY, ON THE OTHER HAND...
AND AFTER I GAVE HIM THIS GREAT SETUP...
PASSITA! IF YOU CAN'T DO BETTER THAN THAT, WE'RE GOING.
ZA
ZA (SHUF)
ZA
DAMMIT ...
DAMMIT !!
MMF...
NNNN...

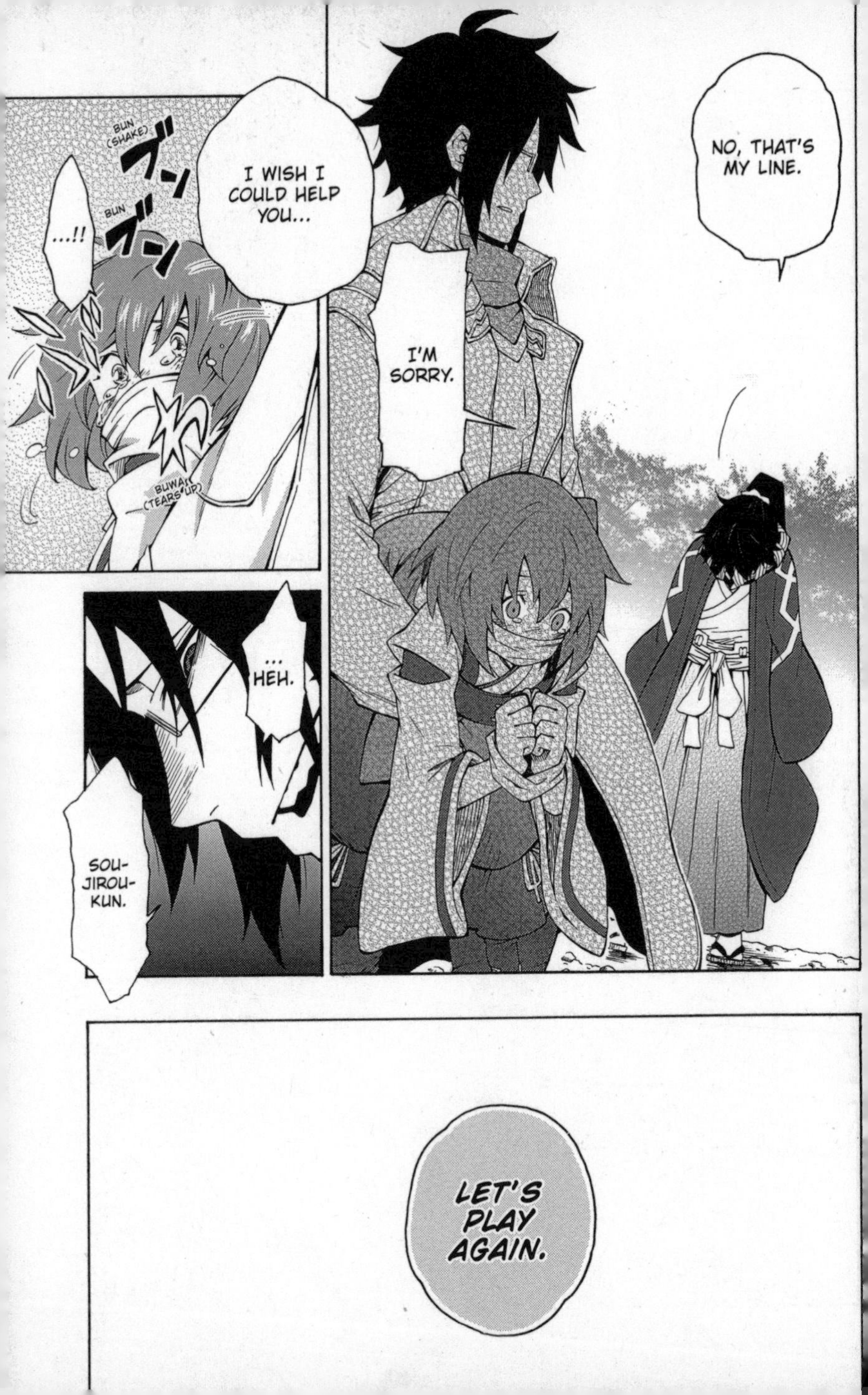
NO, THAT'S MY LINE.
I'M SORRY.
I WISH I COULD HELP YOU...
BUN (SHAKE)
ブン
BUN
ブン
...!!
BUWA (TEARS UP)
... HEH.
SOU-JIROU-KUN.
LET'S PLAY AGAIN.

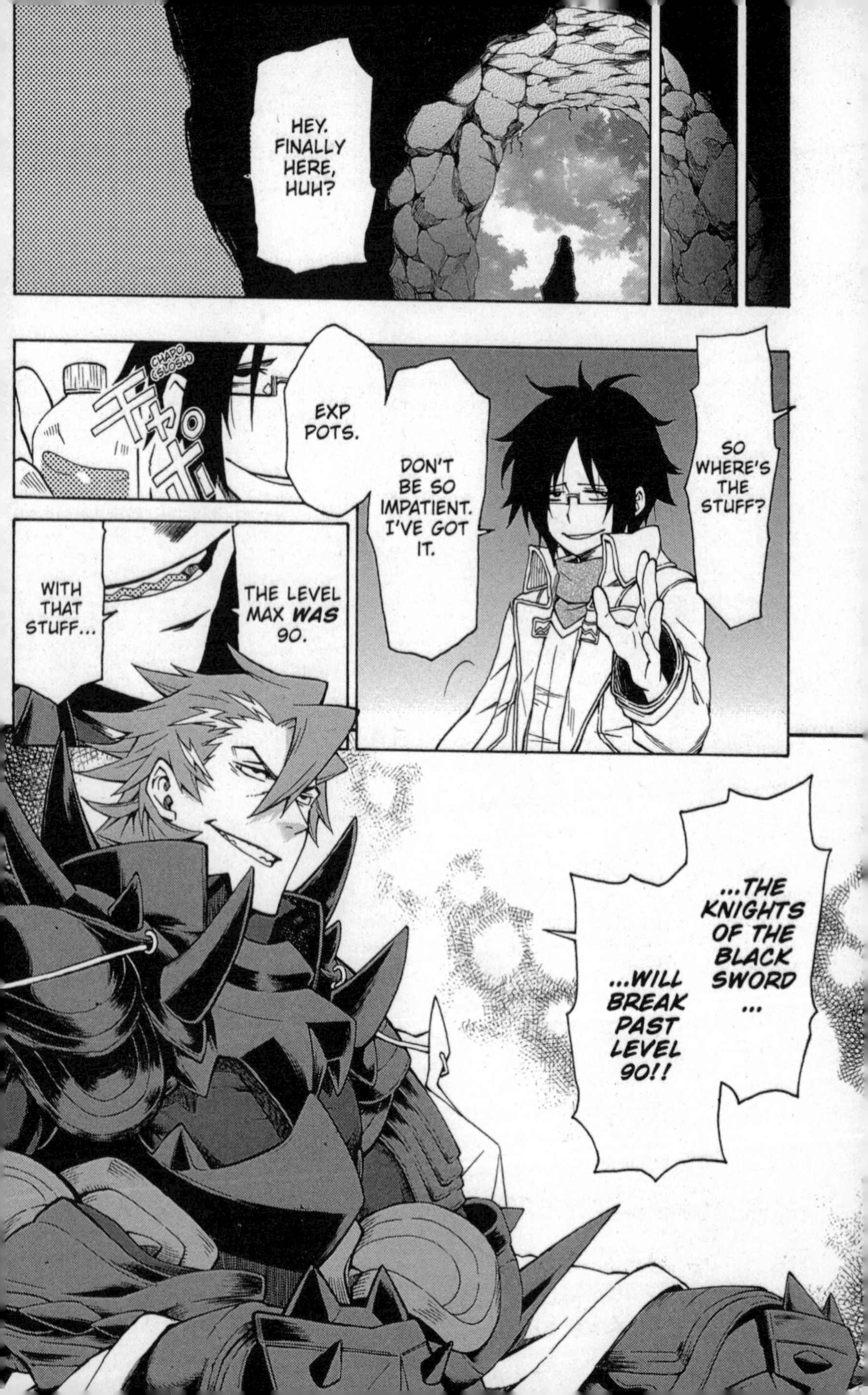
HEY. FINALLY HERE, HUH?
SO WHERE'S THE STUFF?
DON'T BE SO IMPATIENT. I'VE GOT IT.
CHAPO (SLOSH)
EXP POTS.
THE LEVEL MAX **WAS** 90.
WITH THAT STUFF...
...THE KNIGHTS OF THE BLACK SWORD ...
...WILL BREAK PAST LEVEL 90!!

LOG HORIZON

THE WEST WIND BRIGADE

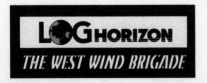

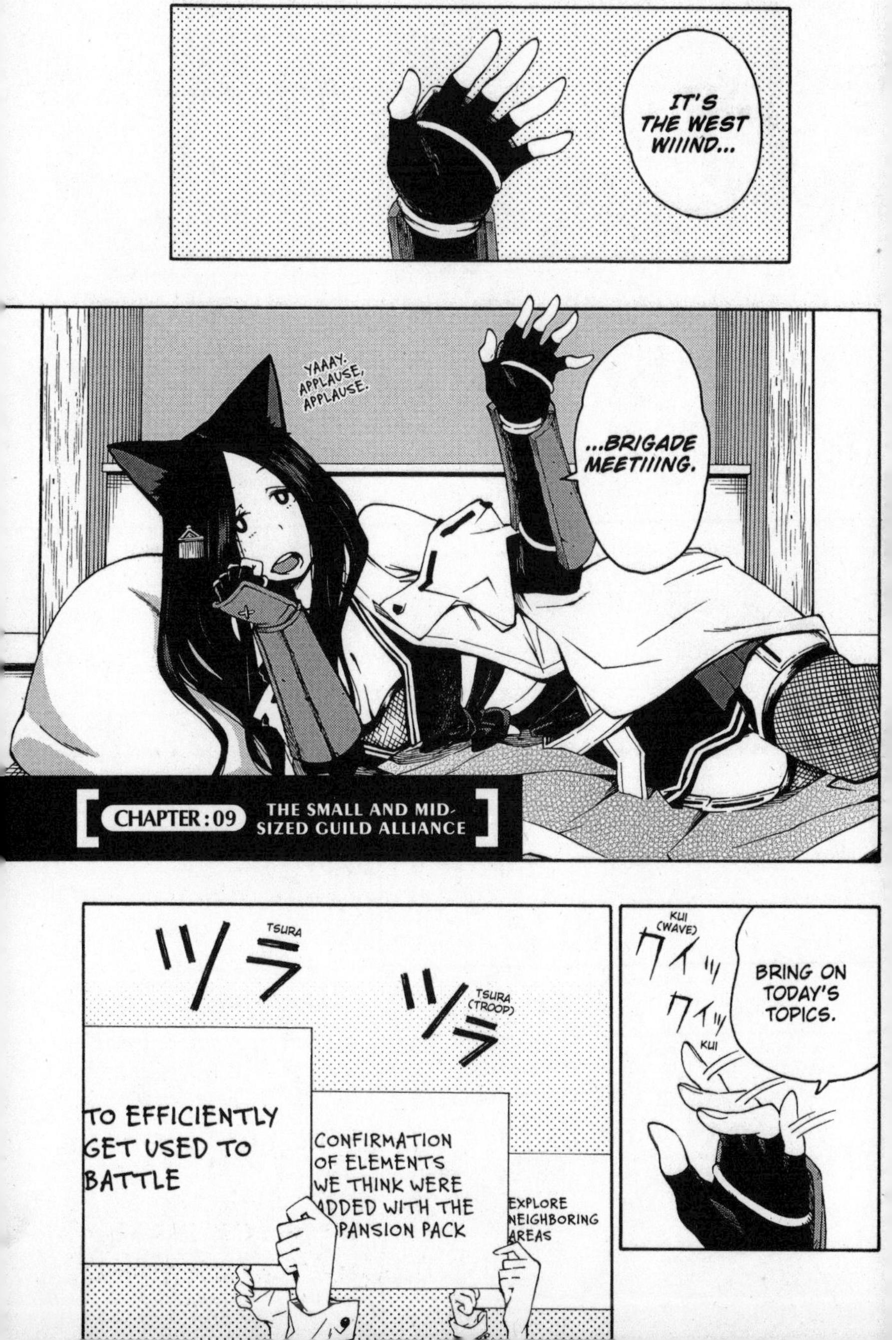
IT'S THE WEST WIIIND...
...BRIGADE MEETIIING.
YAAAY. APPLAUSE, APPLAUSE.
CHAPTER : 09
THE SMALL AND MID-SIZED GUILD ALLIANCE
クイッ KUI (WAVE)
クイッ KUI
BRING ON TODAY'S TOPICS.
ツラ TSURA
ツラ TSURA (TROOP)
EXPLORE NEIGHBORING AREAS
CONFIRMATION OF ELEMENTS WE THINK WERE DDED WITH THE PANSION PACK
TO EFFICIENTLY GET USED TO BATTLE

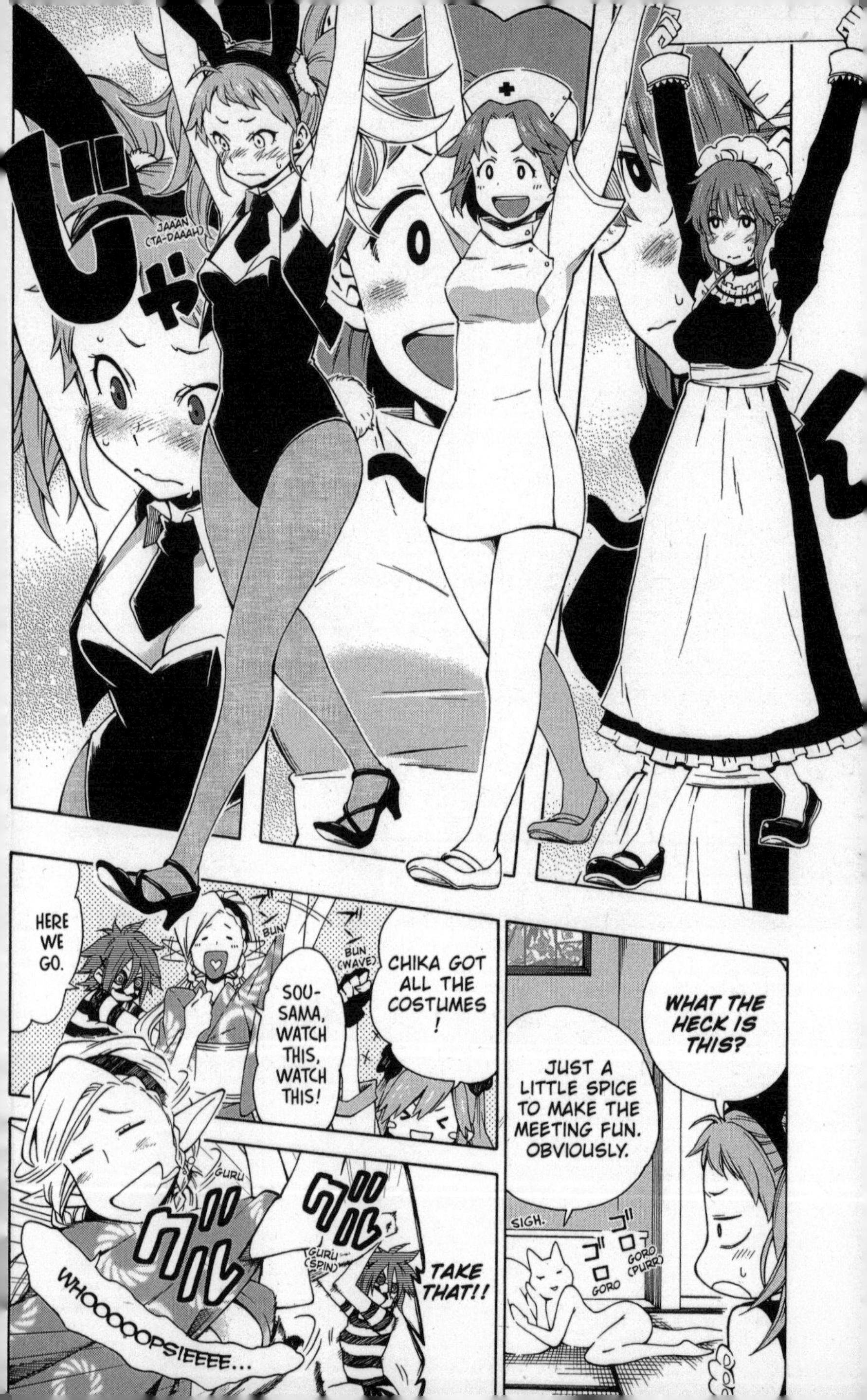
JAAAN (TA-DAAAH)
WHAT THE HECK IS THIS?
JUST A LITTLE SPICE TO MAKE THE MEETING FUN. OBVIOUSLY.
SIGH.
GORO (PURR)
GORO
CHIKA GOT ALL THE COSTUMES!
BUN (WAVE)
SOU-SAMA, WATCH THIS, WATCH THIS!
BUN
HERE WE GO.
TAKE THAT!!
GURU (SPIN)
GURU
WHOOOOOOPSIEEEE...

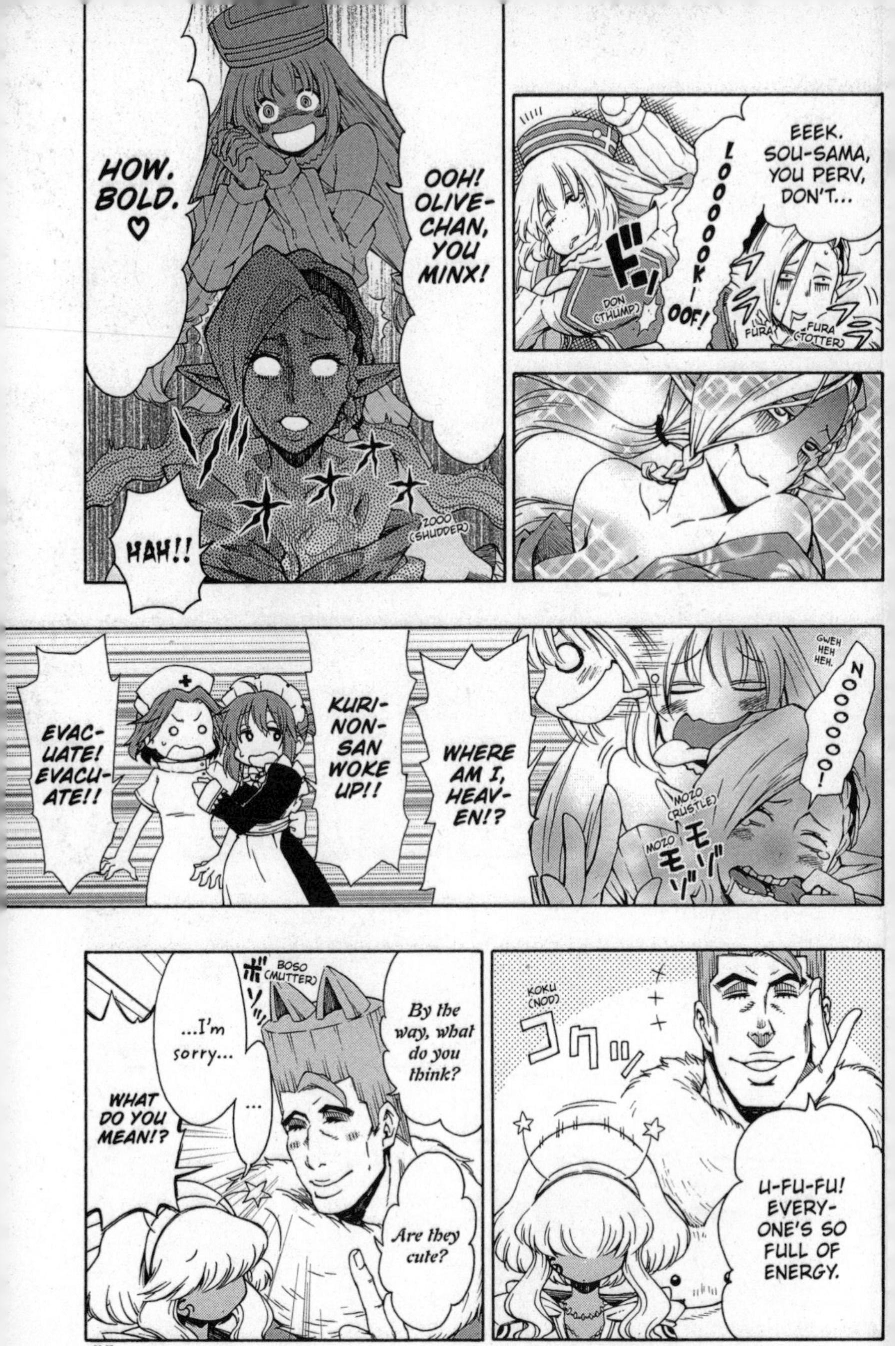
EEEK. SOU-SAMA, YOU PERV, DON'T...
LOOOOOOK!
DON (THUMP)
OOF!
FURA
FURA (TOTTER)
OOH! OLIVE-CHAN, YOU MINX!
HOW. BOLD. ♡
ZOOO (SHUDDER)
HAH!!
GWEH HEH HEH.
NOOOOOOO!
MOZO (RUSTLE)
MOZO
WHERE AM I, HEAVEN!?
KURI-NON-SAN WOKE UP!!
EVACUATE! EVACUATE!!
KOKU (NOD)
U-FU-FU! EVERYONE'S SO FULL OF ENERGY.
By the way, what do you think?
Are they cute?
BOSO (MUTTER)
...I'm sorry...
...
WHAT DO YOU MEAN!?

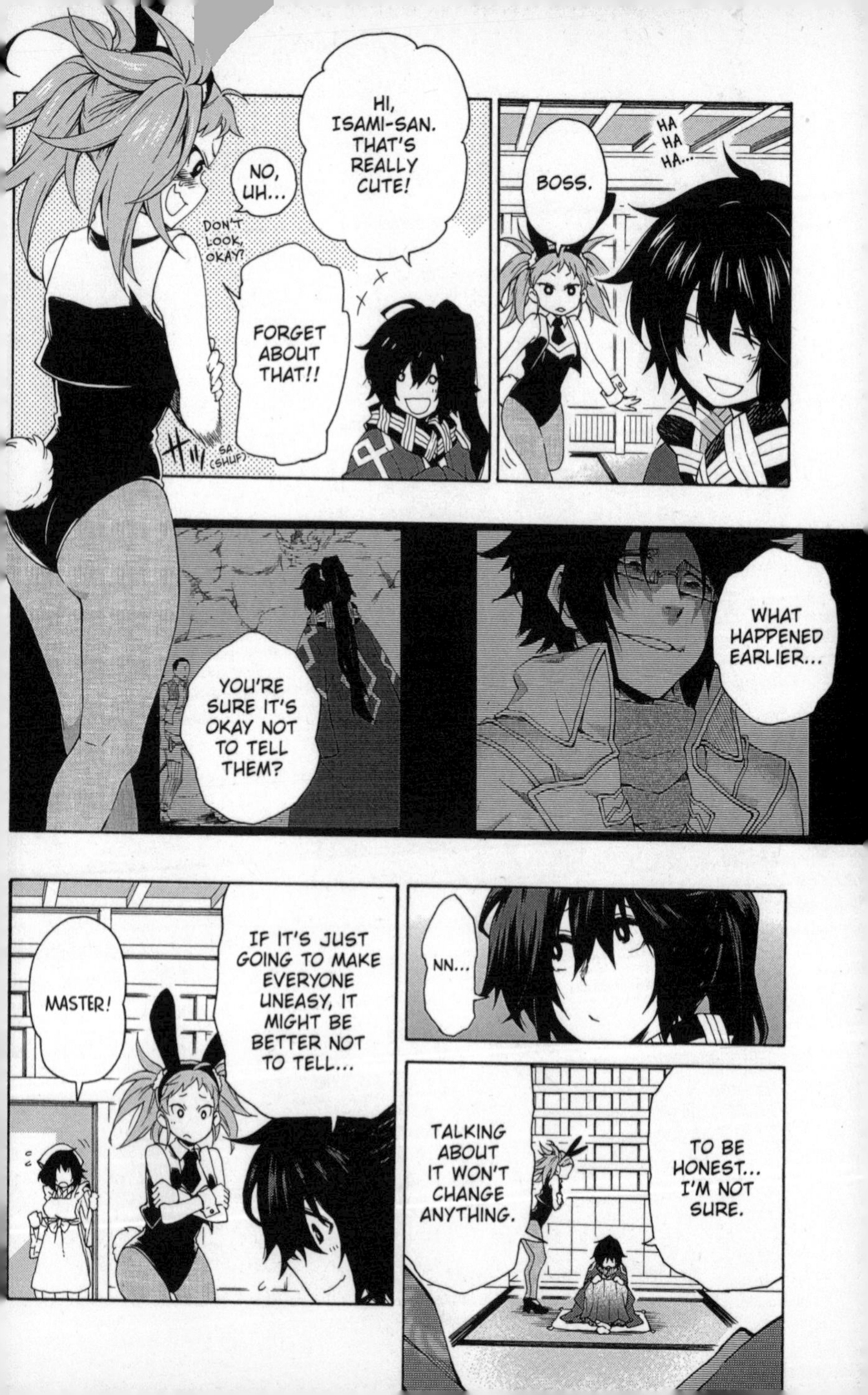
HA HA HA...
BOSS.
HI, ISAMI-SAN. THAT'S REALLY CUTE!
NO, UH...
DON'T LOOK, OKAY?
FORGET ABOUT THAT!!
SA (SHUF)
WHAT HAPPENED EARLIER...
YOU'RE SURE IT'S OKAY NOT TO TELL THEM?
NN...
TO BE HONEST... I'M NOT SURE.
TALKING ABOUT IT WON'T CHANGE ANYTHING.
IF IT'S JUST GOING TO MAKE EVERYONE UNEASY, IT MIGHT BE BETTER NOT TO TELL...
MASTER!

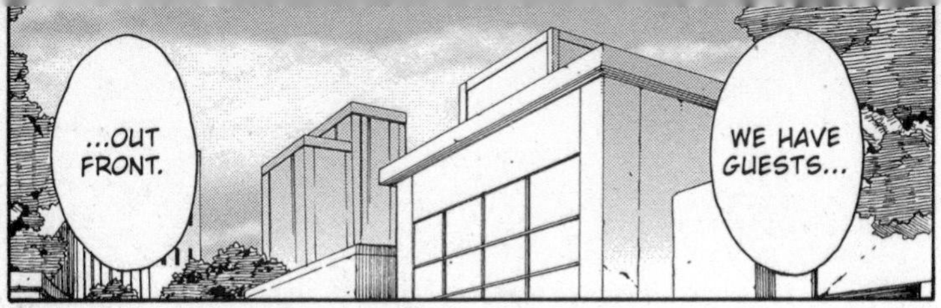
WE HAVE GUESTS...
...OUT FRONT.

**CHAPTER: 09** **THE SMALL AND MID-SIZED GUILD ALLIANCE**

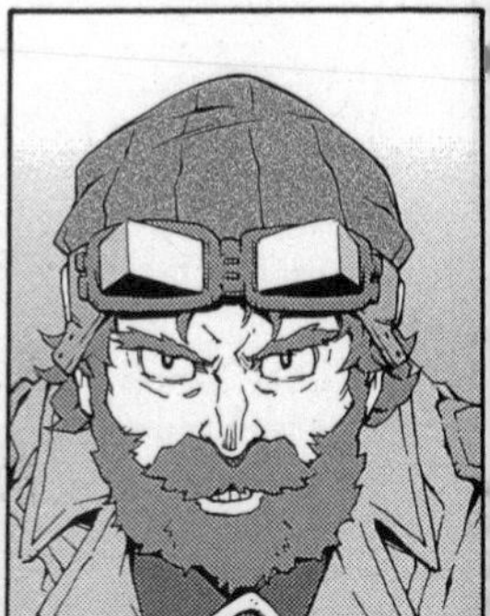
GUILD
<GRANDALE>
WOODSTOCK W.
FORMER MEMBER OF THE KNIGHTS OF THE BLACK SWORD

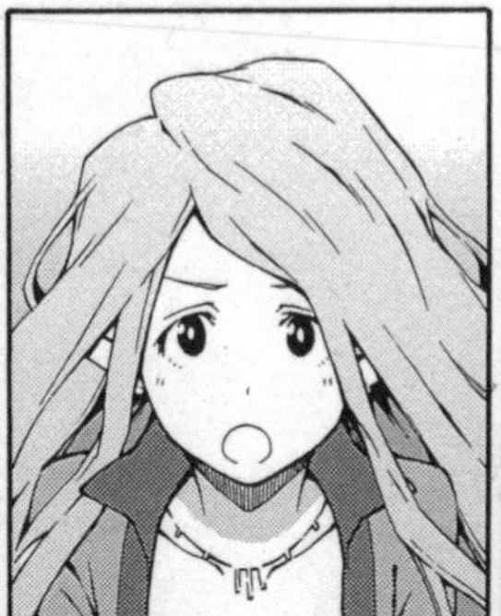
GUILD
<CRESCENT MOON LEAGUE>
MARIELLE
AKIBA'S GENEROUS "SUNFLOWER"

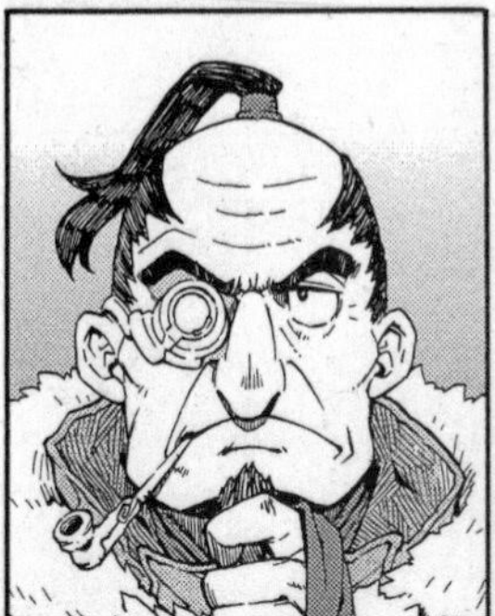
GUILD
<RADIO MARKET>
AKANEYA ICHIMONJINOSUKE
A VETERAN WHO'S BEEN AROUND LONGER THAN SHIROE

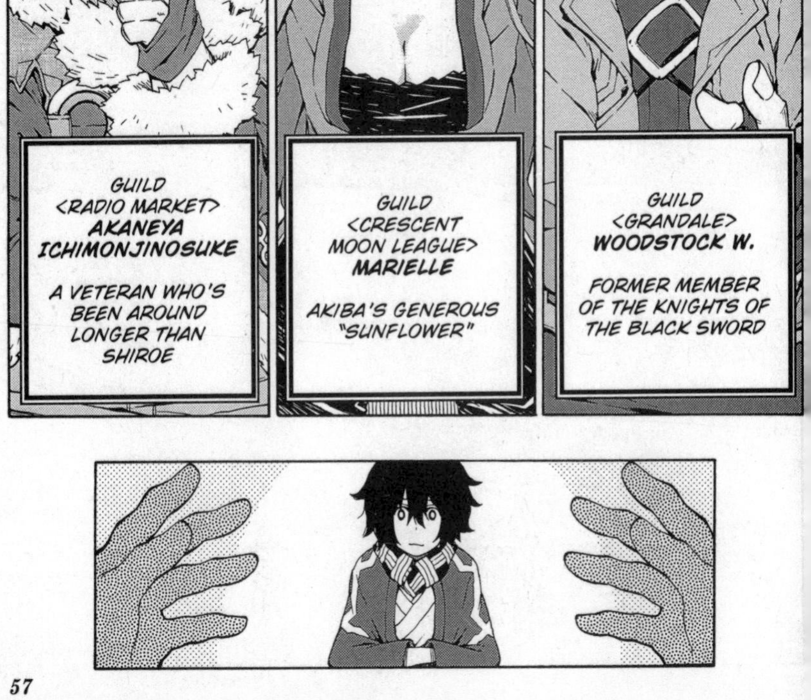

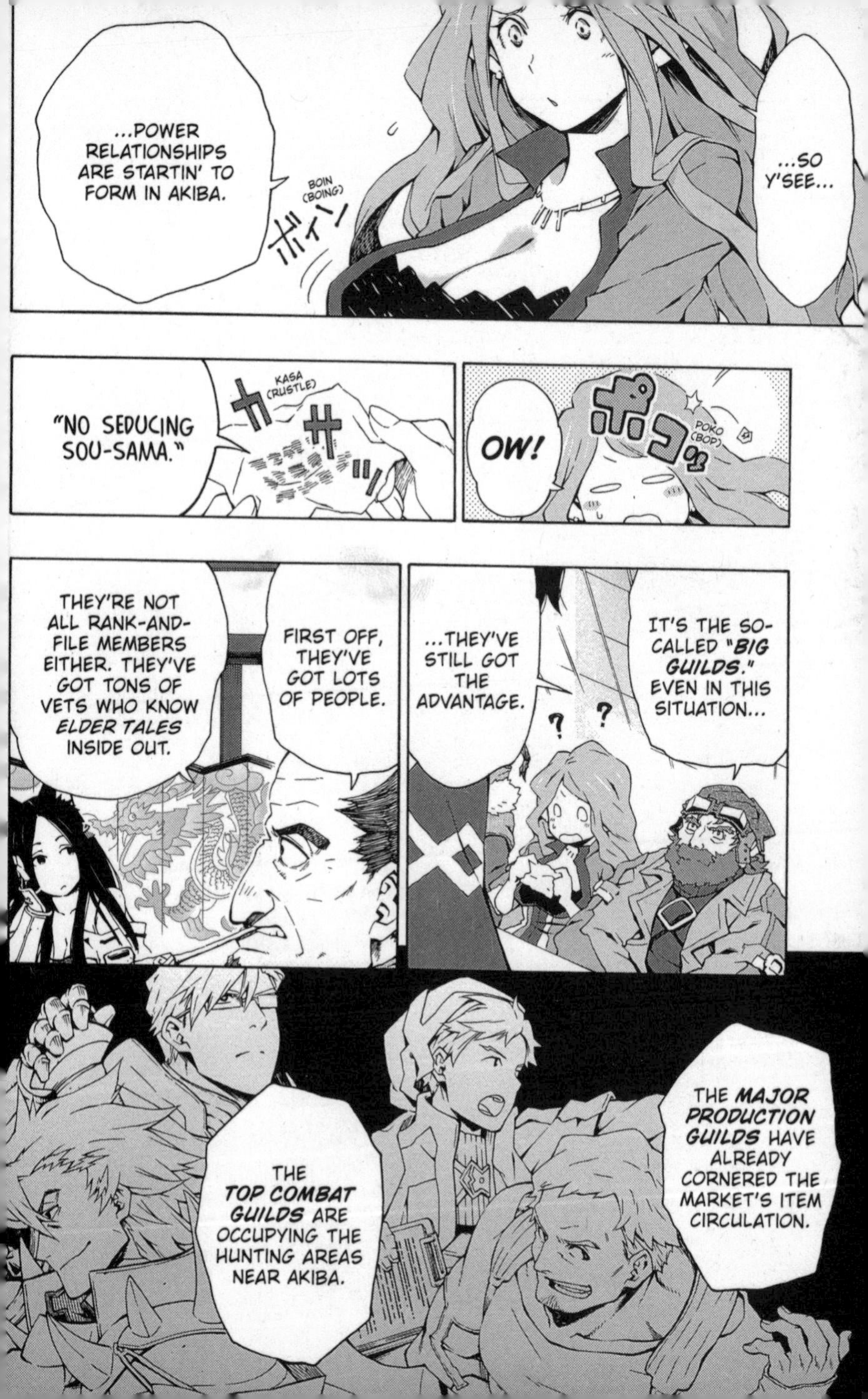
...SO Y'SEE...
...POWER RELATIONSHIPS ARE STARTIN' TO FORM IN AKIBA.
BOIN (BOING)
POKO (BOP)
OW!
KASA (RUSTLE)
"NO SEDUCING SOU-SAMA."
IT'S THE SO-CALLED "BIG GUILDS." EVEN IN THIS SITUATION...
...THEY'VE STILL GOT THE ADVANTAGE.
? ?
FIRST OFF, THEY'VE GOT LOTS OF PEOPLE.
THEY'RE NOT ALL RANK-AND-FILE MEMBERS EITHER. THEY'VE GOT TONS OF VETS WHO KNOW *ELDER TALES* INSIDE OUT.
THE ***MAJOR PRODUCTION GUILDS*** HAVE ALREADY CORNERED THE MARKET'S ITEM CIRCULATION.
THE ***TOP COMBAT GUILDS*** ARE OCCUPYING THE HUNTING AREAS NEAR AKIBA.

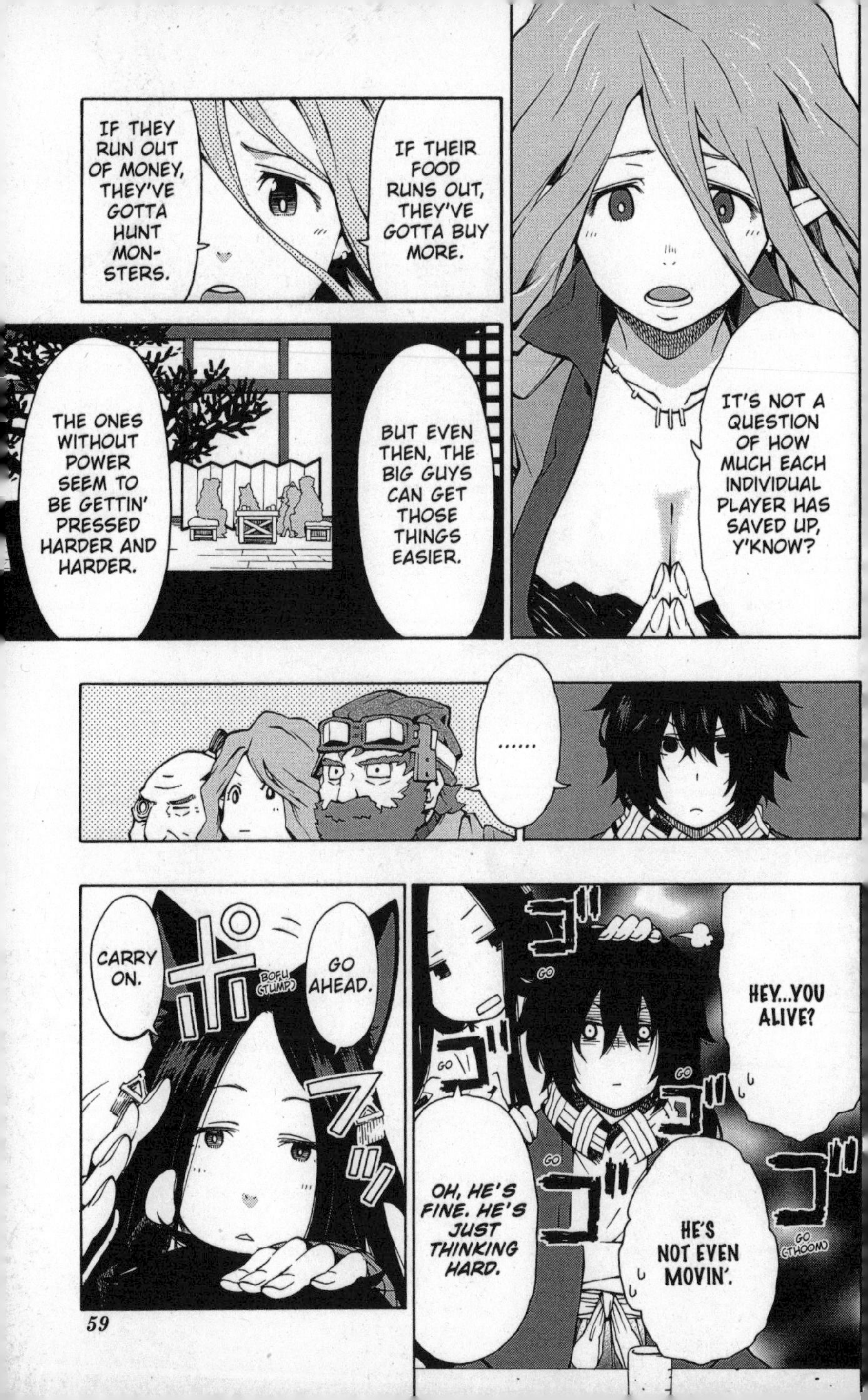
IT'S NOT A QUESTION OF HOW MUCH EACH INDIVIDUAL PLAYER HAS SAVED UP, Y'KNOW?
IF THEIR FOOD RUNS OUT, THEY'VE GOTTA BUY MORE.
IF THEY RUN OUT OF MONEY, THEY'VE GOTTA HUNT MON-STERS.
BUT EVEN THEN, THE BIG GUYS CAN GET THOSE THINGS EASIER.
THE ONES WITHOUT POWER SEEM TO BE GETTIN' PRESSED HARDER AND HARDER.
......
HEY...YOU ALIVE?
GO
GO
HE'S NOT EVEN MOVIN'.
GO (THOOM)
GO
OH, HE'S FINE. HE'S JUST THINKING HARD.
GO
GO AHEAD.
BOFU (STUMP)
CARRY ON.

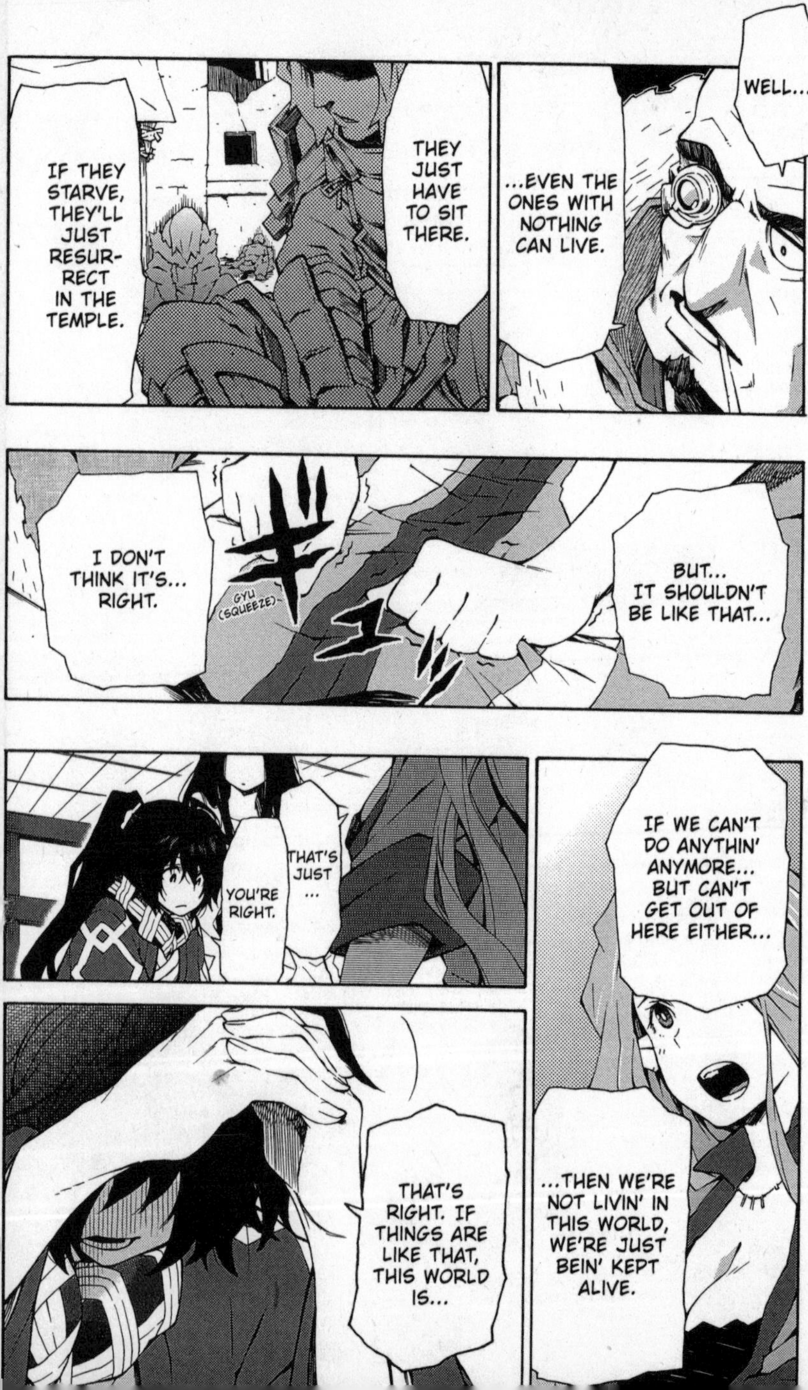
WELL...
...EVEN THE ONES WITH NOTHING CAN LIVE.
THEY JUST HAVE TO SIT THERE.
IF THEY STARVE, THEY'LL JUST RESURRECT IN THE TEMPLE.
BUT... IT SHOULDN'T BE LIKE THAT...
GYU (SQUEEZE)
I DON'T THINK IT'S... RIGHT.
IF WE CAN'T DO ANYTHIN' ANYMORE... BUT CAN'T GET OUT OF HERE EITHER...
...THEN WE'RE NOT LIVIN' IN THIS WORLD, WE'RE JUST BEIN' KEPT ALIVE.
THAT'S JUST ...
YOU'RE RIGHT.
THAT'S RIGHT. IF THINGS ARE LIKE THAT, THIS WORLD IS...

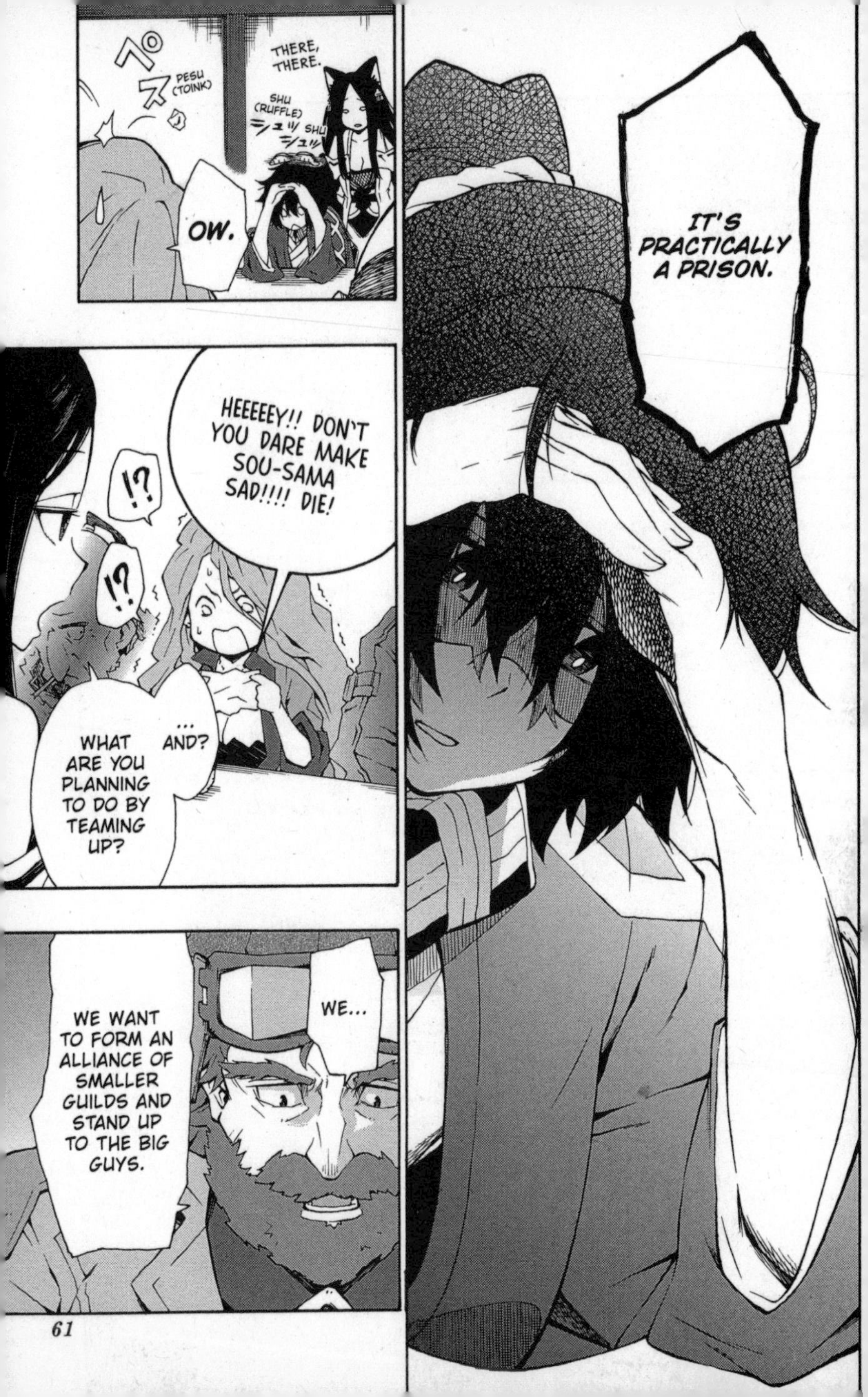
IT'S PRACTICALLY A PRISON.
THERE, THERE.
SHU (RUFFLE)
シュッ SHU シュッ
ペス
PESU (TOINK)
OW.
HEEEEEY!! DON'T YOU DARE MAKE SOU-SAMA SAD!!!! DIE!
!?
!?
... AND?
WHAT ARE YOU PLANNING TO DO BY TEAMING UP?
WE...
WE WANT TO FORM AN ALLIANCE OF SMALLER GUILDS AND STAND UP TO THE BIG GUYS.

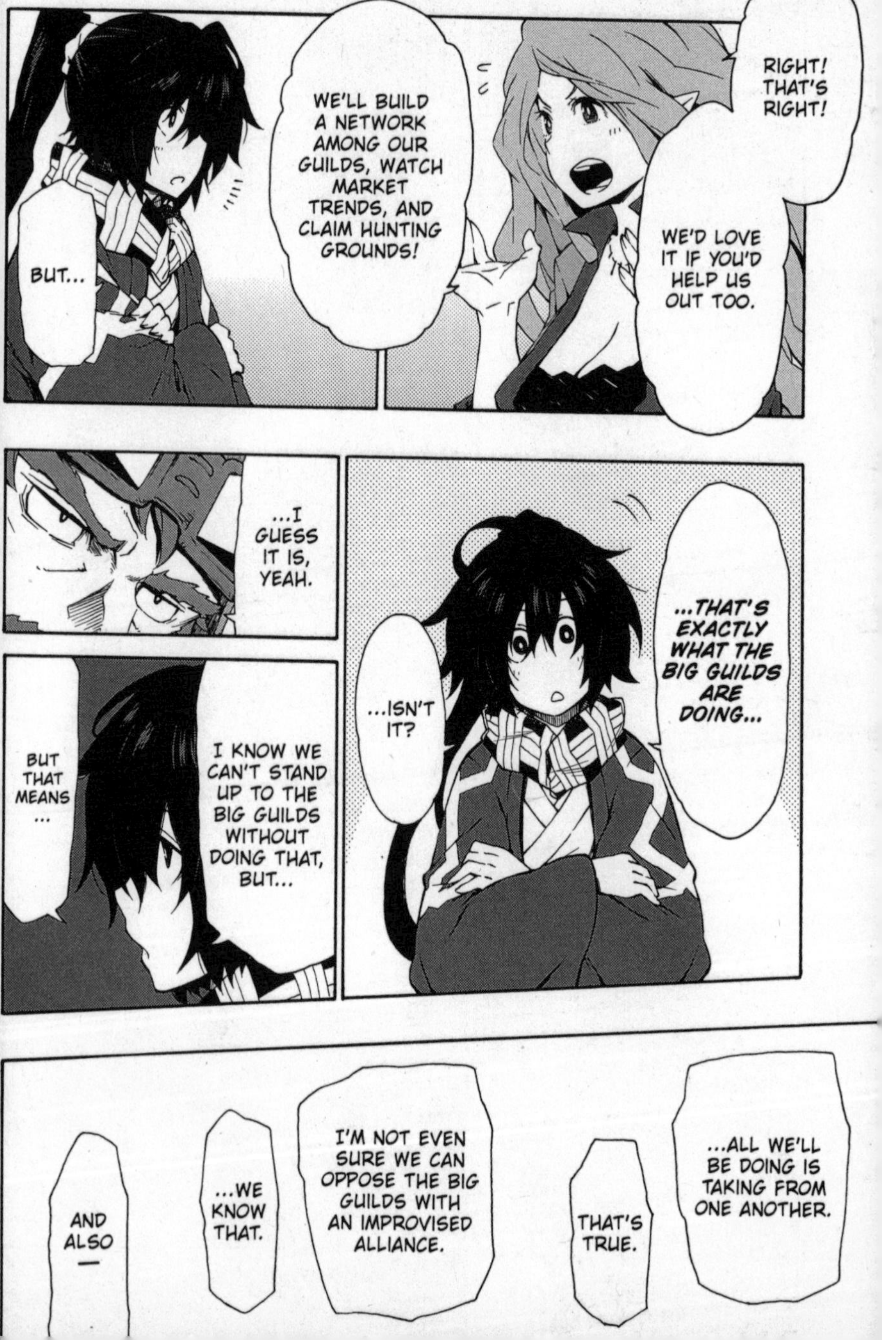
RIGHT! THAT'S RIGHT!
WE'LL BUILD A NETWORK AMONG OUR GUILDS, WATCH MARKET TRENDS, AND CLAIM HUNTING GROUNDS!
WE'D LOVE IT IF YOU'D HELP US OUT TOO.
BUT...
...THAT'S EXACTLY WHAT THE BIG GUILDS ARE DOING...
...ISN'T IT?
...I GUESS IT IS, YEAH.
I KNOW WE CAN'T STAND UP TO THE BIG GUILDS WITHOUT DOING THAT, BUT...
BUT THAT MEANS...
...ALL WE'LL BE DOING IS TAKING FROM ONE ANOTHER.
THAT'S TRUE.
I'M NOT EVEN SURE WE CAN OPPOSE THE BIG GUILDS WITH AN IMPROVISED ALLIANCE.
...WE KNOW THAT.
AND ALSO —

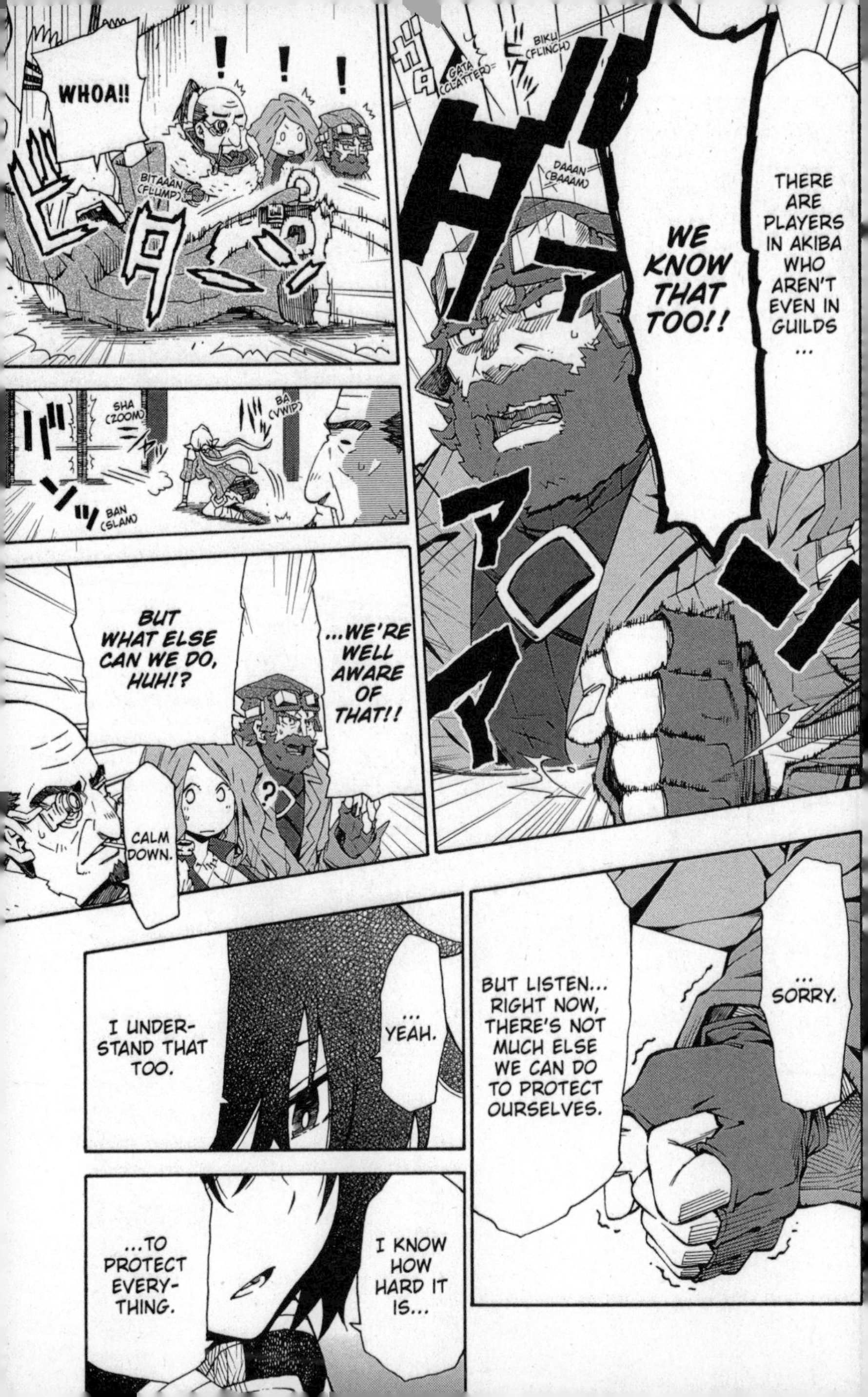
THERE ARE PLAYERS IN AKIBA WHO AREN'T EVEN IN GUILDS ...
BIKU (FLINCH)
GATA (CLATTER)
WE KNOW THAT TOO!!
DAAAN (BAAAM)
WHOA!!
BITAAAN (FLUMP)
BA (VWIP)
SHA (ZOOM)
BAN (SLAM)
...WE'RE WELL AWARE OF THAT!!
BUT WHAT ELSE CAN WE DO, HUH!?
CALM DOWN.
... SORRY.
BUT LISTEN... RIGHT NOW, THERE'S NOT MUCH ELSE WE CAN DO TO PROTECT OURSELVES.
... YEAH.
I UNDER-STAND THAT TOO.
I KNOW HOW HARD IT IS...
...TO PROTECT EVERY-THING.

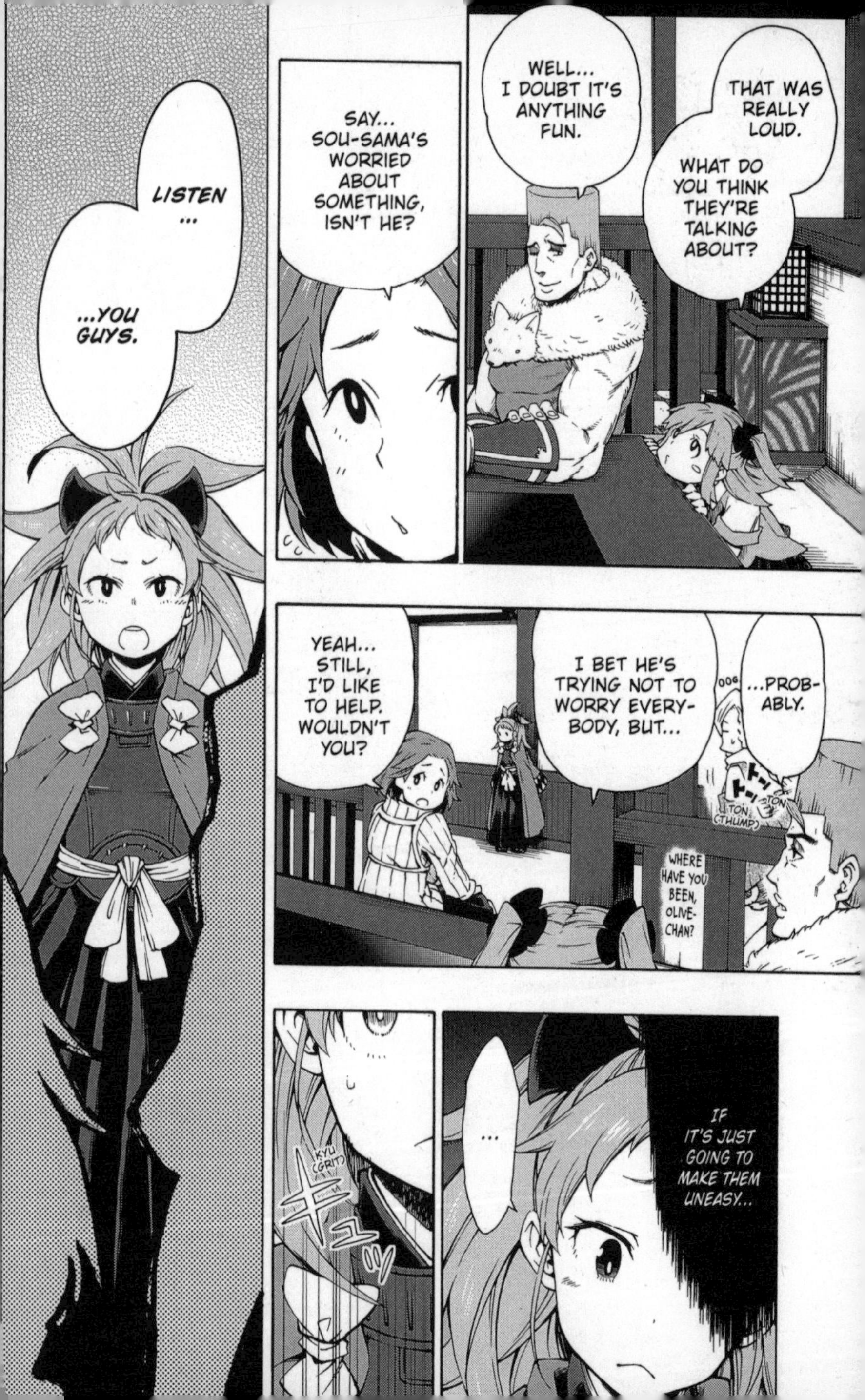
THAT WAS REALLY LOUD.
WHAT DO YOU THINK THEY'RE TALKING ABOUT?
WELL... I DOUBT IT'S ANYTHING FUN.
SAY... SOU-SAMA'S WORRIED ABOUT SOMETHING, ISN'T HE?
...PROB-ABLY.
OOG
TON TON (THUMP)
I BET HE'S TRYING NOT TO WORRY EVERY-BODY, BUT...
WHERE HAVE YOU BEEN, OLIVE-CHAN?
YEAH... STILL, I'D LIKE TO HELP. WOULDN'T YOU?
IF IT'S JUST GOING TO MAKE THEM UNEASY...
...
...
KYU (GRIT)
LISTEN...
...YOU GUYS.

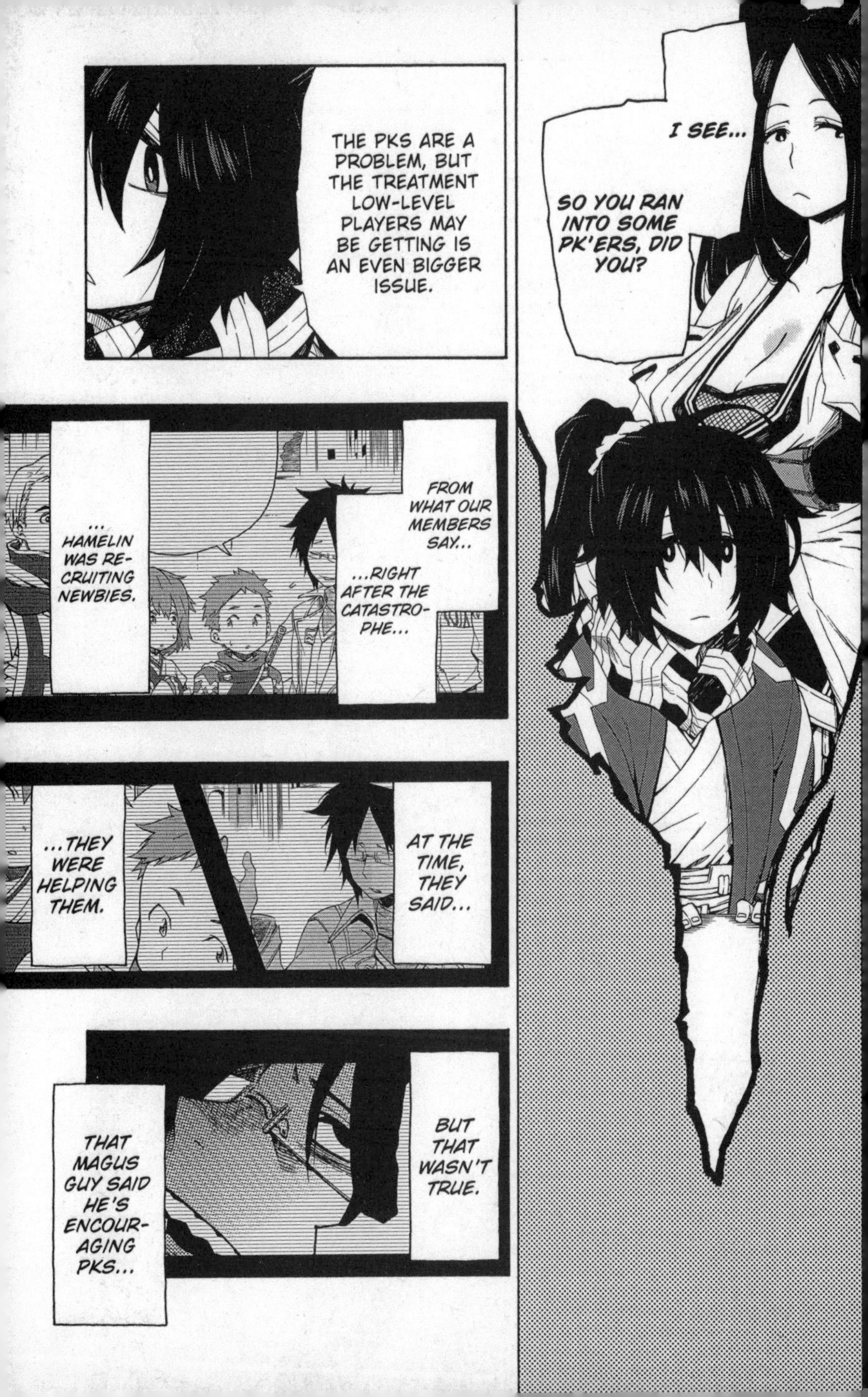
I SEE...
SO YOU RAN INTO SOME PK'ERS, DID YOU?
THE PKS ARE A PROBLEM, BUT THE TREATMENT LOW-LEVEL PLAYERS MAY BE GETTING IS AN EVEN BIGGER ISSUE.
FROM WHAT OUR MEMBERS SAY...
...RIGHT AFTER THE CATASTROPHE...
...HAMELIN WAS RECRUITING NEWBIES.
AT THE TIME, THEY SAID...
...THEY WERE HELPING THEM.
BUT THAT WASN'T TRUE.
THAT MAGUS GUY SAID HE'S ENCOURAGING PKS...

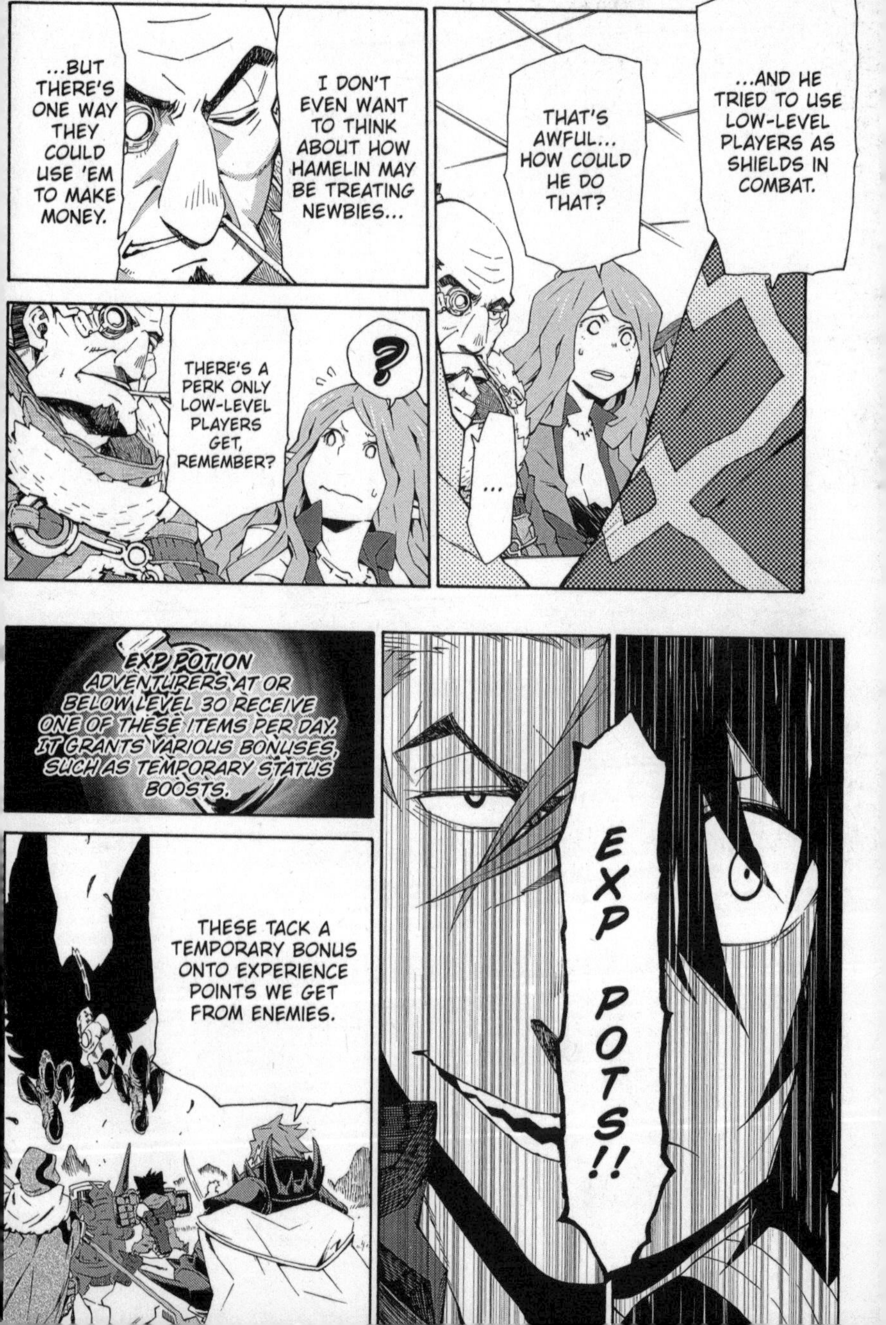
...AND HE TRIED TO USE LOW-LEVEL PLAYERS AS SHIELDS IN COMBAT.
THAT'S AWFUL... HOW COULD HE DO THAT?
...
I DON'T EVEN WANT TO THINK ABOUT HOW HAMELIN MAY BE TREATING NEWBIES...
...BUT THERE'S ONE WAY THEY COULD USE 'EM TO MAKE MONEY.
?
THERE'S A PERK ONLY LOW-LEVEL PLAYERS GET, REMEMBER?
EXP POTS!!
EXP POTION
ADVENTURERS AT OR BELOW LEVEL 30 RECEIVE ONE OF THESE ITEMS PER DAY. IT GRANTS VARIOUS BONUSES, SUCH AS TEMPORARY STATUS BOOSTS.
THESE TACK A TEMPORARY BONUS ONTO EXPERIENCE POINTS WE GET FROM ENEMIES.

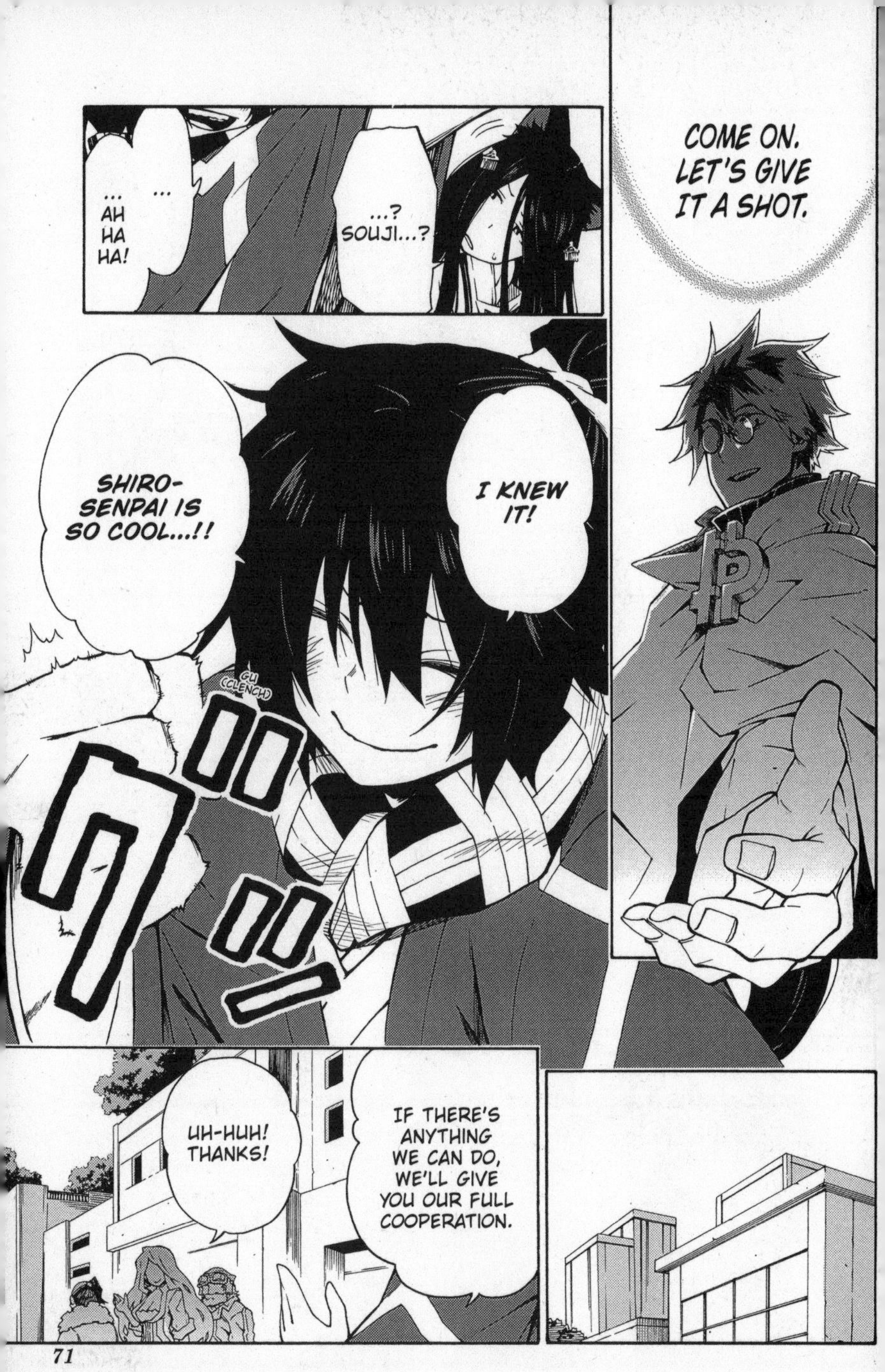
COME ON. LET'S GIVE IT A SHOT.
...? SOUJI...?
... ... AH HA HA!
I KNEW IT!
SHIRO-SENPAI IS SO COOL...!!
GU (CLENCH)
IF THERE'S ANYTHING WE CAN DO, WE'LL GIVE YOU OUR FULL COOPERATION.
UH-HUH! THANKS!

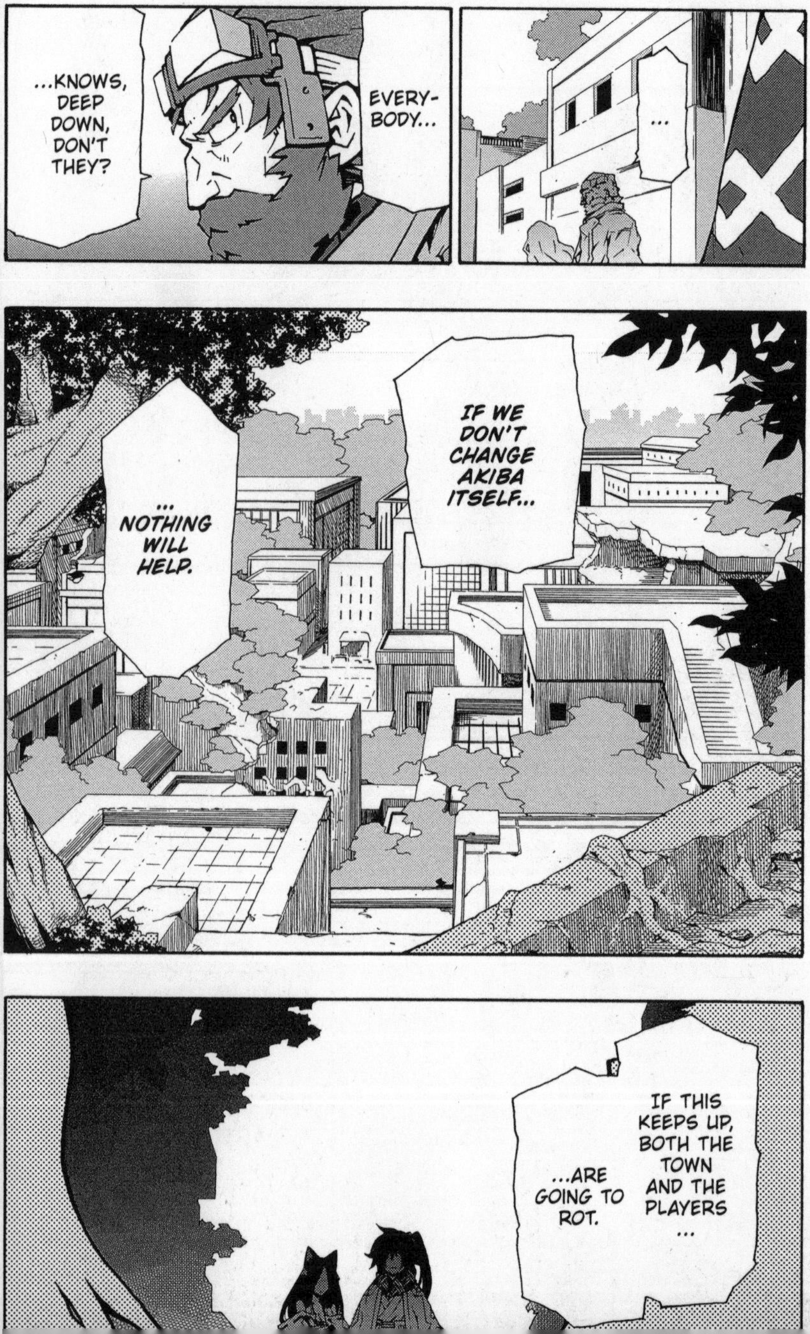
...
EVERYBODY...
...KNOWS, DEEP DOWN, DON'T THEY?
IF WE DON'T CHANGE AKIBA ITSELF...
...NOTHING WILL HELP.
IF THIS KEEPS UP, BOTH THE TOWN AND THE PLAYERS...
...ARE GOING TO ROT.

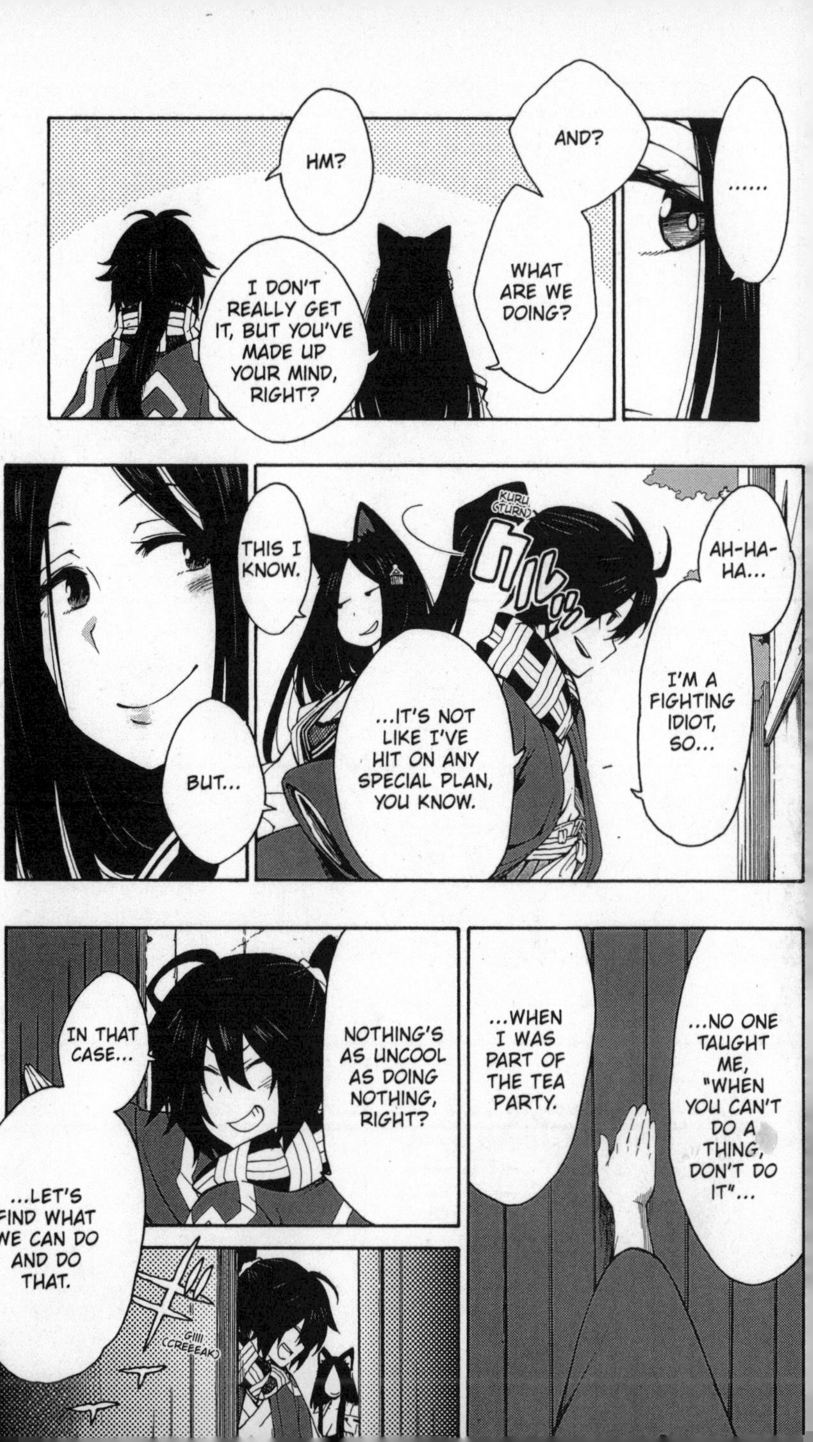
......
AND?
HM?
WHAT ARE WE DOING?
I DON'T REALLY GET IT, BUT YOU'VE MADE UP YOUR MIND, RIGHT?
KURU (TURN)
AH-HA-HA...
I'M A FIGHTING IDIOT, SO...
...IT'S NOT LIKE I'VE HIT ON ANY SPECIAL PLAN, YOU KNOW.
THIS I KNOW.
BUT...
...NO ONE TAUGHT ME, "WHEN YOU CAN'T DO A THING, DON'T DO IT"...
...WHEN I WAS PART OF THE TEA PARTY.
NOTHING'S AS UNCOOL AS DOING NOTHING, RIGHT?
IN THAT CASE...
...LET'S FIND WHAT WE CAN DO AND DO THAT.
GIIII (CREEEAK)

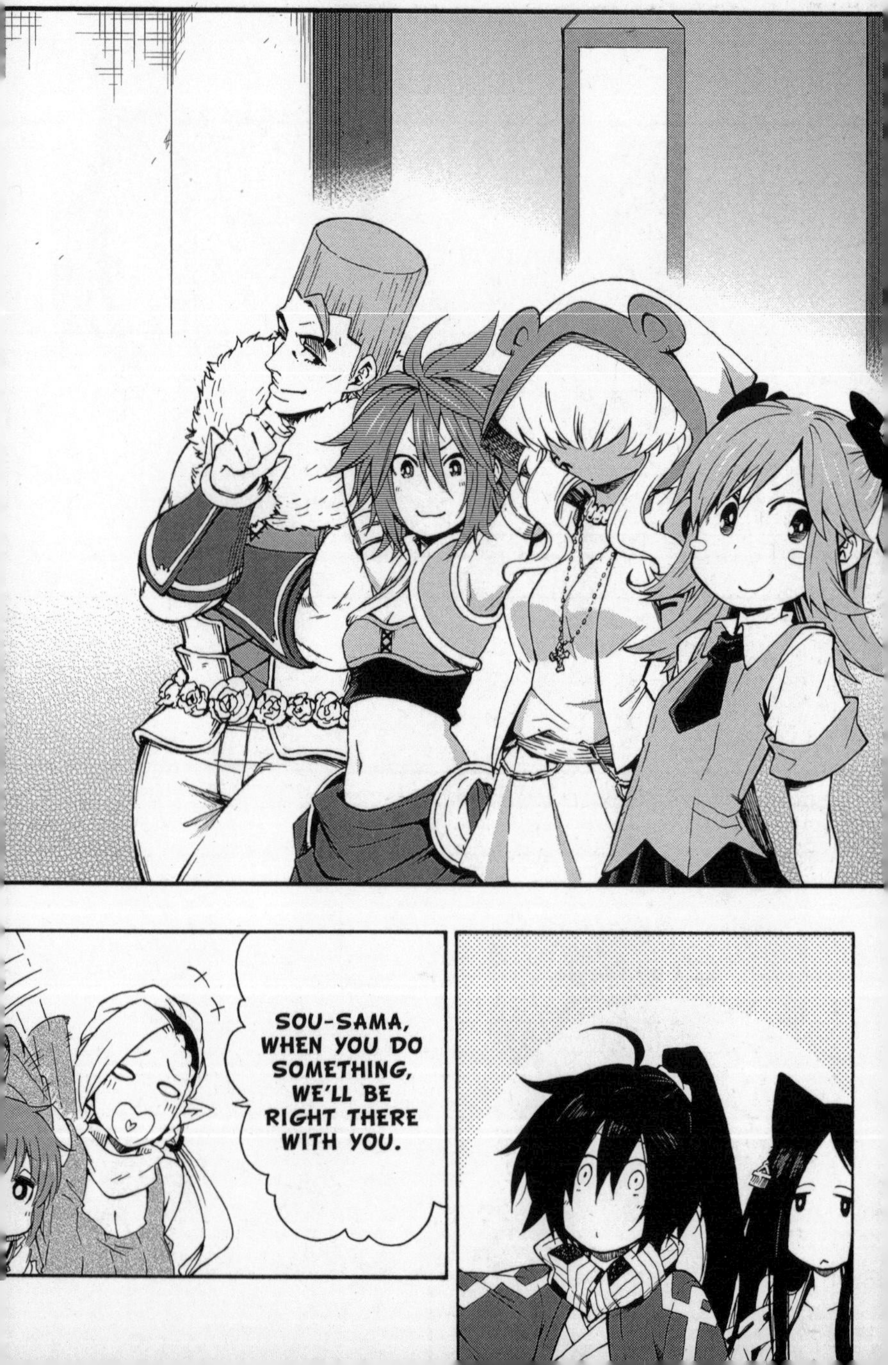
SOU-SAMA, WHEN YOU DO SOMETHING, WE'LL BE RIGHT THERE WITH YOU.

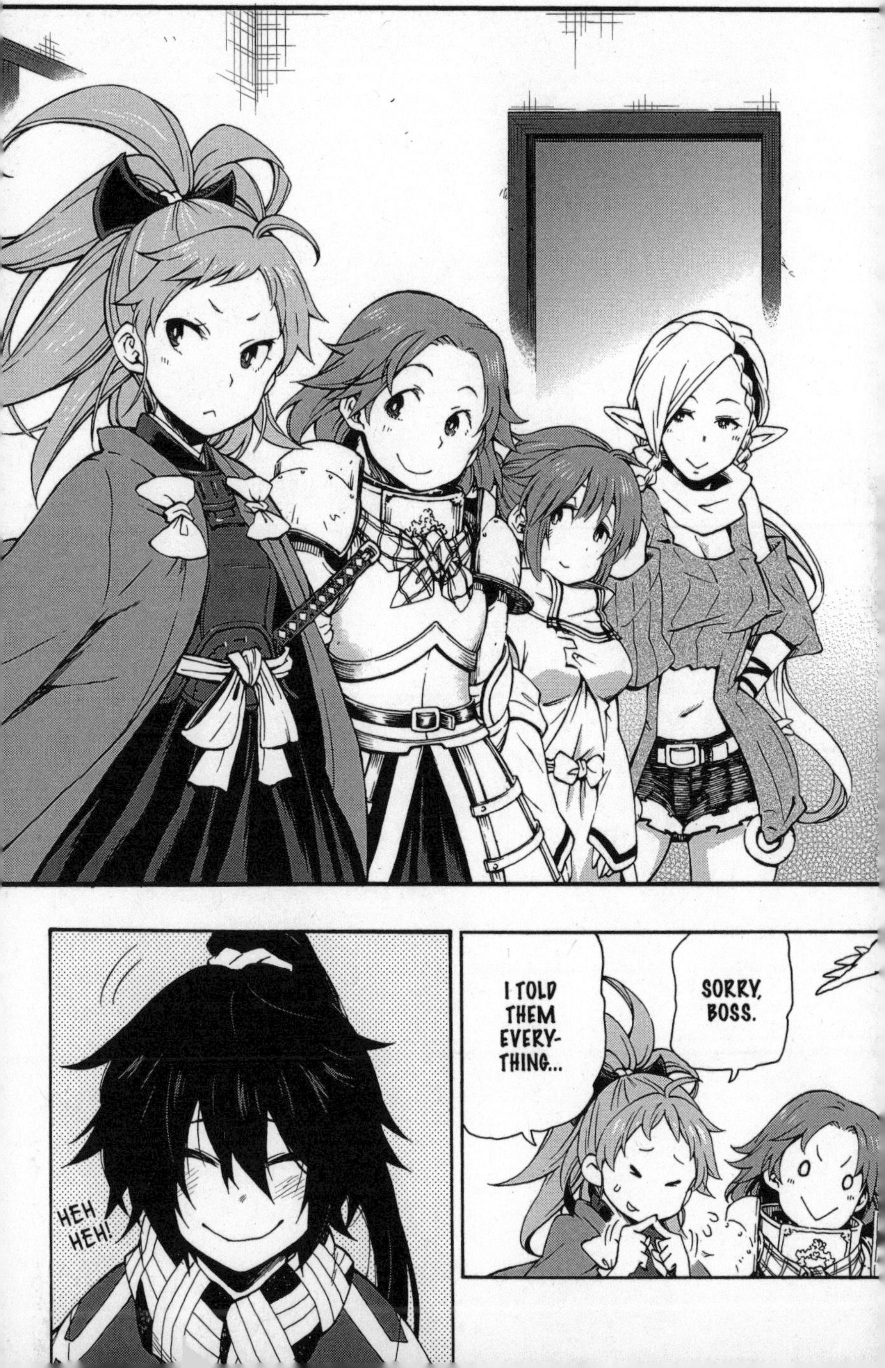
SORRY, BOSS.
I TOLD THEM EVERY-THING...
HEH HEH!

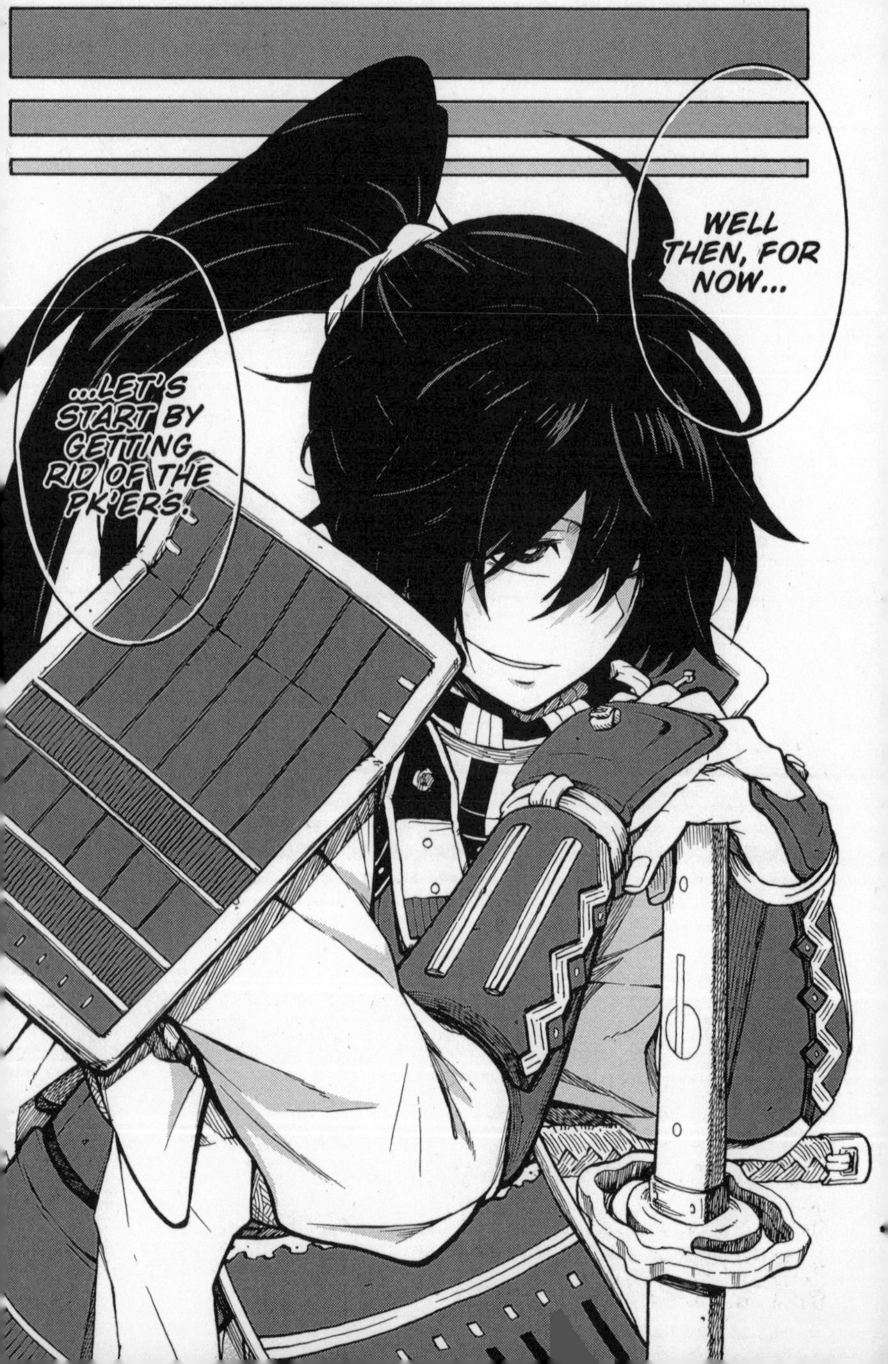
WELL THEN, FOR NOW...
...LET'S START BY GETTING RID OF THE PK'ERS!

LOG HORIZON
THE WEST WIND BRIGADE

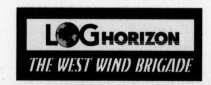

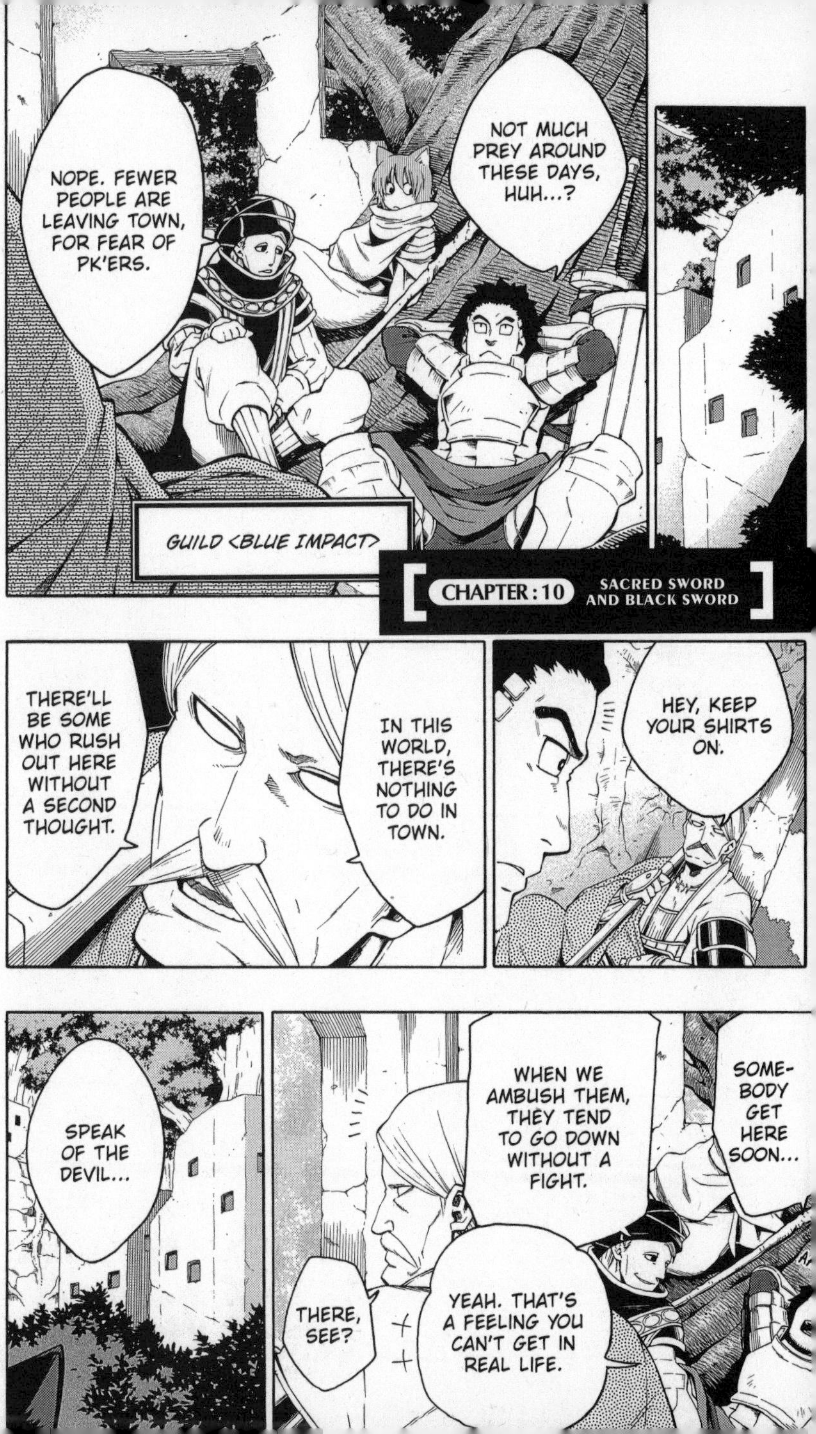
NOT MUCH PREY AROUND THESE DAYS, HUH...?
NOPE. FEWER PEOPLE ARE LEAVING TOWN, FOR FEAR OF PK'ERS.
GUILD <BLUE IMPACT>
CHAPTER : 10 SACRED SWORD AND BLACK SWORD
HEY, KEEP YOUR SHIRTS ON.
IN THIS WORLD, THERE'S NOTHING TO DO IN TOWN.
THERE'LL BE SOME WHO RUSH OUT HERE WITHOUT A SECOND THOUGHT.
SOME-BODY GET HERE SOON...
WHEN WE AMBUSH THEM, THEY TEND TO GO DOWN WITHOUT A FIGHT.
YEAH. THAT'S A FEELING YOU CAN'T GET IN REAL LIFE.
THERE, SEE?
SPEAK OF THE DEVIL...

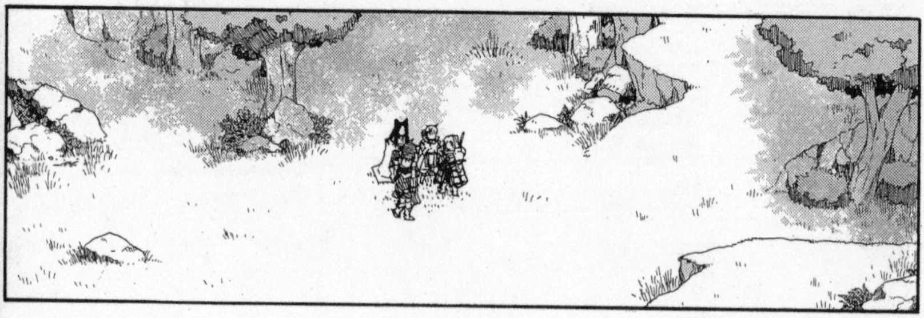

## CHAPTER : 10 SACRED SWORD AND BLACK SWORD

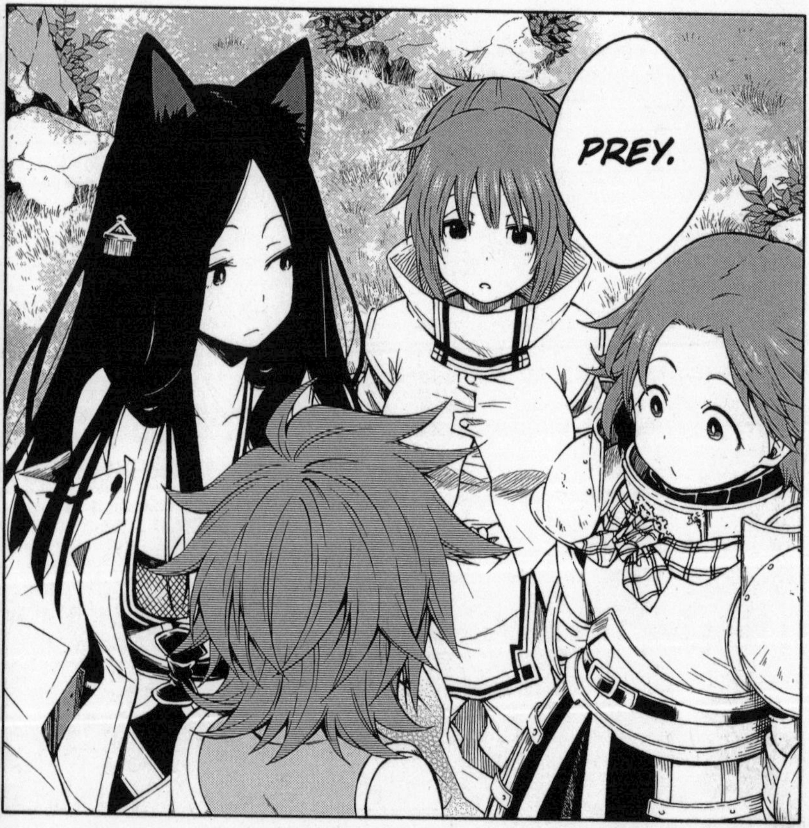
PREY.

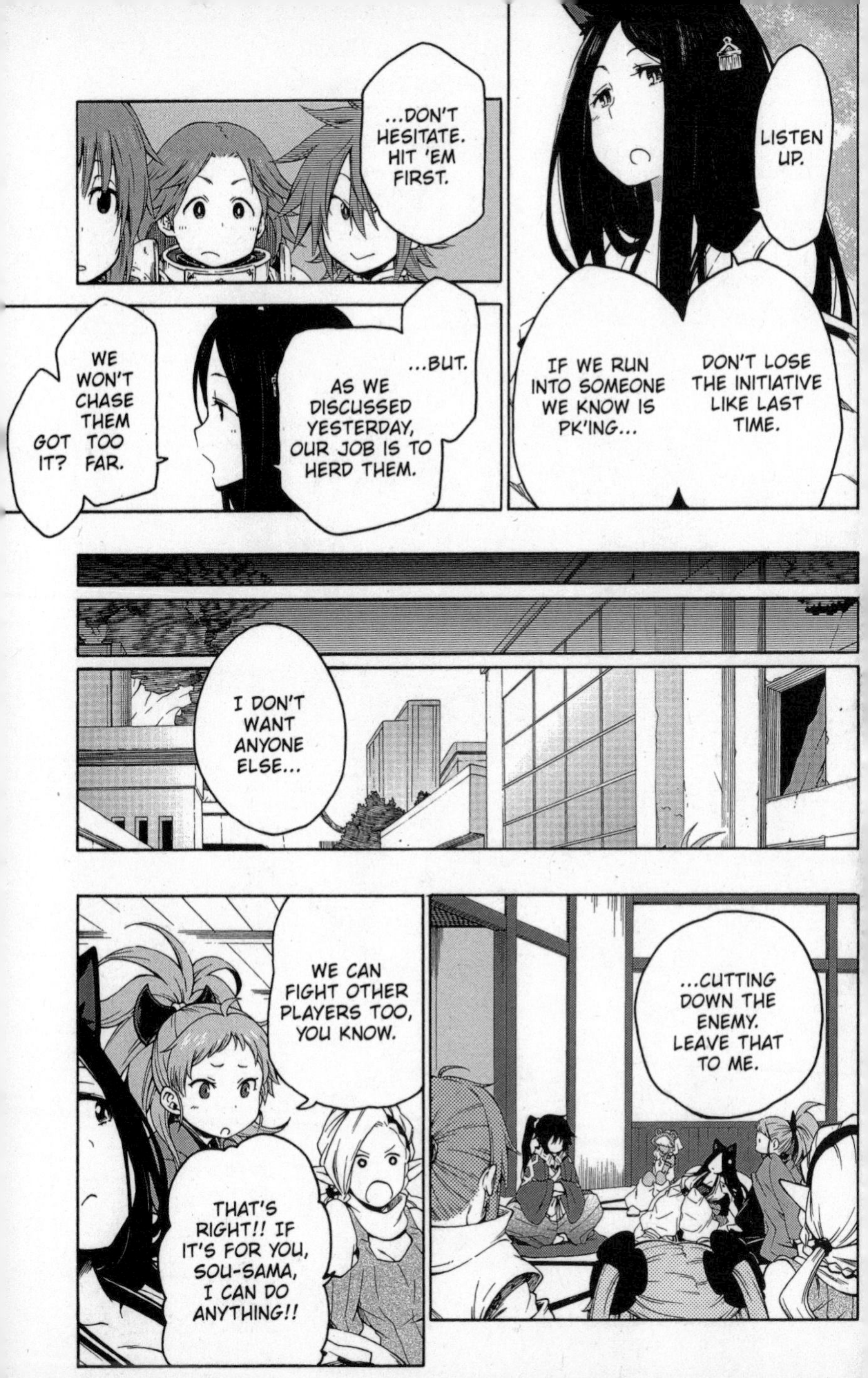
LISTEN UP.
DON'T LOSE THE INITIATIVE LIKE LAST TIME.
IF WE RUN INTO SOMEONE WE KNOW IS PK'ING...
...DON'T HESITATE. HIT 'EM FIRST.
...BUT.
AS WE DISCUSSED YESTERDAY, OUR JOB IS TO HERD THEM.
WE WON'T CHASE THEM TOO FAR. GOT IT?
I DON'T WANT ANYONE ELSE...
...CUTTING DOWN THE ENEMY. LEAVE THAT TO ME.
WE CAN FIGHT OTHER PLAYERS TOO, YOU KNOW.
THAT'S RIGHT!! IF IT'S FOR YOU, SOU-SAMA, I CAN DO ANYTHING!!

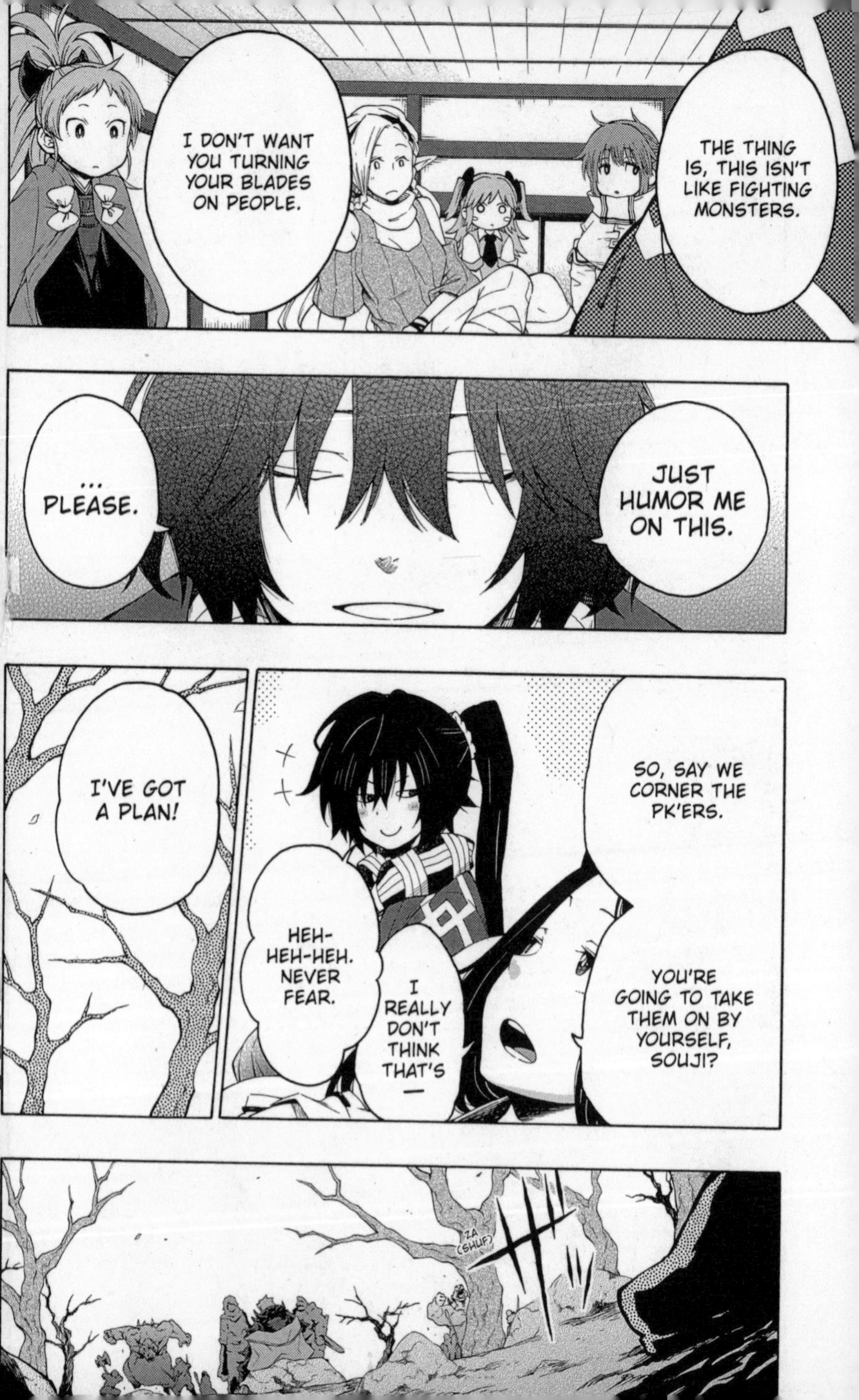
THE THING IS, THIS ISN'T LIKE FIGHTING MONSTERS.
I DON'T WANT YOU TURNING YOUR BLADES ON PEOPLE.
JUST HUMOR ME ON THIS.
... PLEASE.
SO, SAY WE CORNER THE PK'ERS.
YOU'RE GOING TO TAKE THEM ON BY YOURSELF, SOUJI?
I REALLY DON'T THINK THAT'S—
HEH-HEH-HEH. NEVER FEAR.
I'VE GOT A PLAN!
ZA (SHUF)

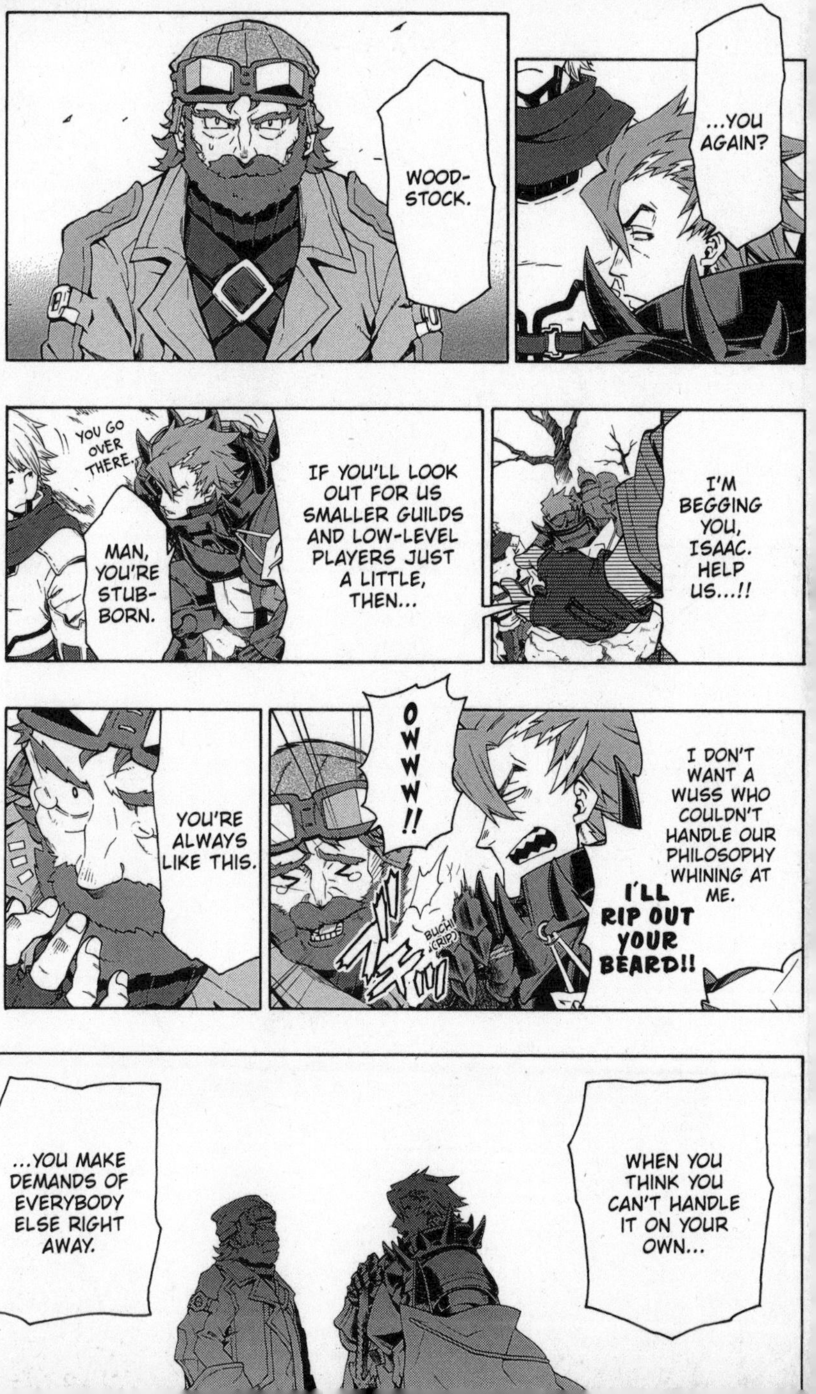
...YOU AGAIN?
WOOD-STOCK.
I'M BEGGING YOU, ISAAC. HELP US...!!
IF YOU'LL LOOK OUT FOR US SMALLER GUILDS AND LOW-LEVEL PLAYERS JUST A LITTLE, THEN...
YOU GO OVER THERE.
MAN, YOU'RE STUB-BORN.
I DON'T WANT A WUSS WHO COULDN'T HANDLE OUR PHILOSOPHY WHINING AT ME.
OWWW!!
I'LL RIP OUT YOUR BEARD!!
BUCHI (RIP)
YOU'RE ALWAYS LIKE THIS.
WHEN YOU THINK YOU CAN'T HANDLE IT ON YOUR OWN...
...YOU MAKE DEMANDS OF EVERYBODY ELSE RIGHT AWAY.

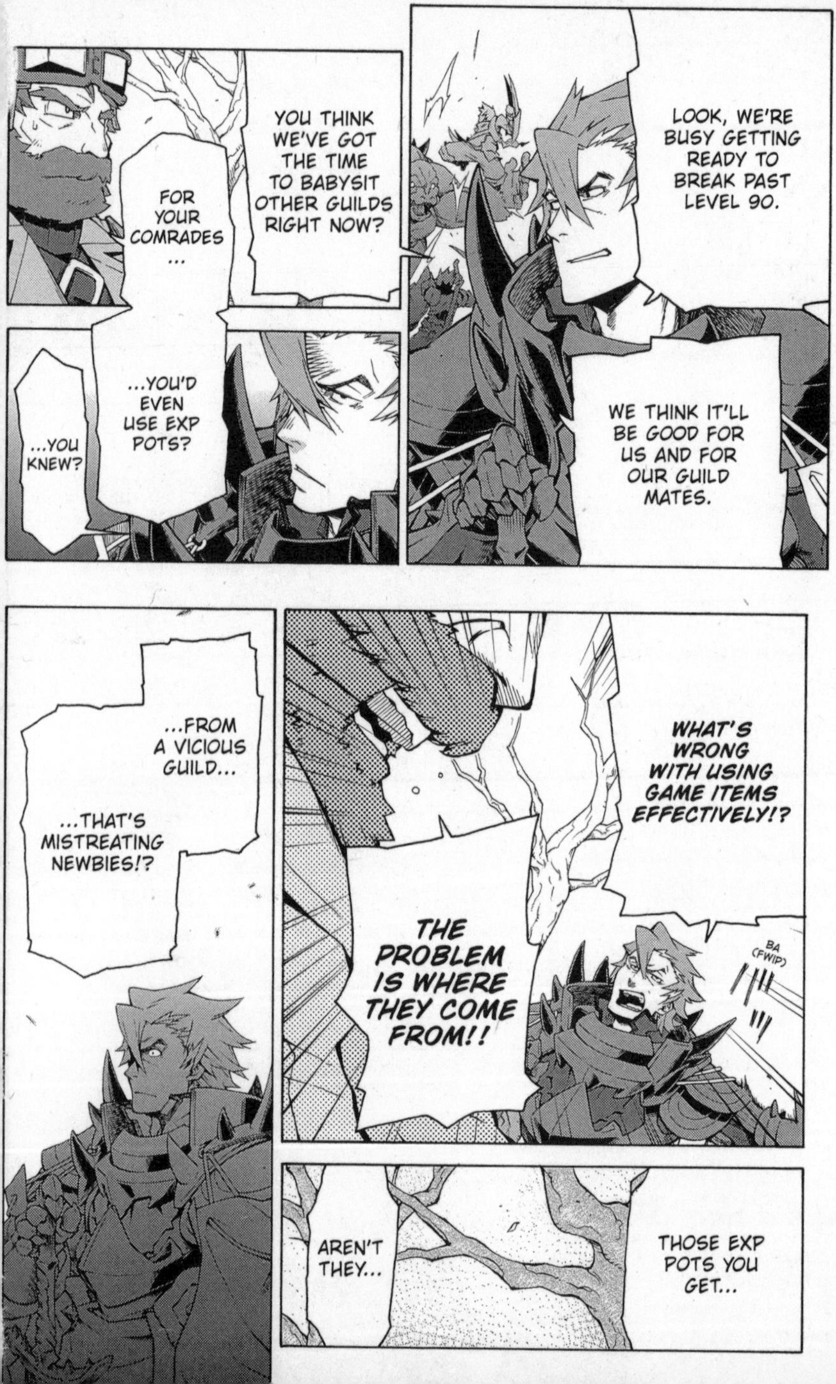
LOOK, WE'RE BUSY GETTING READY TO BREAK PAST LEVEL 90.
WE THINK IT'LL BE GOOD FOR US AND FOR OUR GUILD MATES.
YOU THINK WE'VE GOT THE TIME TO BABYSIT OTHER GUILDS RIGHT NOW?
FOR YOUR COMRADES ...
...YOU'D EVEN USE EXP POTS?
...YOU KNEW?
WHAT'S WRONG WITH USING GAME ITEMS EFFECTIVELY!?
BA (FWIP)
THE PROBLEM IS WHERE THEY COME FROM!!
THOSE EXP POTS YOU GET...
AREN'T THEY...
...FROM A VICIOUS GUILD...
...THAT'S MISTREATING NEWBIES!?

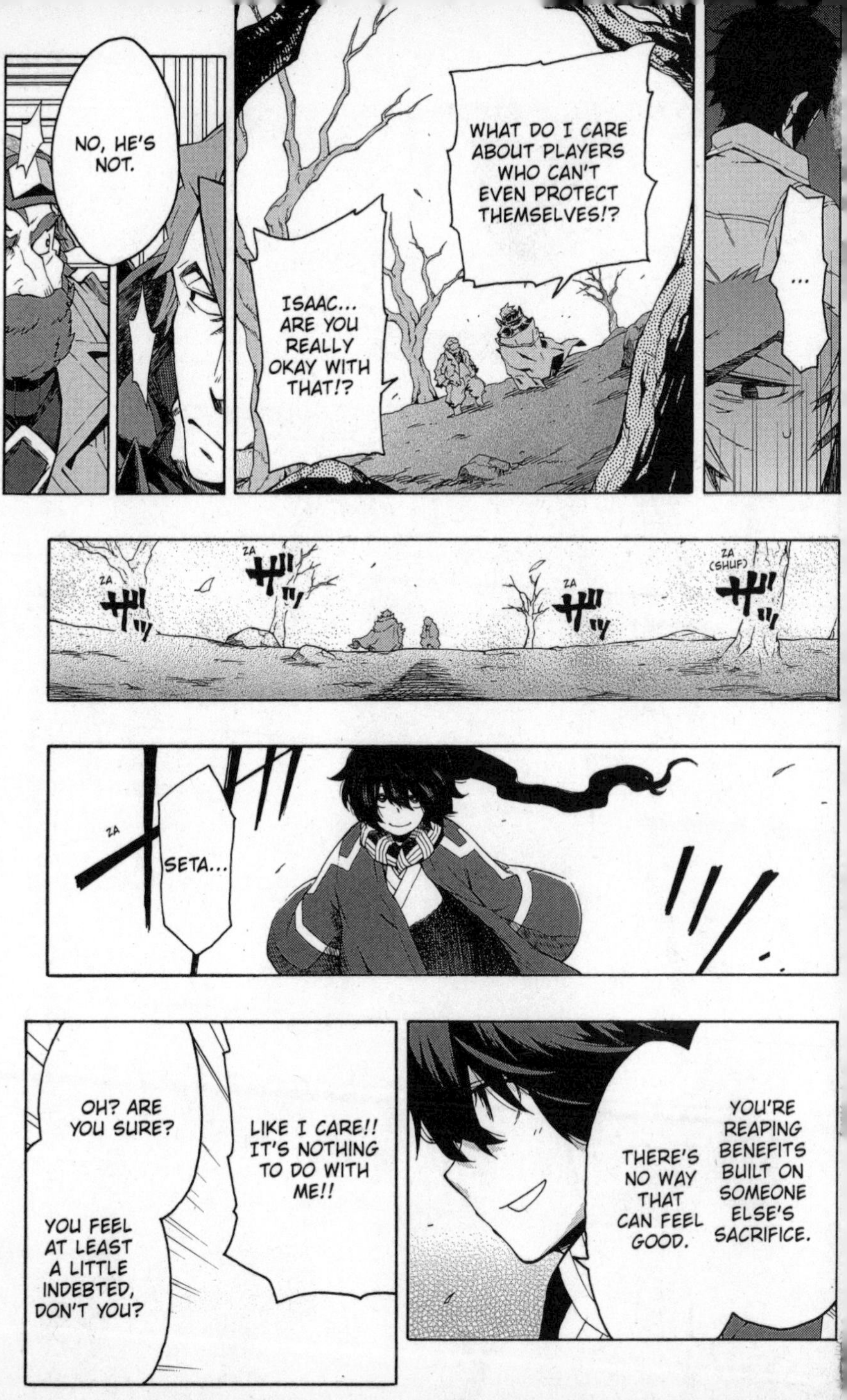
...
WHAT DO I CARE ABOUT PLAYERS WHO CAN'T EVEN PROTECT THEMSELVES!?
ISAAC... ARE YOU REALLY OKAY WITH THAT!?
NO, HE'S NOT.
ZA (SHUF)
ZA
ZA
ZA
ZA
SETA...
YOU'RE REAPING BENEFITS BUILT ON SOMEONE ELSE'S SACRIFICE.
THERE'S NO WAY THAT CAN FEEL GOOD.
LIKE I CARE!! IT'S NOTHING TO DO WITH ME!!
OH? ARE YOU SURE?
YOU FEEL AT LEAST A LITTLE INDEBTED, DON'T YOU?

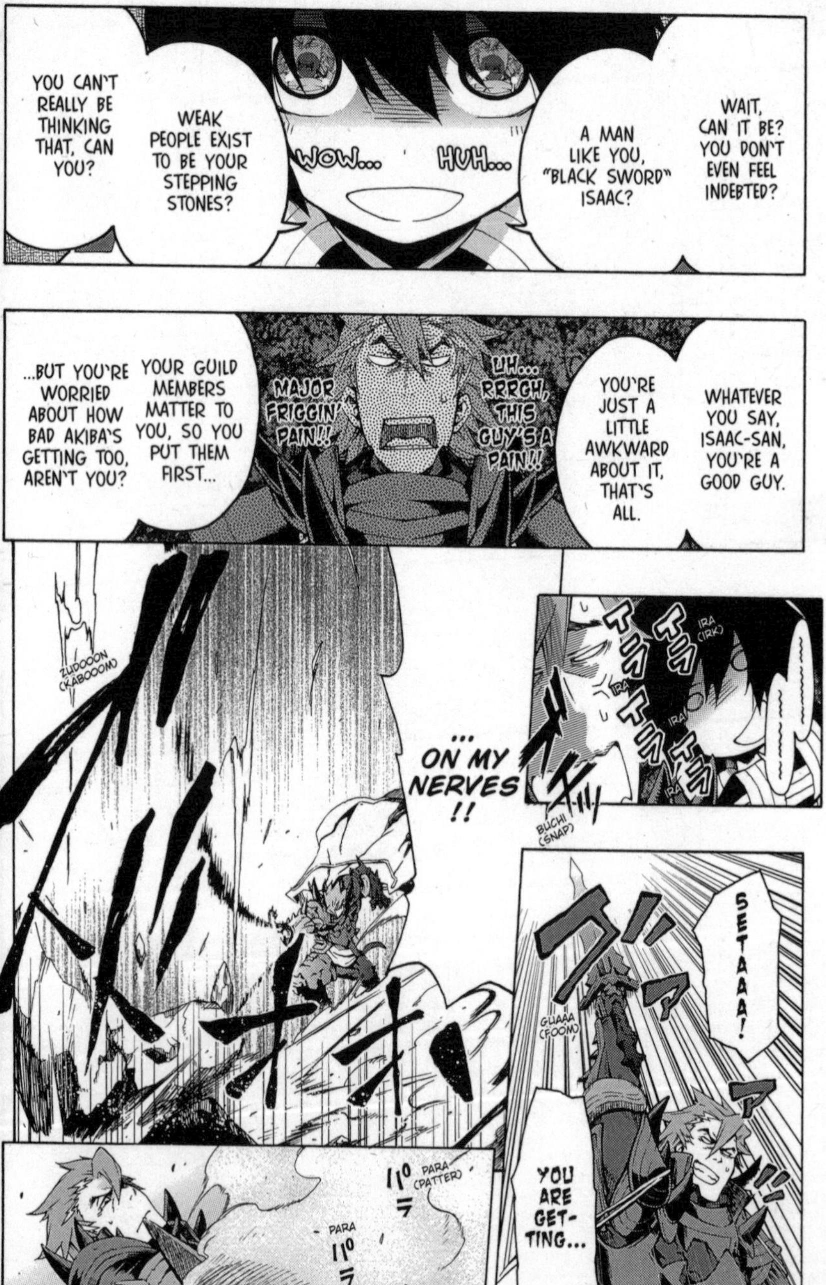
WAIT, CAN IT BE? YOU DON'T EVEN FEEL INDEBTED?
A MAN LIKE YOU, "BLACK SWORD" ISAAC?
HUH...
WOW...
WEAK PEOPLE EXIST TO BE YOUR STEPPING STONES?
YOU CAN'T REALLY BE THINKING THAT, CAN YOU?
WHATEVER YOU SAY, ISAAC-SAN, YOU'RE A GOOD GUY.
YOU'RE JUST A LITTLE AWKWARD ABOUT IT, THAT'S ALL.
UH... RRRGH, THIS GUY'S A PAIN!!
MAJOR FRIGGIN' PAIN!!
YOUR GUILD MEMBERS MATTER TO YOU, SO YOU PUT THEM FIRST...
...BUT YOU'RE WORRIED ABOUT HOW BAD AKIBA'S GETTING TOO, AREN'T YOU?
IRA (IRK)
IRA
IRA
IRA
BUCHI (SNAP)
SETAAAA!
YOU ARE GETTING...
GUAAA (FOOM)
... ON MY NERVES !!
ZUDOOON (KABOOOM)
PARA (PATTER)
PARA

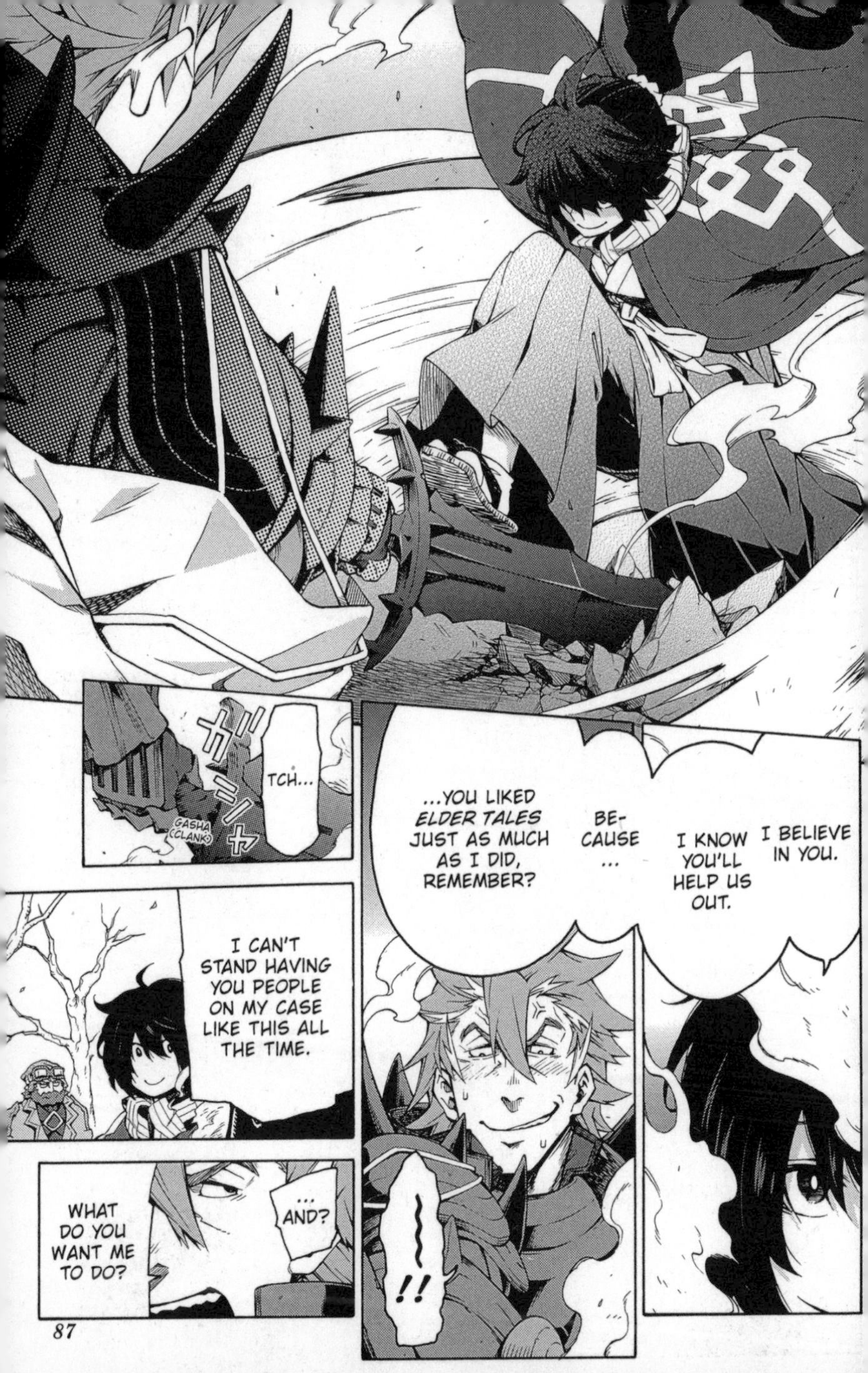
I BELIEVE IN YOU.
I KNOW YOU'LL HELP US OUT.
BE-CAUSE...
...YOU LIKED *ELDER TALES* JUST AS MUCH AS I DID, REMEMBER?
~~!!
TCH...
GASHA (CLANK)
I CAN'T STAND HAVING YOU PEOPLE ON MY CASE LIKE THIS ALL THE TIME.
...AND?
WHAT DO YOU WANT ME TO DO?

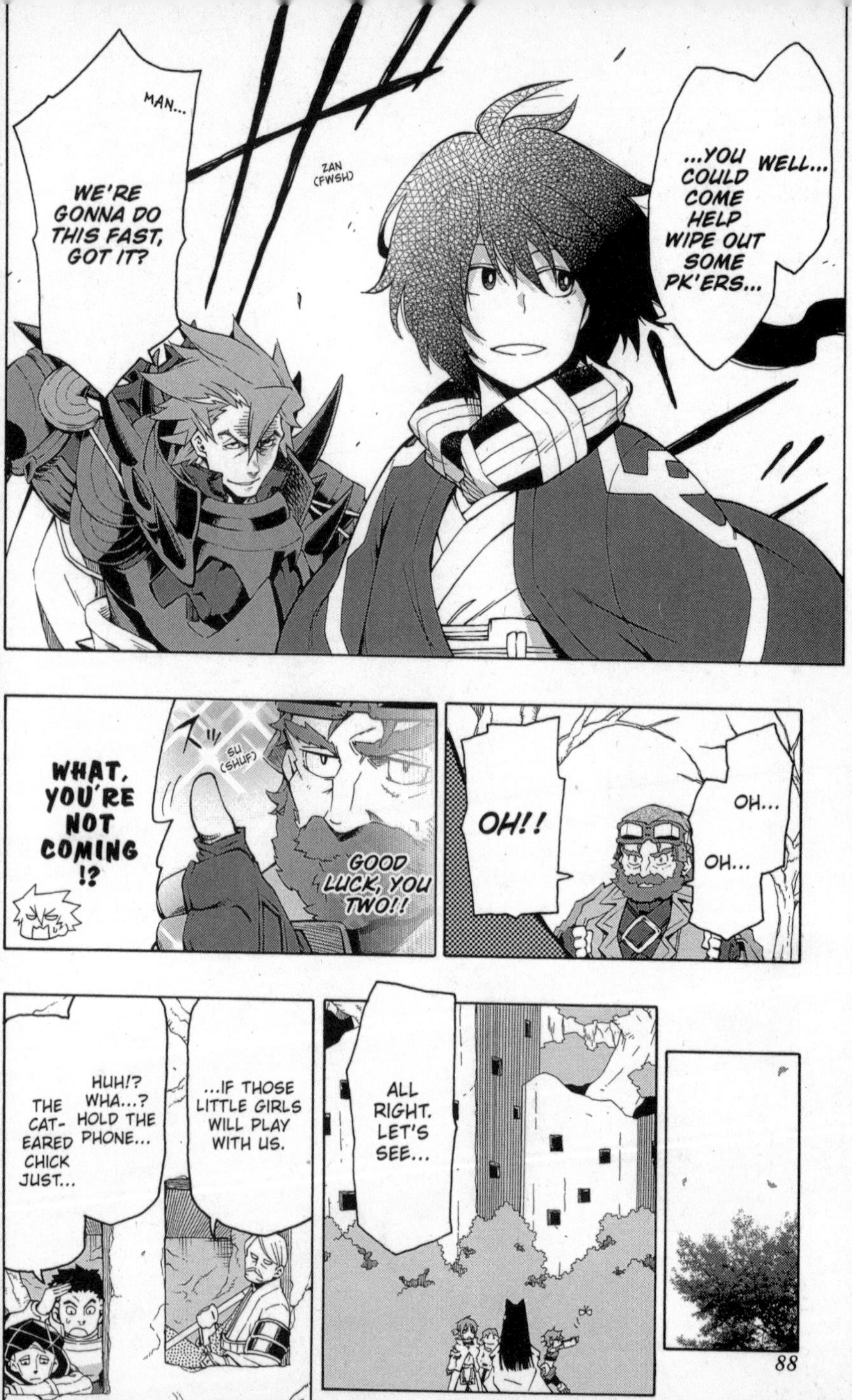
WELL...
...YOU COULD COME HELP WIPE OUT SOME PK'ERS...
ZAN (FWSH)
MAN...
WE'RE GONNA DO THIS FAST, GOT IT?
OH...
OH...
OH!!
GOOD LUCK, YOU TWO!!
SU (SHUF)
WHAT, YOU'RE NOT COMING!?
ALL RIGHT. LET'S SEE...
...IF THOSE LITTLE GIRLS WILL PLAY WITH US.
HUH!? WHA...? HOLD THE PHONE...
THE CAT-EARED CHICK JUST...

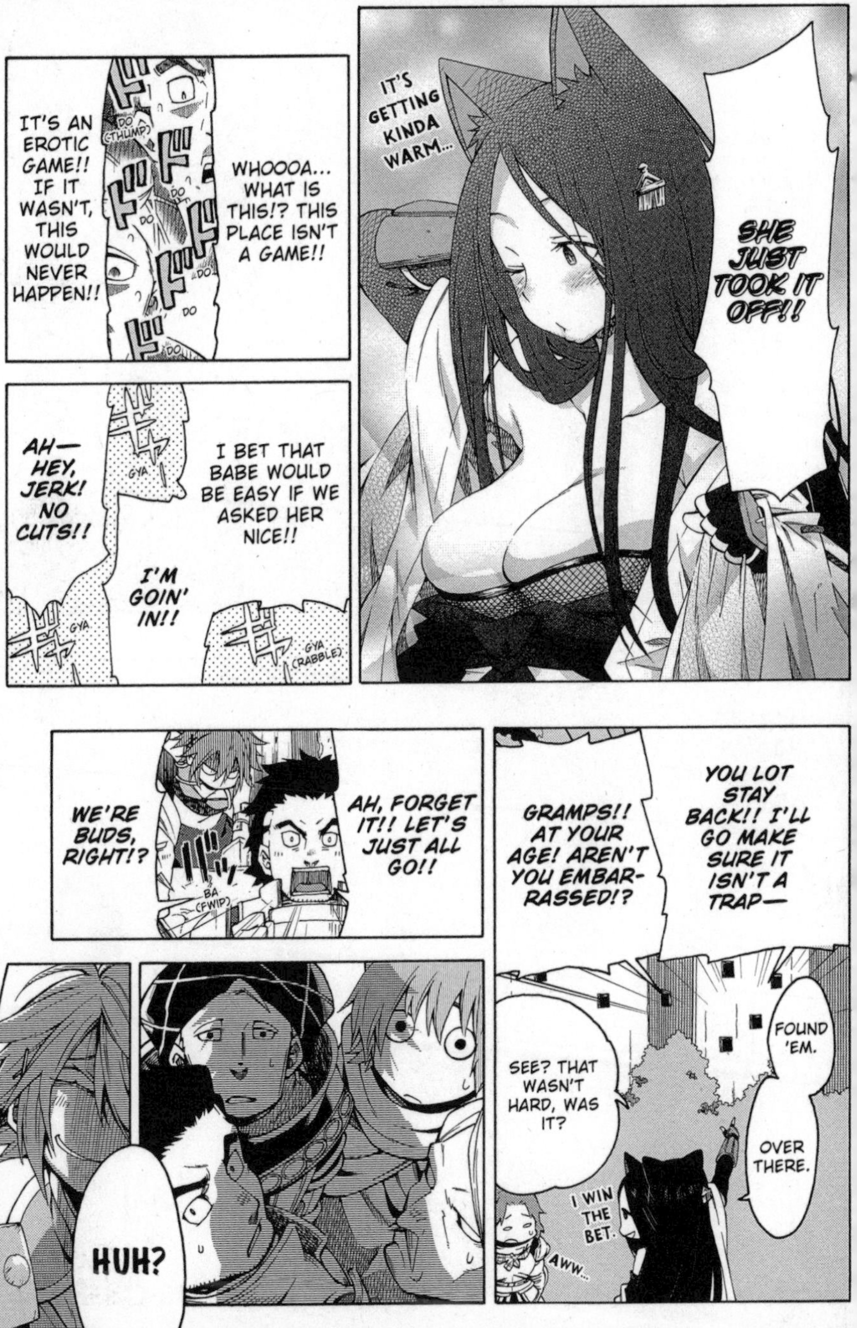

SHE JUST TOOK IT OFF!!
IT'S GETTING KINDA WARM...
WHOOOA... WHAT IS THIS!? THIS PLACE ISN'T A GAME!!
DO (THUMP)
DO
DO
DO
DO
DO
IT'S AN EROTIC GAME!! IF IT WASN'T, THIS WOULD NEVER HAPPEN!!
I BET THAT BABE WOULD BE EASY IF WE ASKED HER NICE!!
GYA
AH— HEY, JERK! NO CUTS!!
I'M GOIN' IN!!
GYA (RABBLE)
GYA
YOU LOT STAY BACK!! I'LL GO MAKE SURE IT ISN'T A TRAP—
GRAMPS!! AT YOUR AGE! AREN'T YOU EMBARRASSED!?
AH, FORGET IT!! LET'S JUST ALL GO!!
WE'RE BUDS, RIGHT!?
BA (FWIP)
FOUND 'EM.
OVER THERE.
SEE? THAT WASN'T HARD, WAS IT?
I WIN THE BET.
AWW...
HUH?

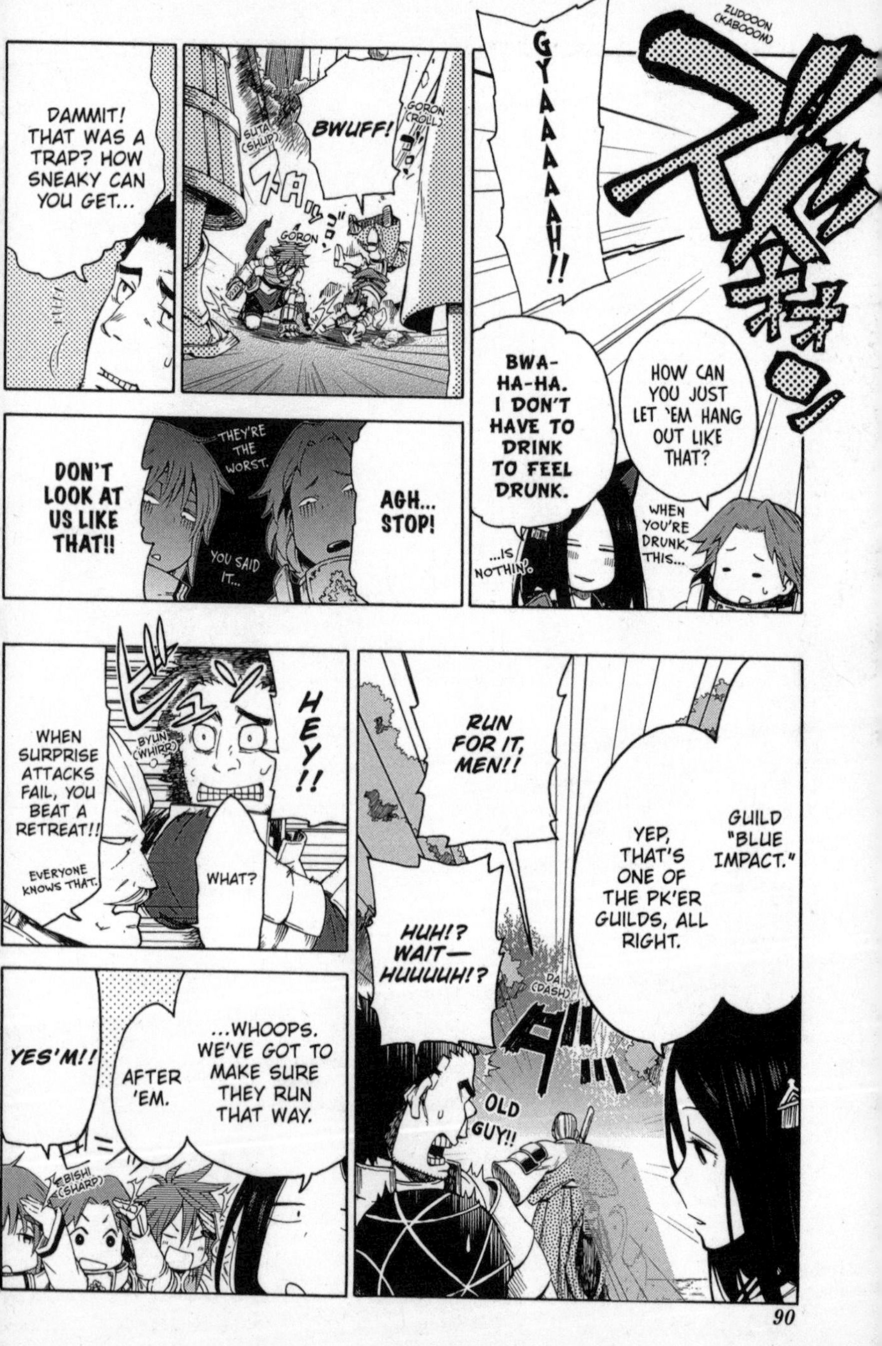
ZUDOOON (KABOOOM)
GYAAAAAH!!
HOW CAN YOU JUST LET 'EM HANG OUT LIKE THAT?
WHEN YOU'RE DRUNK, THIS...
BWA-HA-HA. I DON'T HAVE TO DRINK TO FEEL DRUNK.
...IS NOTHIN'.
GORON (ROLL)
BWUFF!
SUTA (SHUP)
GORON
DAMMIT! THAT WAS A TRAP? HOW SNEAKY CAN YOU GET...
AGH... STOP!
THEY'RE THE WORST.
YOU SAID IT...
DON'T LOOK AT US LIKE THAT!!
GUILD "BLUE IMPACT."
YEP, THAT'S ONE OF THE PK'ER GUILDS, ALL RIGHT.
RUN FOR IT, MEN!!
HUH!? WAIT—HUUUUH!?
DA (DASH)
OLD GUY!!
HEY!!
BYUN (WHIRR)
WHEN SURPRISE ATTACKS FAIL, YOU BEAT A RETREAT!!
EVERYONE KNOWS THAT.
WHAT?
...WHOOPS. WE'VE GOT TO MAKE SURE THEY RUN THAT WAY.
AFTER 'EM.
YES'M!!
EBISHI (SHARP)

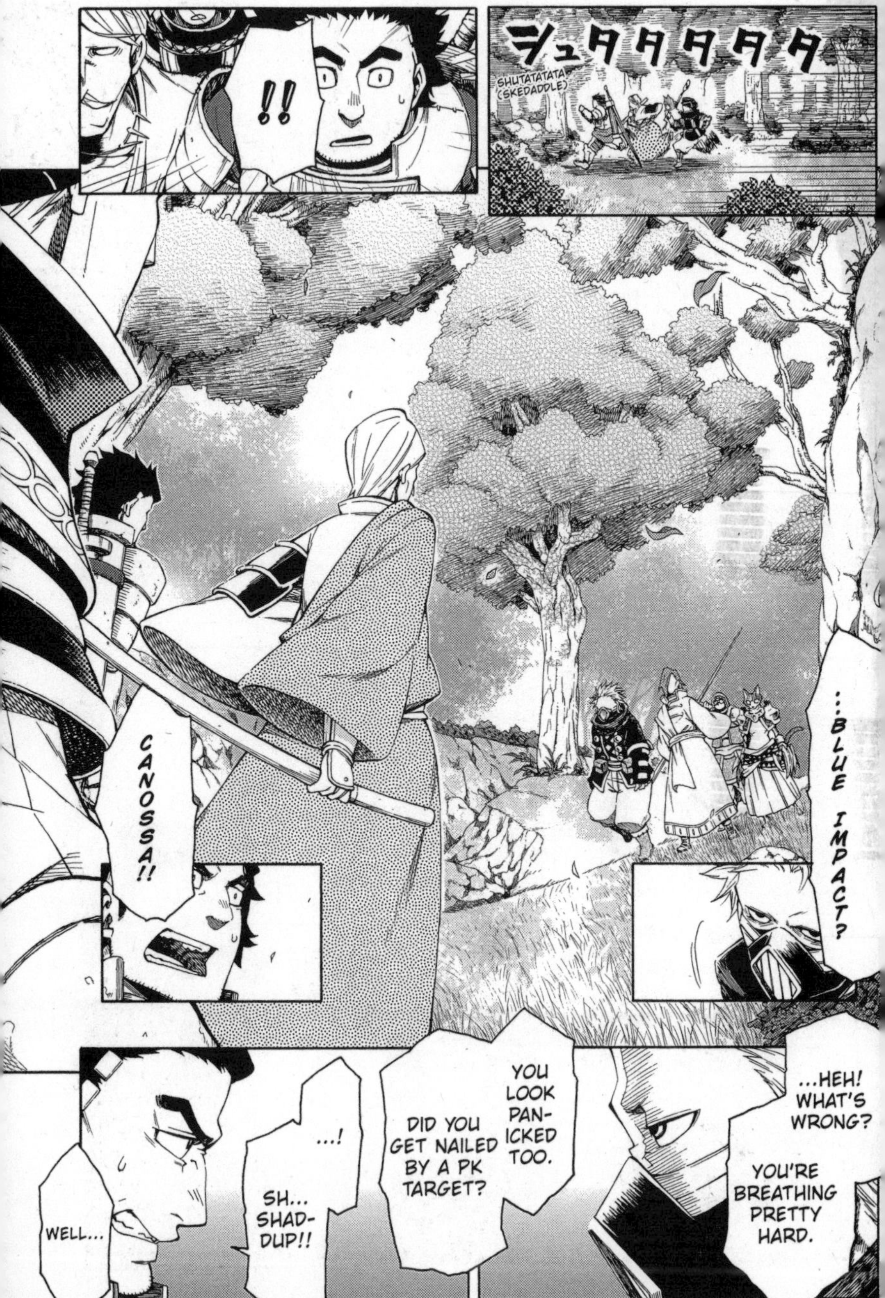
シュタタタタタ
SHUTATATATA (SKEDADDLE)
!!
...BLUE IMPACT?
CANOSSA!!
...HEH! WHAT'S WRONG?
YOU'RE BREATHING PRETTY HARD.
YOU LOOK PAN-ICKED TOO.
DID YOU GET NAILED BY A PK TARGET?
...!
SH... SHAD-DUP!!
WELL...

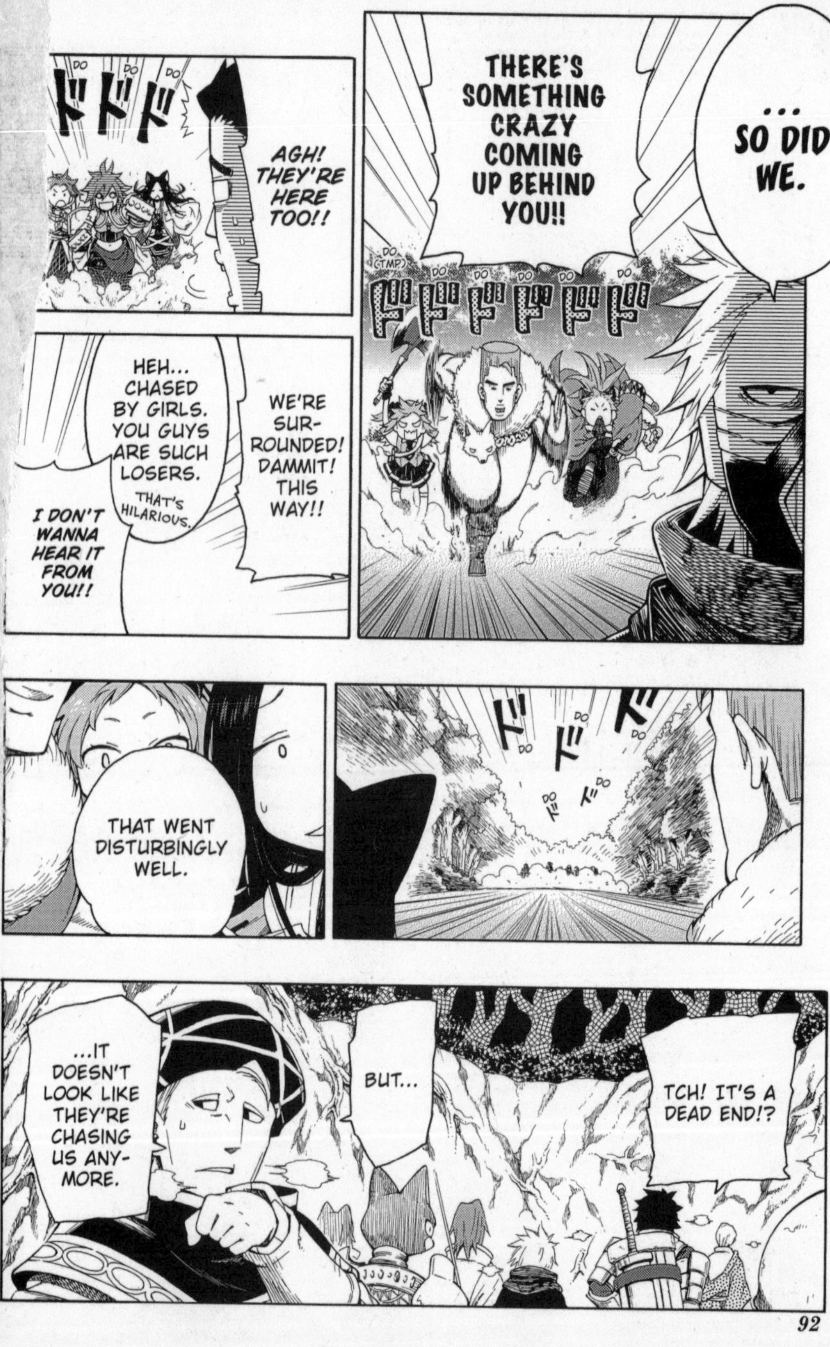
THERE'S SOMETHING CRAZY COMING UP BEHIND YOU!!
... SO DID WE.
DO (TMP) DO DO DO DO DO
DO DO DO
AGH! THEY'RE HERE TOO!!
WE'RE SUR-ROUNDED! DAMMIT! THIS WAY!!
HEH... CHASED BY GIRLS. YOU GUYS ARE SUCH LOSERS.
THAT'S HILARIOUS.
I DON'T WANNA HEAR IT FROM YOU!!
DO DO DO DO
THAT WENT DISTURBINGLY WELL.
TCH! IT'S A DEAD END!?
BUT...
...IT DOESN'T LOOK LIKE THEY'RE CHASING US ANY-MORE.

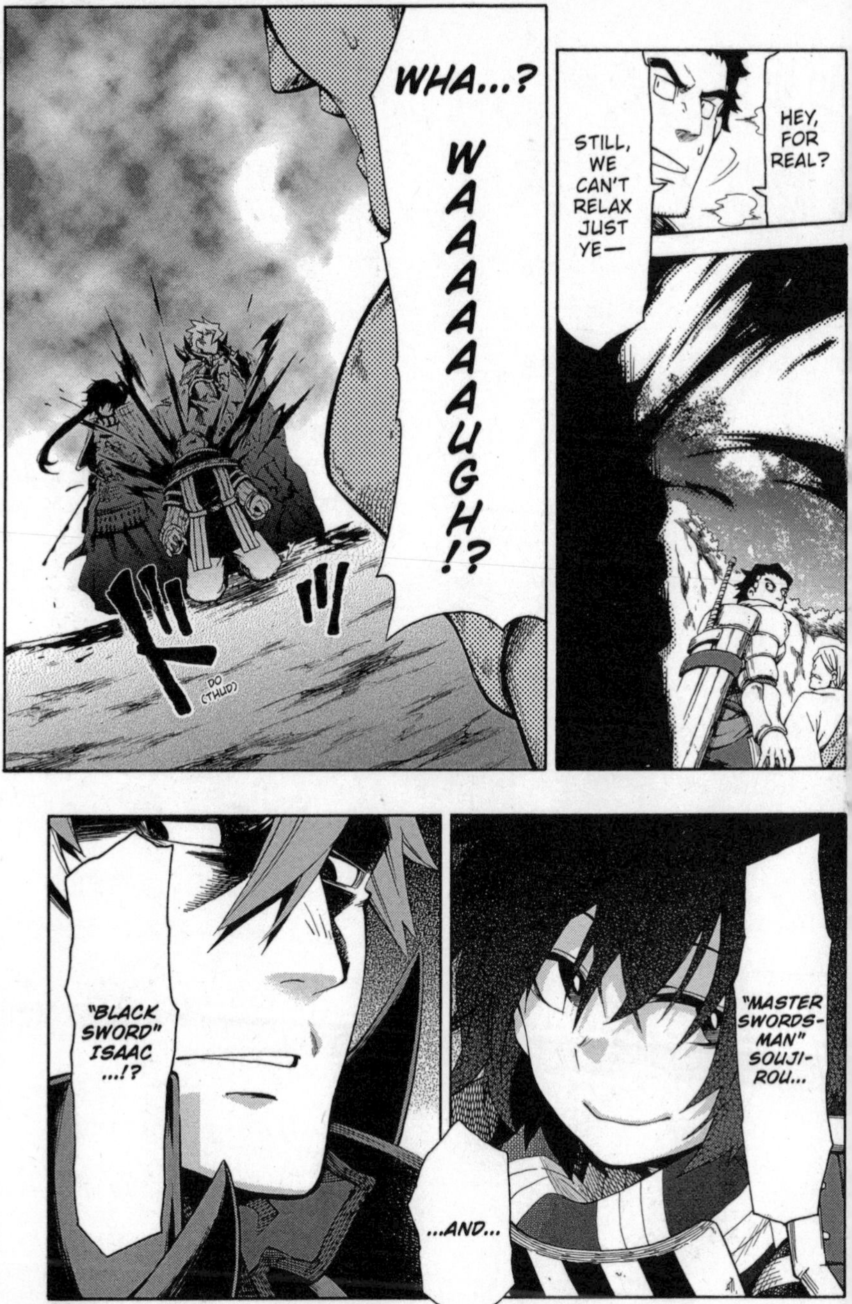
HEY, FOR REAL?
STILL, WE CAN'T RELAX JUST YE—
WHA...?
WAAAAAAAAUGH!?
DO (THUD)
"MASTER SWORDS-MAN" SOUJI-ROU...
...AND...
"BLACK SWORD" ISAAC ...!?

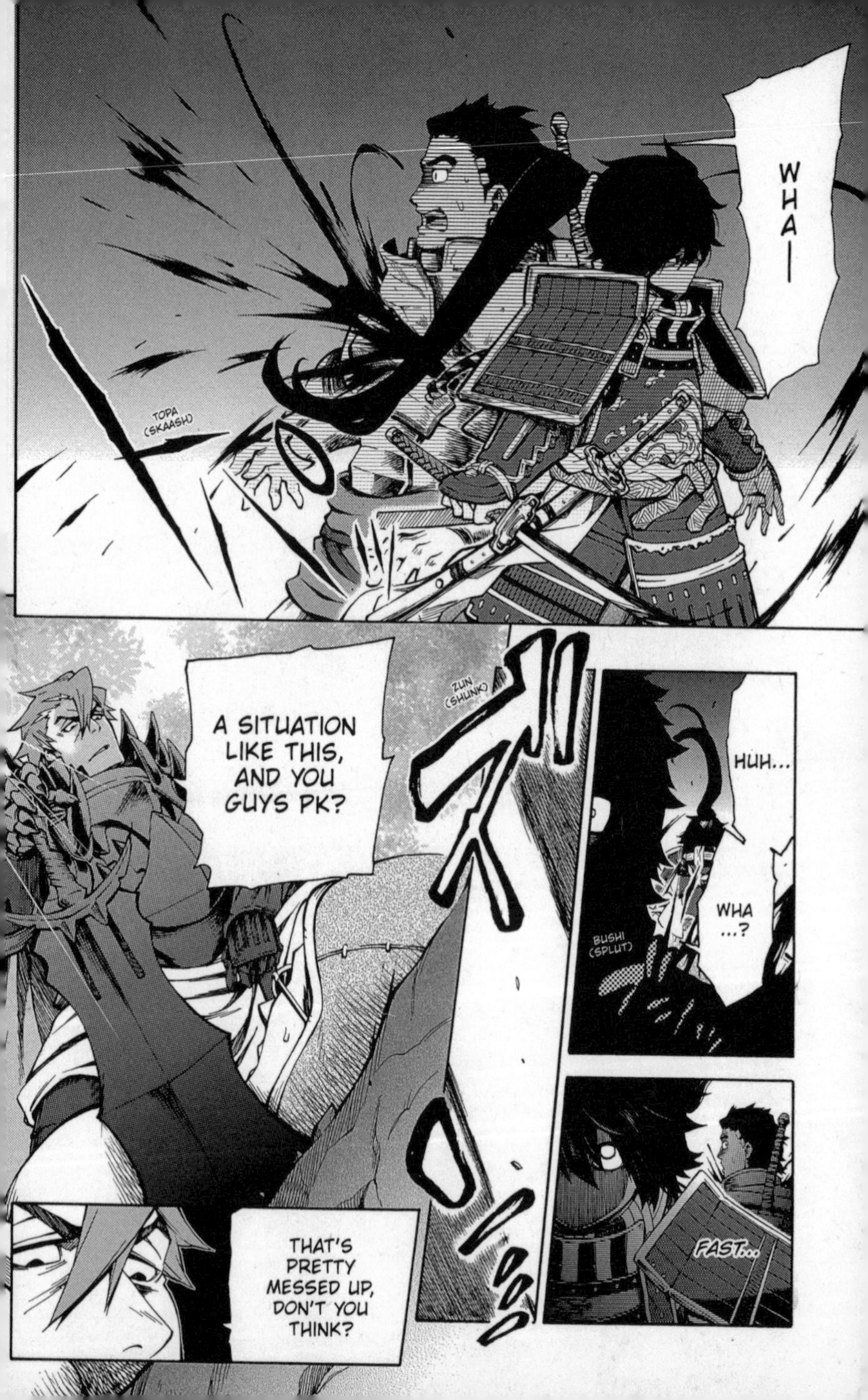
WHA—
TOPA (SKAASH)
HUH...
WHA ...?
BUSHI (SPLUT)
FAST...
ZUN (SHUNK)
A SITUATION LIKE THIS, AND YOU GUYS PK?
THAT'S PRETTY MESSED UP, DON'T YOU THINK?

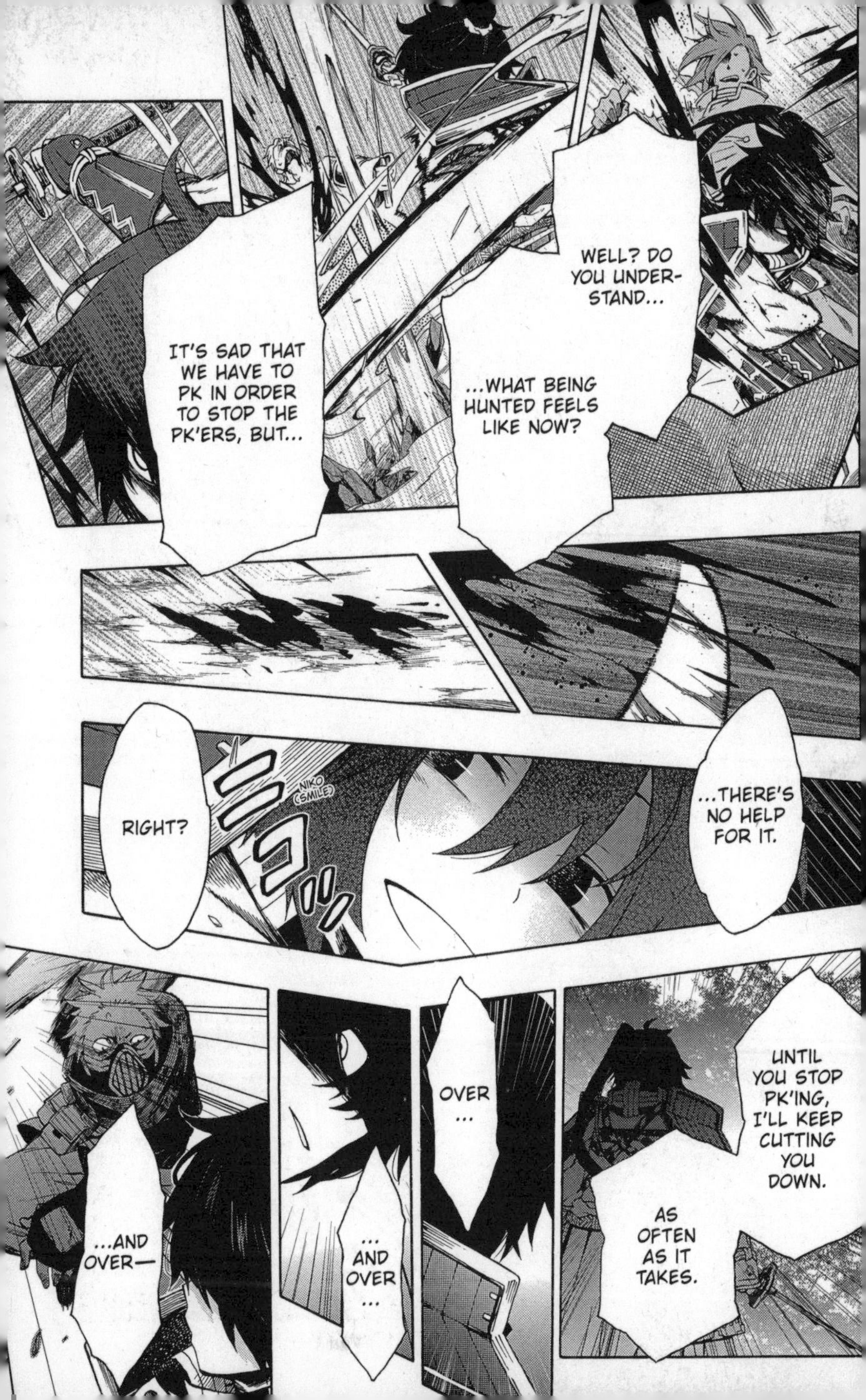
WELL? DO YOU UNDER-STAND...
...WHAT BEING HUNTED FEELS LIKE NOW?
IT'S SAD THAT WE HAVE TO PK IN ORDER TO STOP THE PK'ERS, BUT...
...THERE'S NO HELP FOR IT.
NIKO (SMILE)
RIGHT?
UNTIL YOU STOP PK'ING, I'LL KEEP CUTTING YOU DOWN.
AS OFTEN AS IT TAKES.
OVER...
...AND OVER...
...AND OVER—

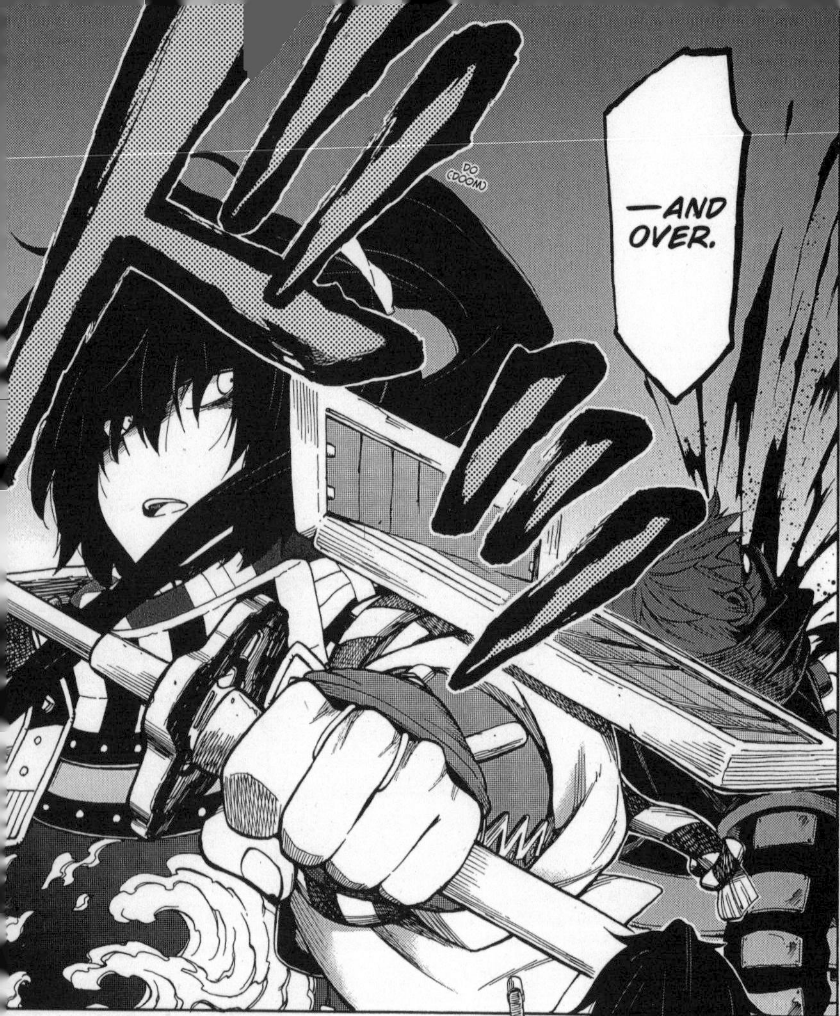
—AND OVER.
DO (DOOM)

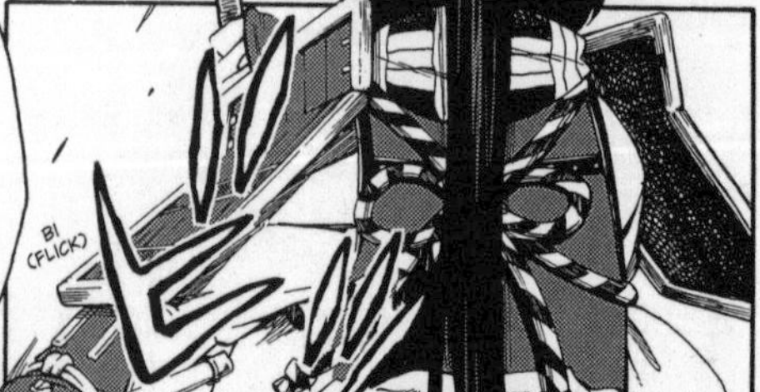
BI (FLICK)

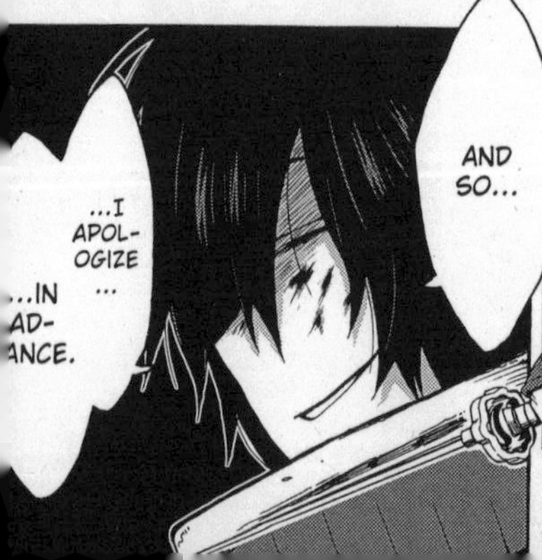
AND SO…
…I APOLOGIZE …
…IN AD-ANCE.

LOG HORIZON
THE WEST WIND BRIGADE

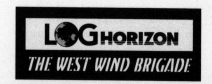

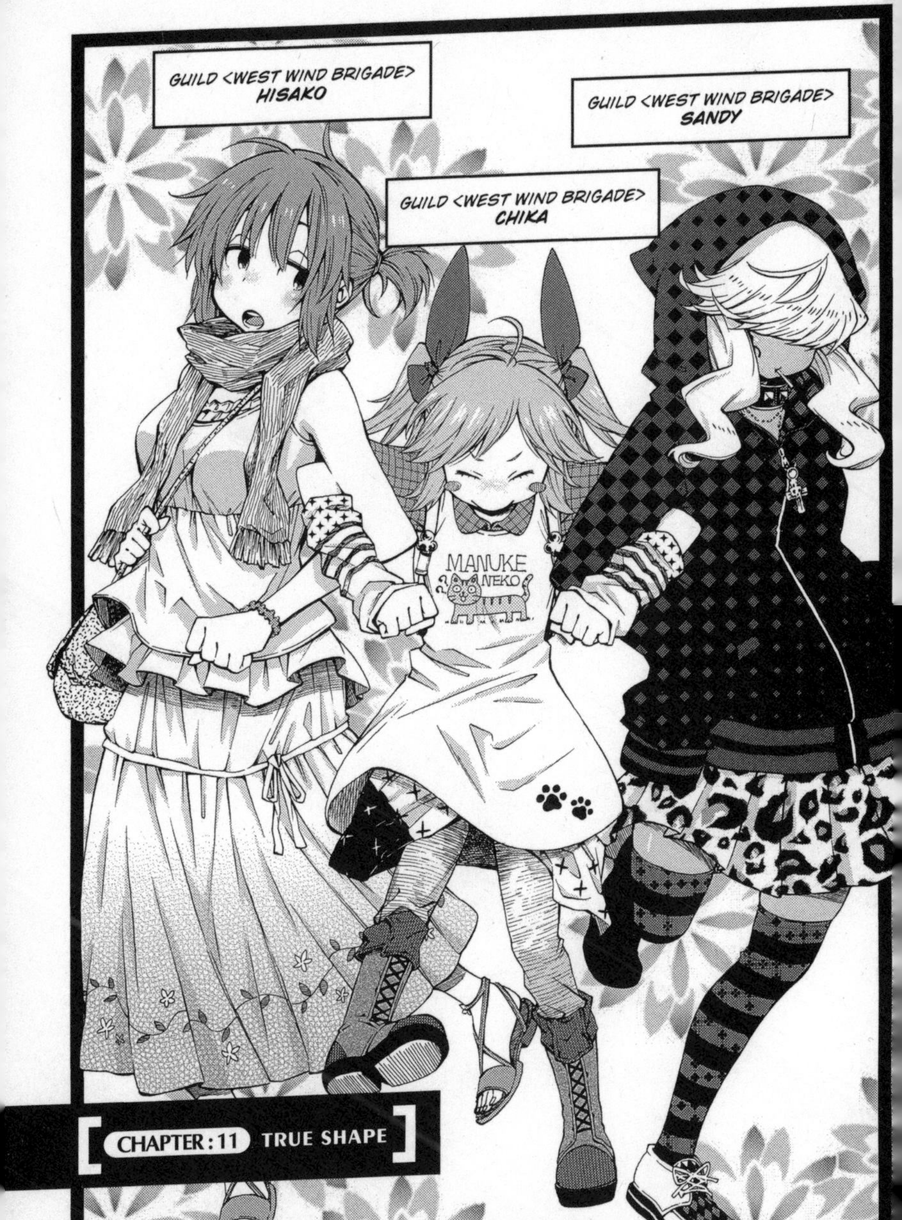
GUILD <WEST WIND BRIGADE>
SANDY
GUILD <WEST WIND BRIGADE>
HISAKO
GUILD <WEST WIND BRIGADE>
CHIKA
MANUKE NEKO

# CHAPTER : 11 TRUE SHAPE

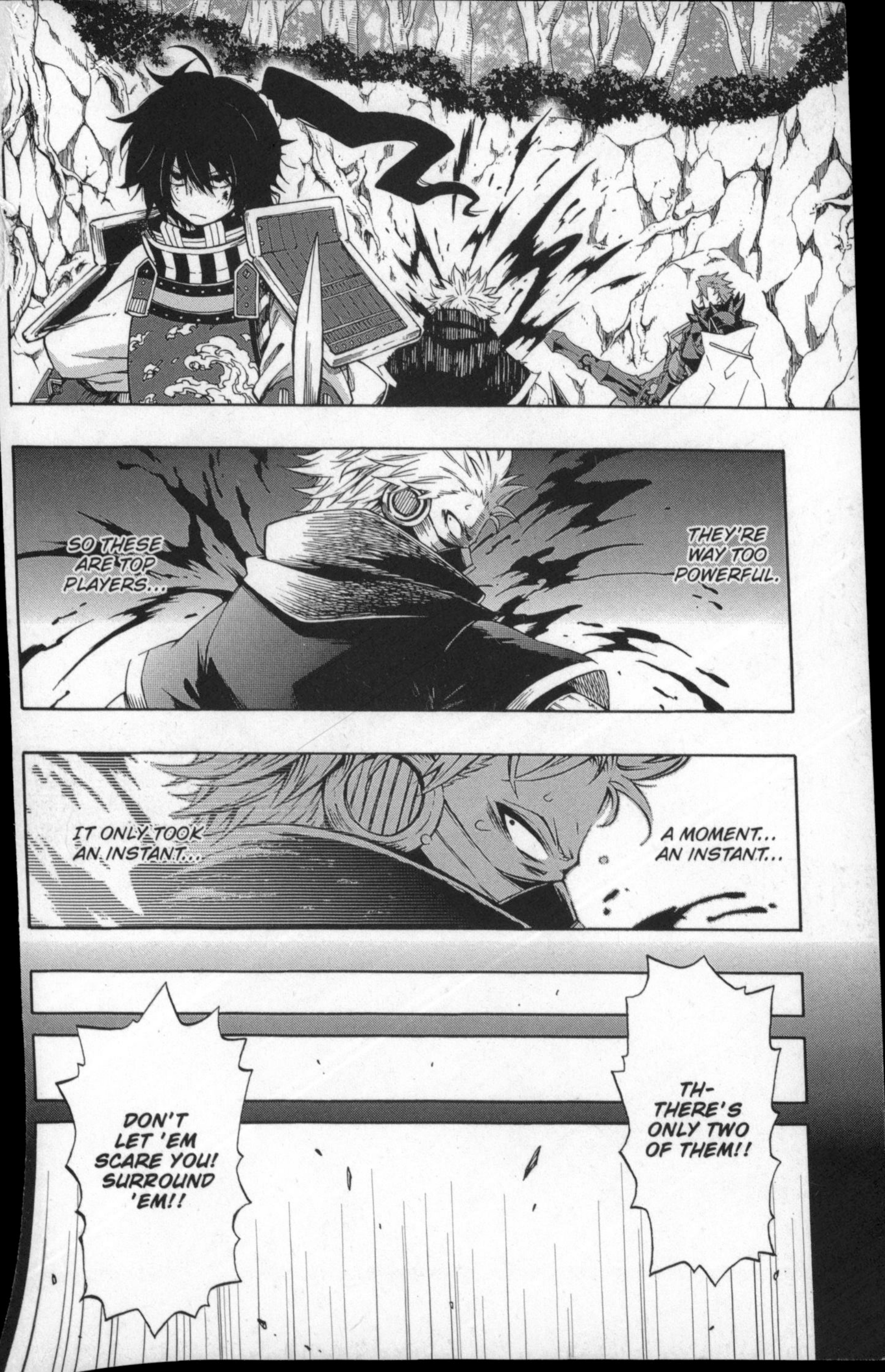
THEY'RE WAY TOO POWERFUL.
SO THESE ARE TOP PLAYERS...
A MOMENT... AN INSTANT...
IT ONLY TOOK AN INSTANT...
TH-THERE'S ONLY TWO OF THEM!!
DON'T LET 'EM SCARE YOU! SURROUND 'EM!!

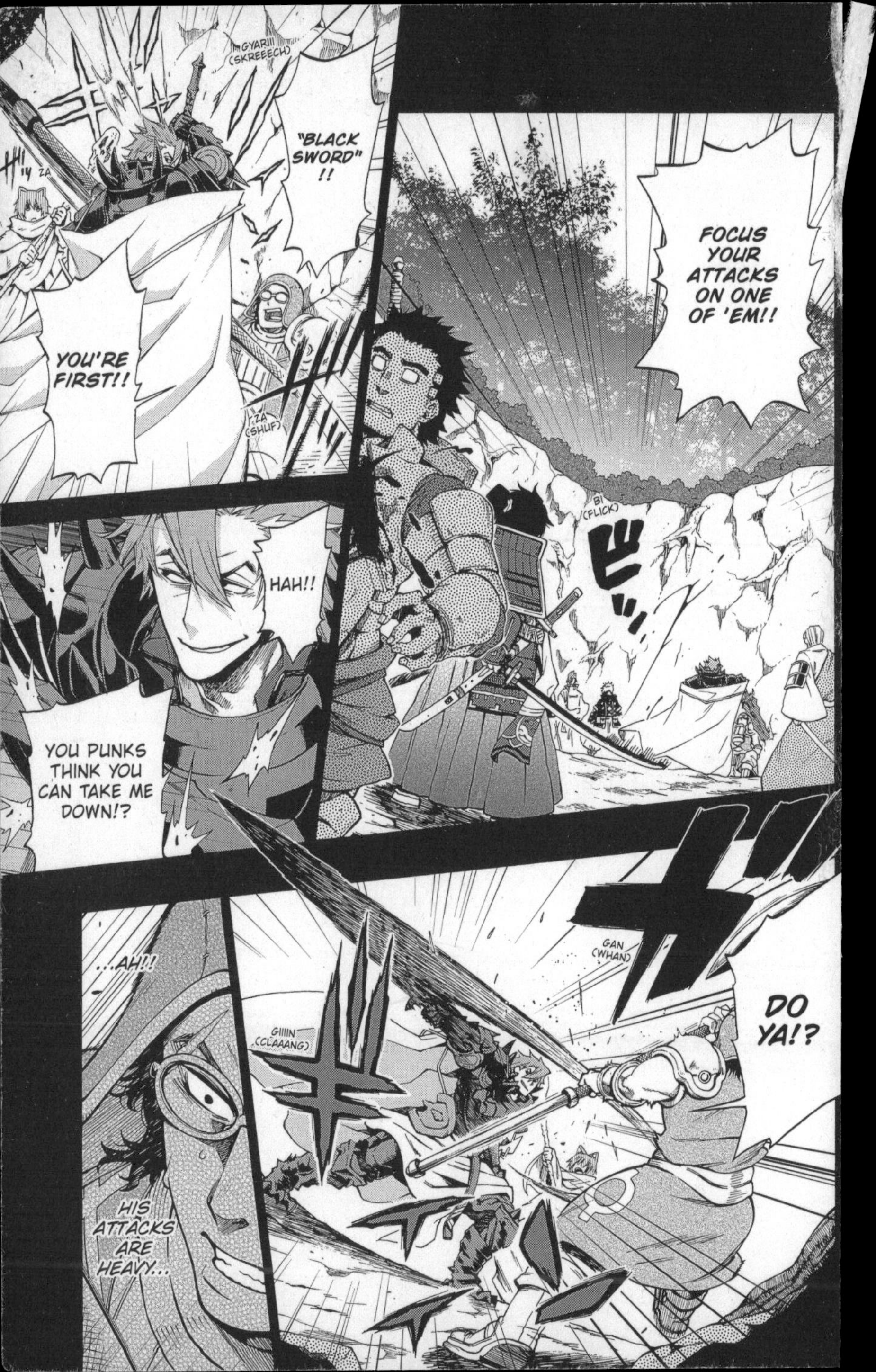
FOCUS YOUR ATTACKS ON ONE OF 'EM!!
BI (FLICK)
GYARIII (SKREEECH)
"BLACK SWORD" !!
ZA
YOU'RE FIRST!!
ZA (SHUF)
HAH!!
YOU PUNKS THINK YOU CAN TAKE ME DOWN!?
GAN (WHAN)
DO YA!?
GIIIN (CLAAANG)
...AH!!
HIS ATTACKS ARE HEAVY...

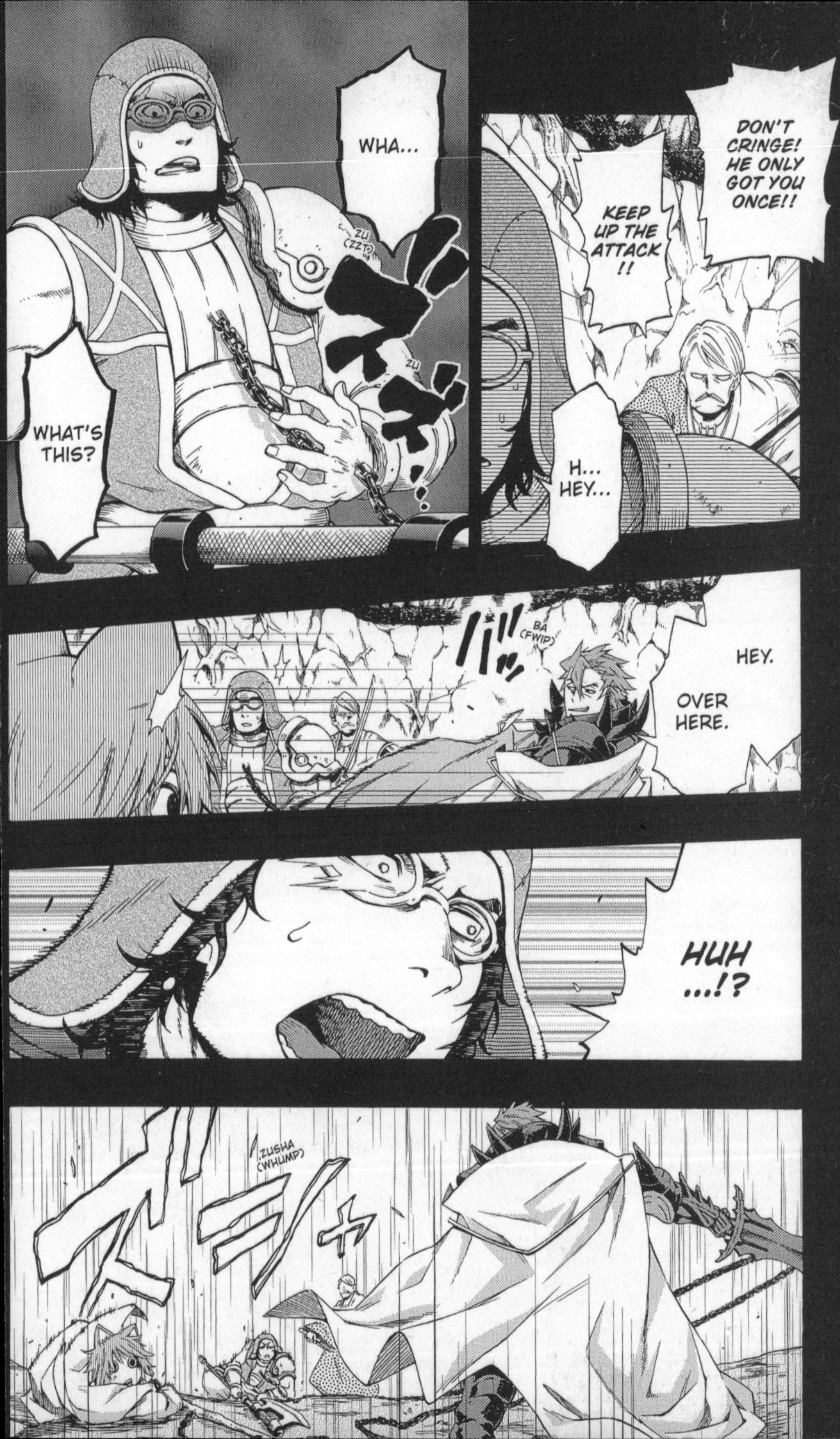
DON'T CRINGE! HE ONLY GOT YOU ONCE!!
KEEP UP THE ATTACK !!
H... HEY...
WHA...
ZU (ZZT)
ZU
WHAT'S THIS?
HEY.
OVER HERE.
BA (FWIP)
HUH ...!?
ZUSHA (WHUMP)

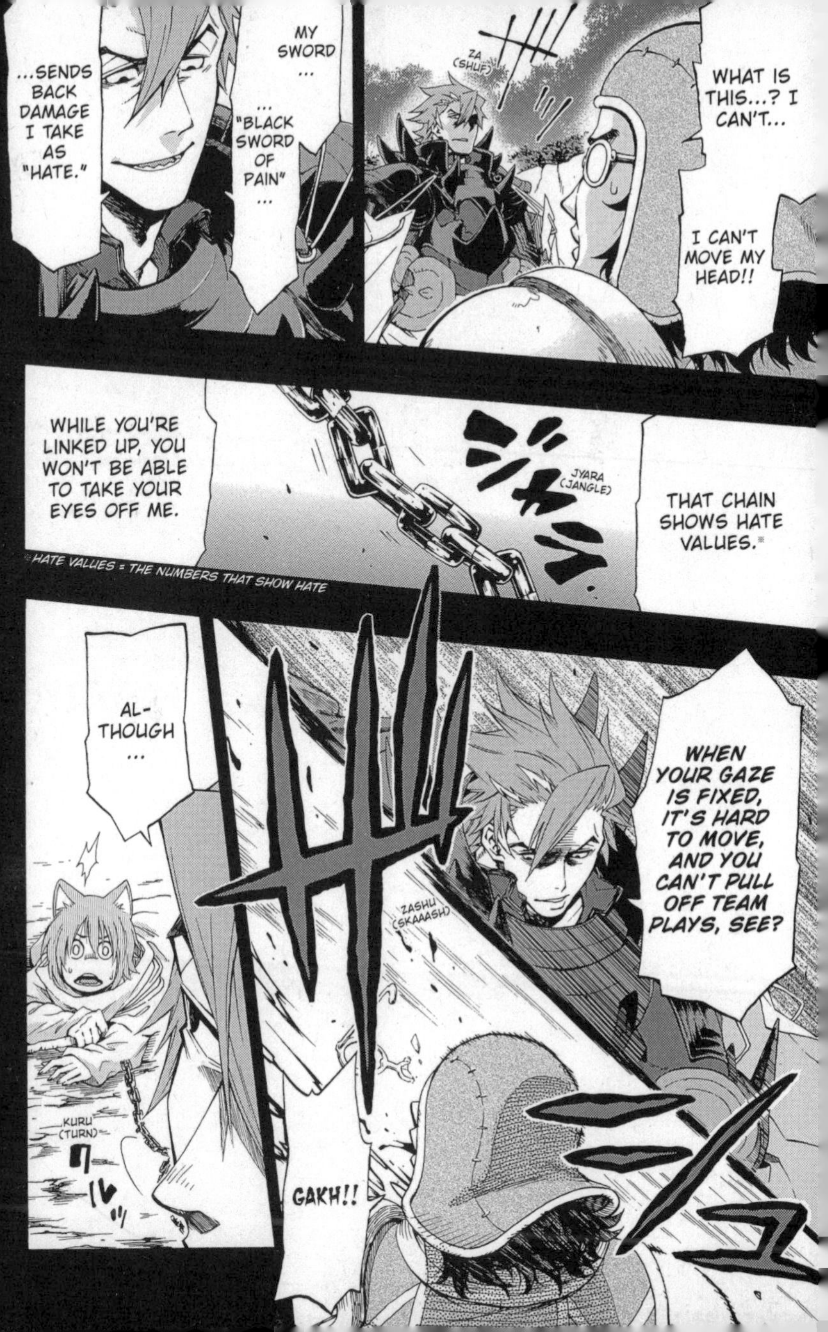

WHAT IS THIS...? I CAN'T...
ZA (SHUF)
I CAN'T MOVE MY HEAD!!
MY SWORD ...
... "BLACK SWORD OF PAIN" ...
...SENDS BACK DAMAGE I TAKE AS "HATE."
THAT CHAIN SHOWS HATE VALUES.*
JYARA (JANGLE)
WHILE YOU'RE LINKED UP, YOU WON'T BE ABLE TO TAKE YOUR EYES OFF ME.
*HATE VALUES = THE NUMBERS THAT SHOW HATE
WHEN YOUR GAZE IS FIXED, IT'S HARD TO MOVE, AND YOU CAN'T PULL OFF TEAM PLAYS, SEE?
ZASHU (SKAAASH)
AL-THOUGH ...
GAKH!!
KURU (TURN)

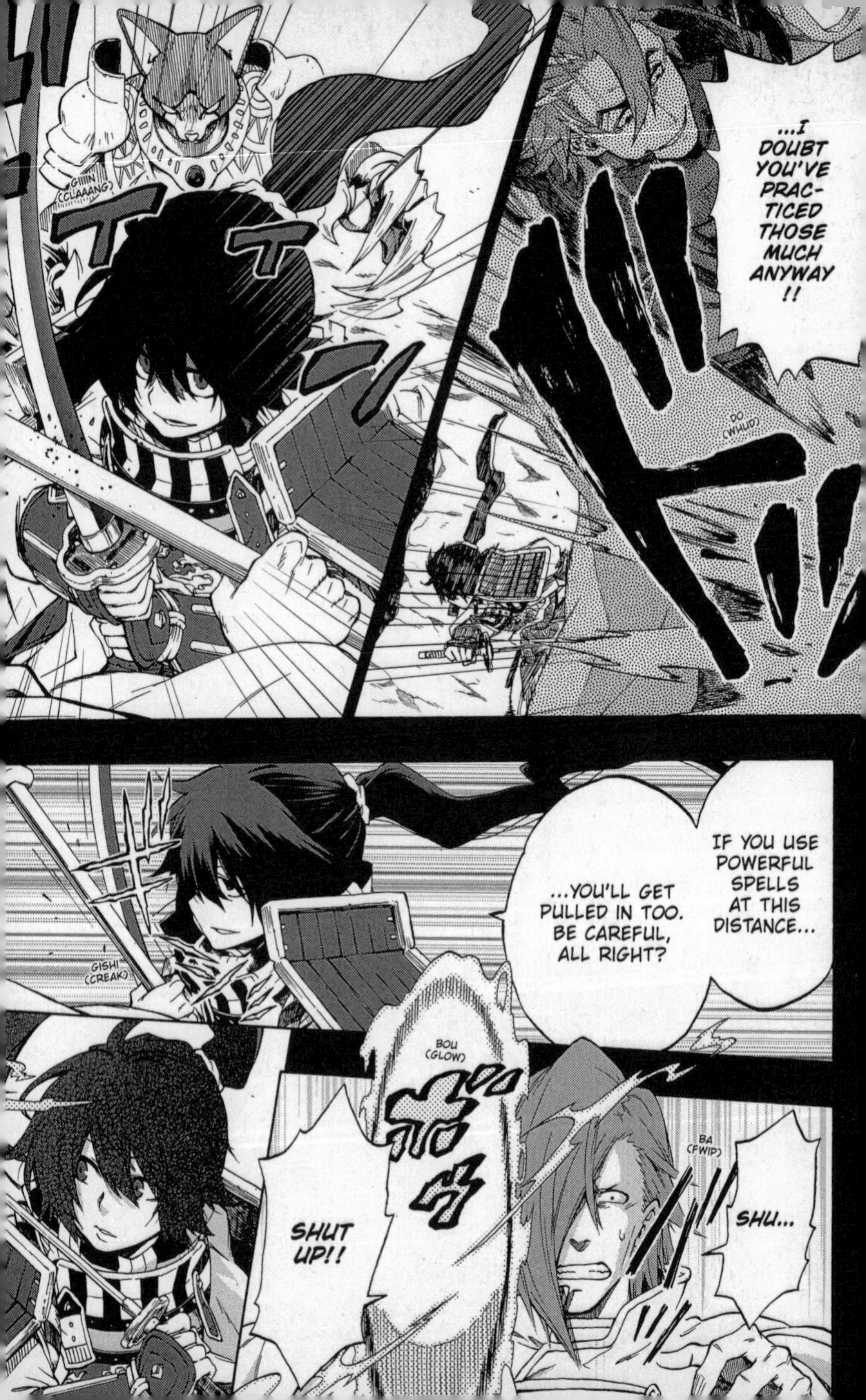
...I DOUBT YOU'VE PRAC-TICED THOSE MUCH ANYWAY!!
DO (WHUD)
GIIIN (CLAAANG)
IF YOU USE POWERFUL SPELLS AT THIS DISTANCE...
...YOU'LL GET PULLED IN TOO. BE CAREFUL, ALL RIGHT?
GISHI (CREAK)
BA (FWIP)
SHU...
BOU (GLOW)
SHUT UP!!

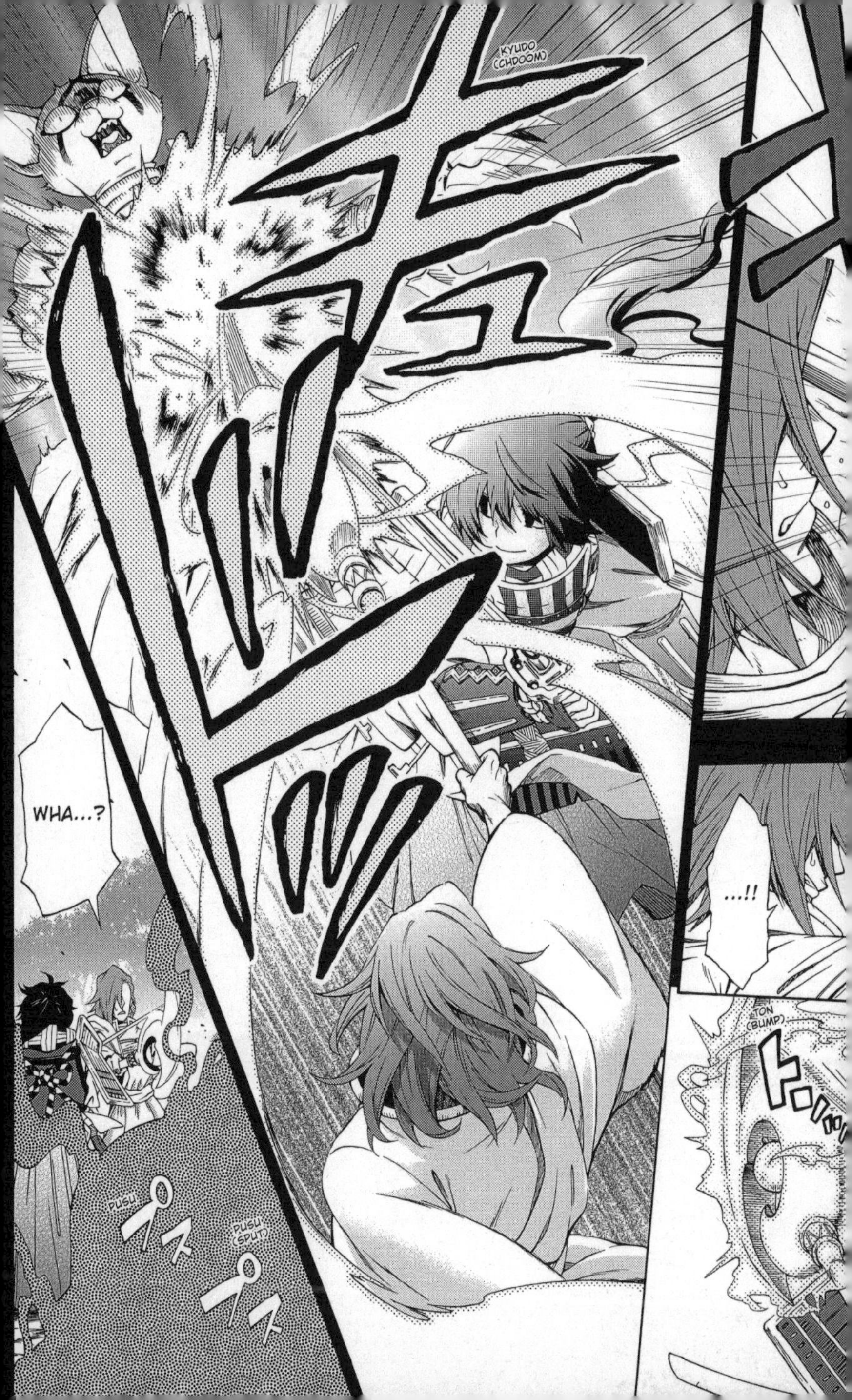
...!!
TON (BUMP)
KYUDO (CHDOOM)
WHA...?
PUSU
PUSU (SPUT)

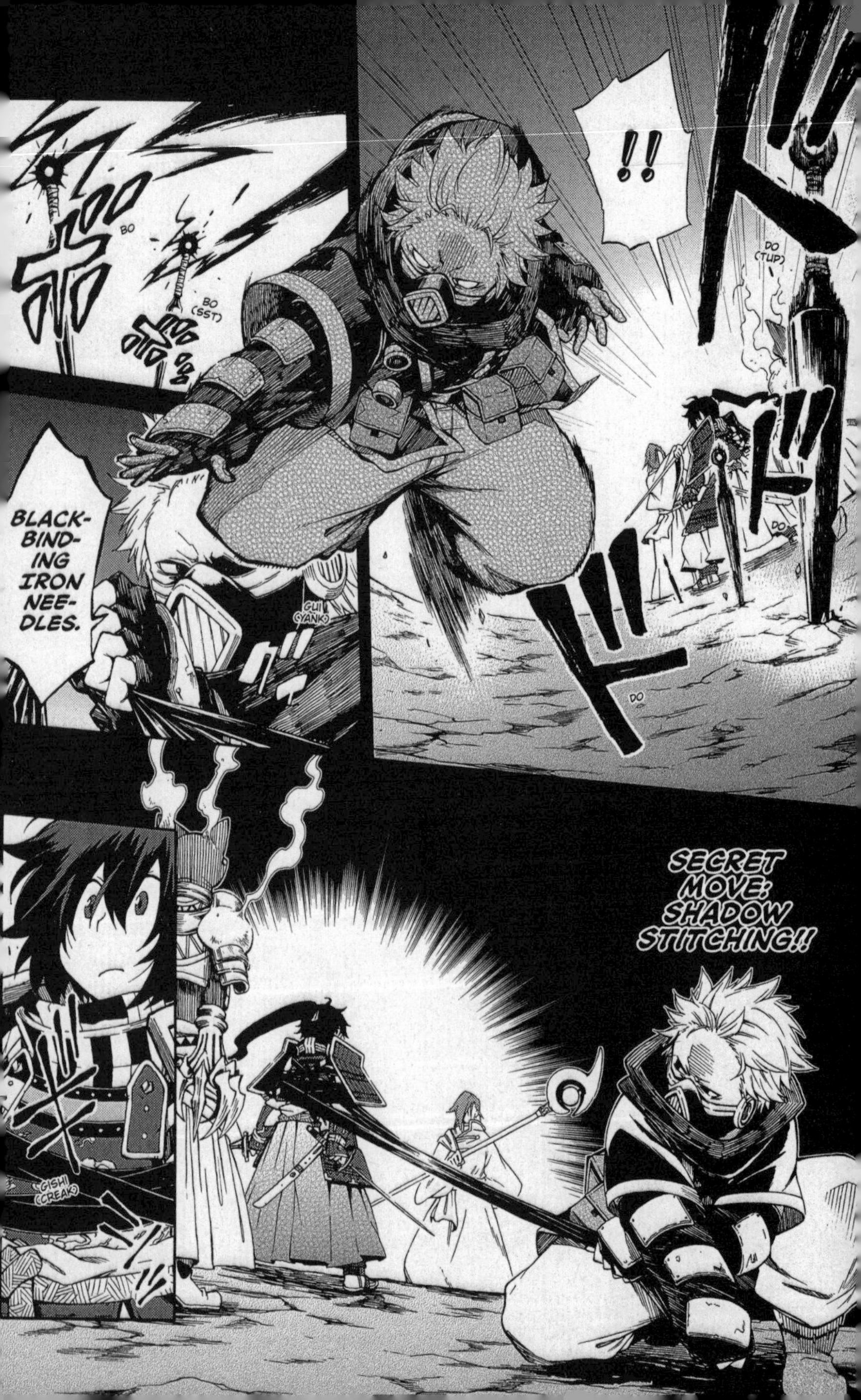
!!
DO (TUP)
DO
DO
BO
BO (SST)
BLACK-BINDING IRON NEEDLES.
GUI (YANK)
SECRET MOVE: SHADOW STITCHING!!
GISHI (CREAK)

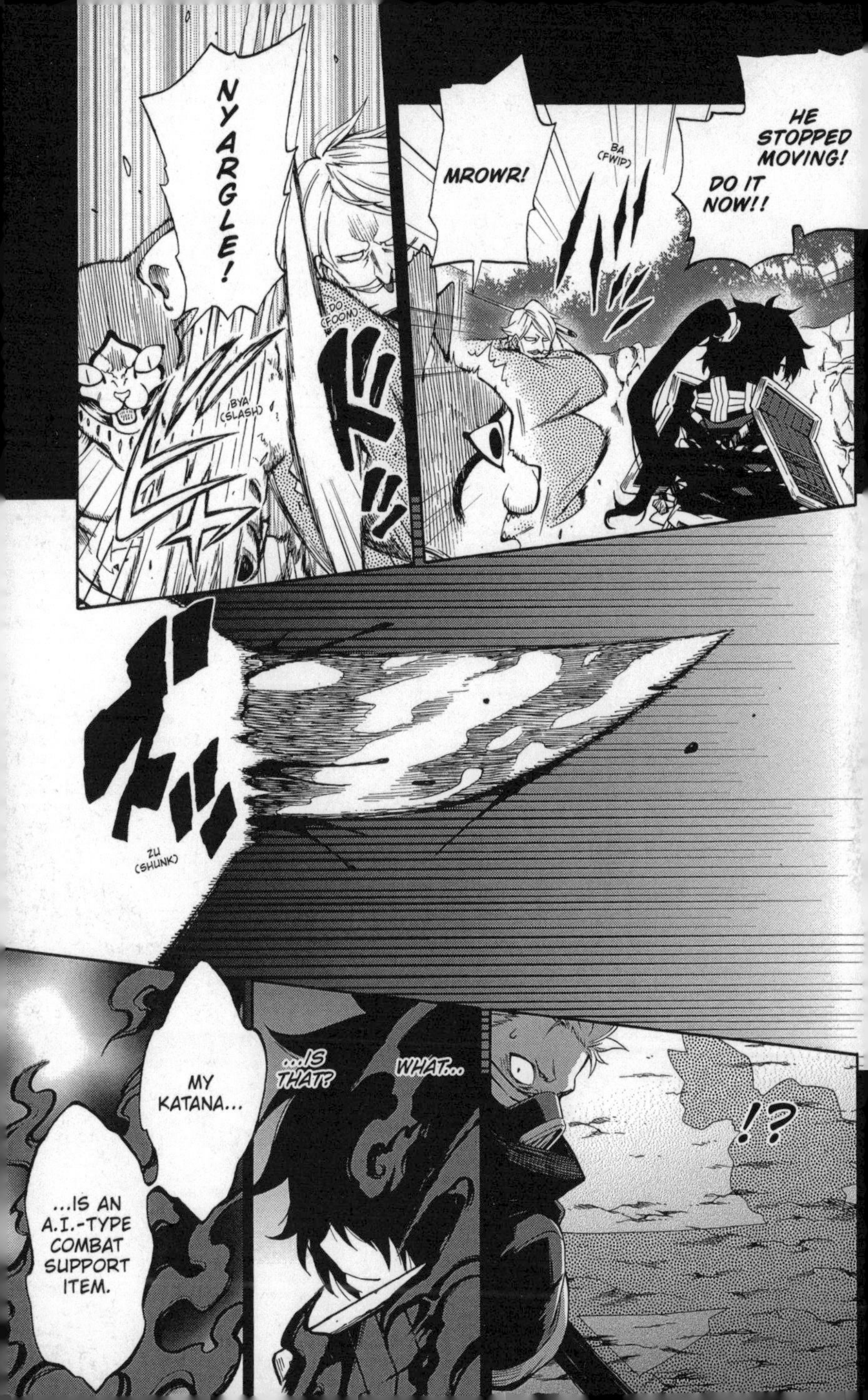
HE STOPPED MOVING!
DO IT NOW!!
BA (FWIP)
MROWR!
NYARGLE!
DO (FOOM)
BYA (SLASH)
ZU (SHUNK)
!?
WHAT...
...IS THAT?
MY KATANA...
...IS AN A.I.-TYPE COMBAT SUPPORT ITEM.

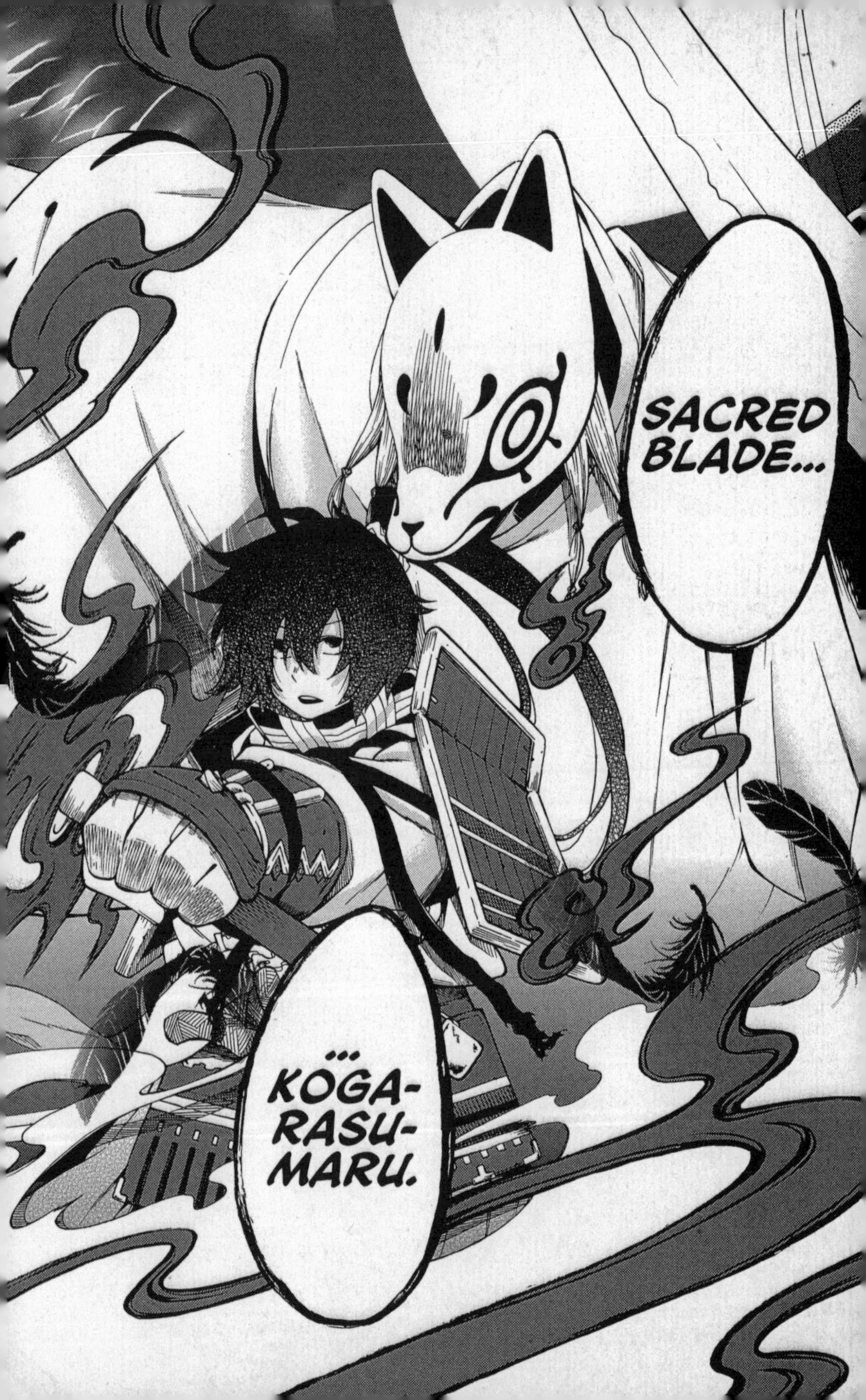
SACRED BLADE...
...KOGA-RASU-MARU.

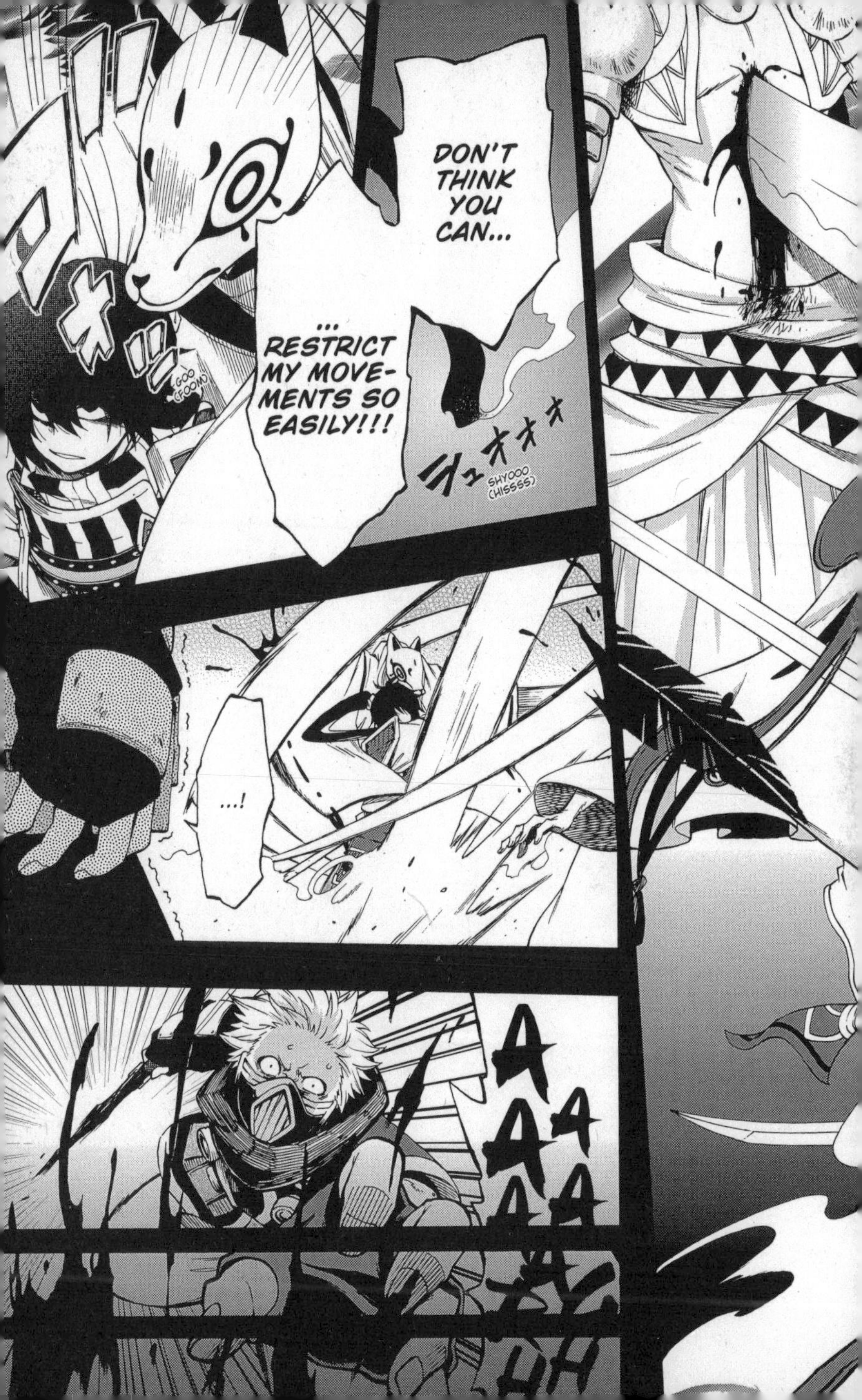
DON'T THINK YOU CAN...
...RESTRICT MY MOVE-MENTS SO EASILY!!!
シュオオオ
SHYOOO (HISSSS)
GOO (FOOM)
...!
AAAAAAH

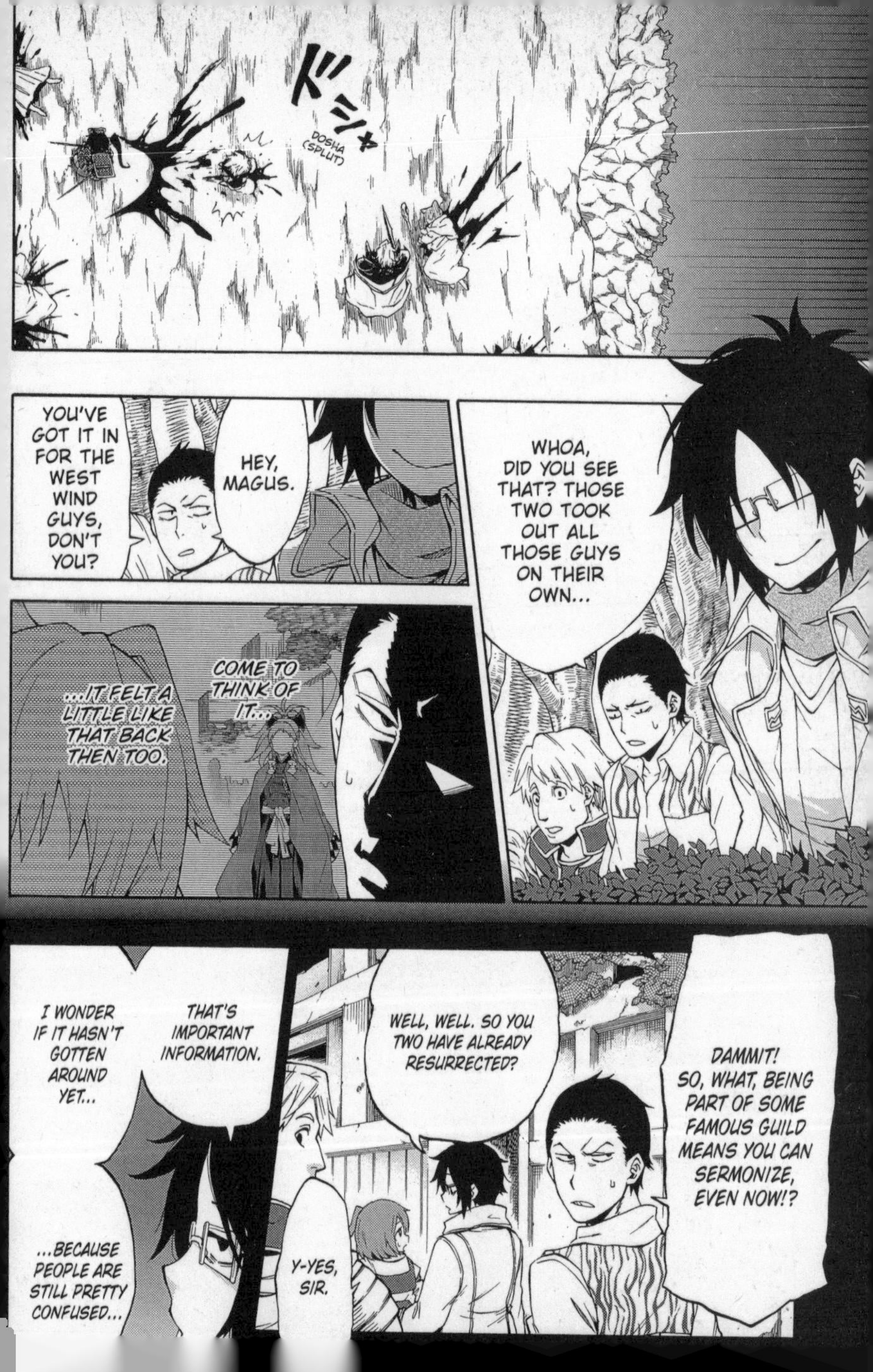
ドシャ
DOSHA (SPLUT)
WHOA, DID YOU SEE THAT? THOSE TWO TOOK OUT ALL THOSE GUYS ON THEIR OWN...
HEY, MAGUS.
YOU'VE GOT IT IN FOR THE WEST WIND GUYS, DON'T YOU?
COME TO THINK OF IT...
...IT FELT A LITTLE LIKE THAT BACK THEN TOO.
DAMMIT! SO, WHAT, BEING PART OF SOME FAMOUS GUILD MEANS YOU CAN SERMONIZE, EVEN NOW!?
WELL, WELL. SO YOU TWO HAVE ALREADY RESURRECTED?
Y-YES, SIR.
THAT'S IMPORTANT INFORMATION.
I WONDER IF IT HASN'T GOTTEN AROUND YET...
...BECAUSE PEOPLE ARE STILL PRETTY CONFUSED...

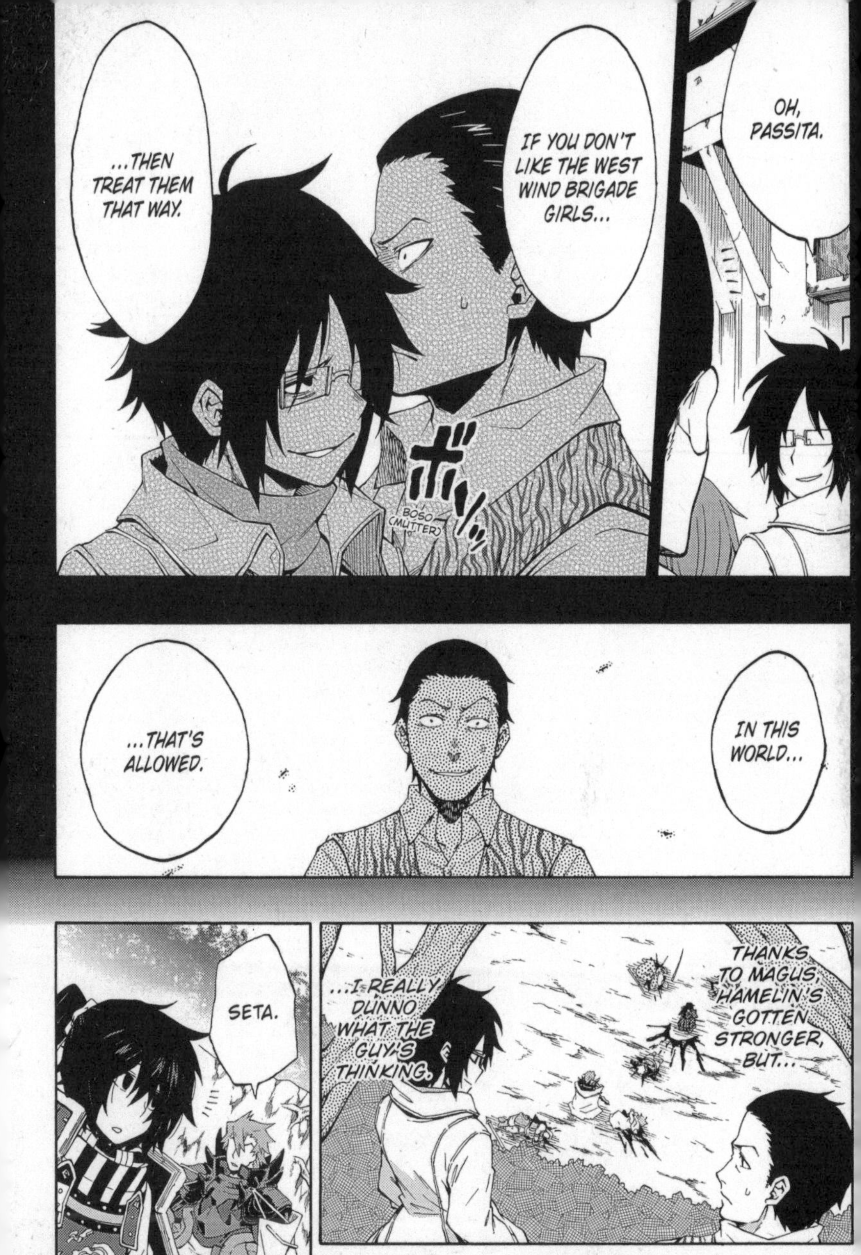
OH, PASSITA.
IF YOU DON'T LIKE THE WEST WIND BRIGADE GIRLS...
...THEN TREAT THEM THAT WAY.
ボソッ
BOSO (MUTTER)
IN THIS WORLD...
...THAT'S ALLOWED.
THANKS TO MAGUS, HAMELIN'S GOTTEN STRONGER, BUT...
...I REALLY DUNNO WHAT THE GUY'S THINKING.
SETA.

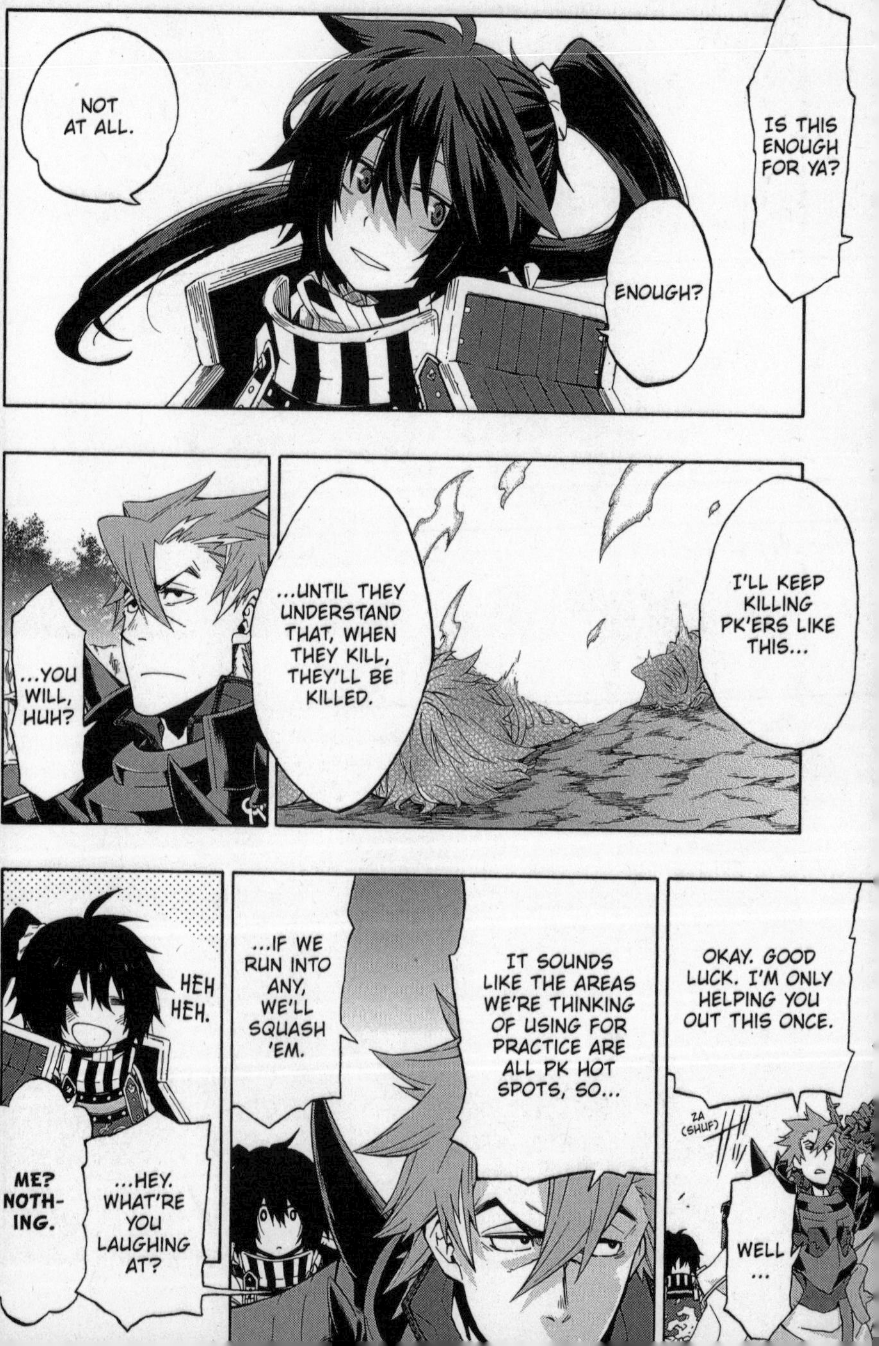
IS THIS ENOUGH FOR YA?
ENOUGH?
NOT AT ALL.
I'LL KEEP KILLING PK'ERS LIKE THIS...
...UNTIL THEY UNDERSTAND THAT, WHEN THEY KILL, THEY'LL BE KILLED.
...YOU WILL, HUH?
OKAY. GOOD LUCK. I'M ONLY HELPING YOU OUT THIS ONCE.
ZA (SHUF)
WELL ...
IT SOUNDS LIKE THE AREAS WE'RE THINKING OF USING FOR PRACTICE ARE ALL PK HOT SPOTS, SO...
...IF WE RUN INTO ANY, WE'LL SQUASH 'EM.
HEH HEH.
...HEY. WHAT'RE YOU LAUGHING AT?
ME? NOTHING.

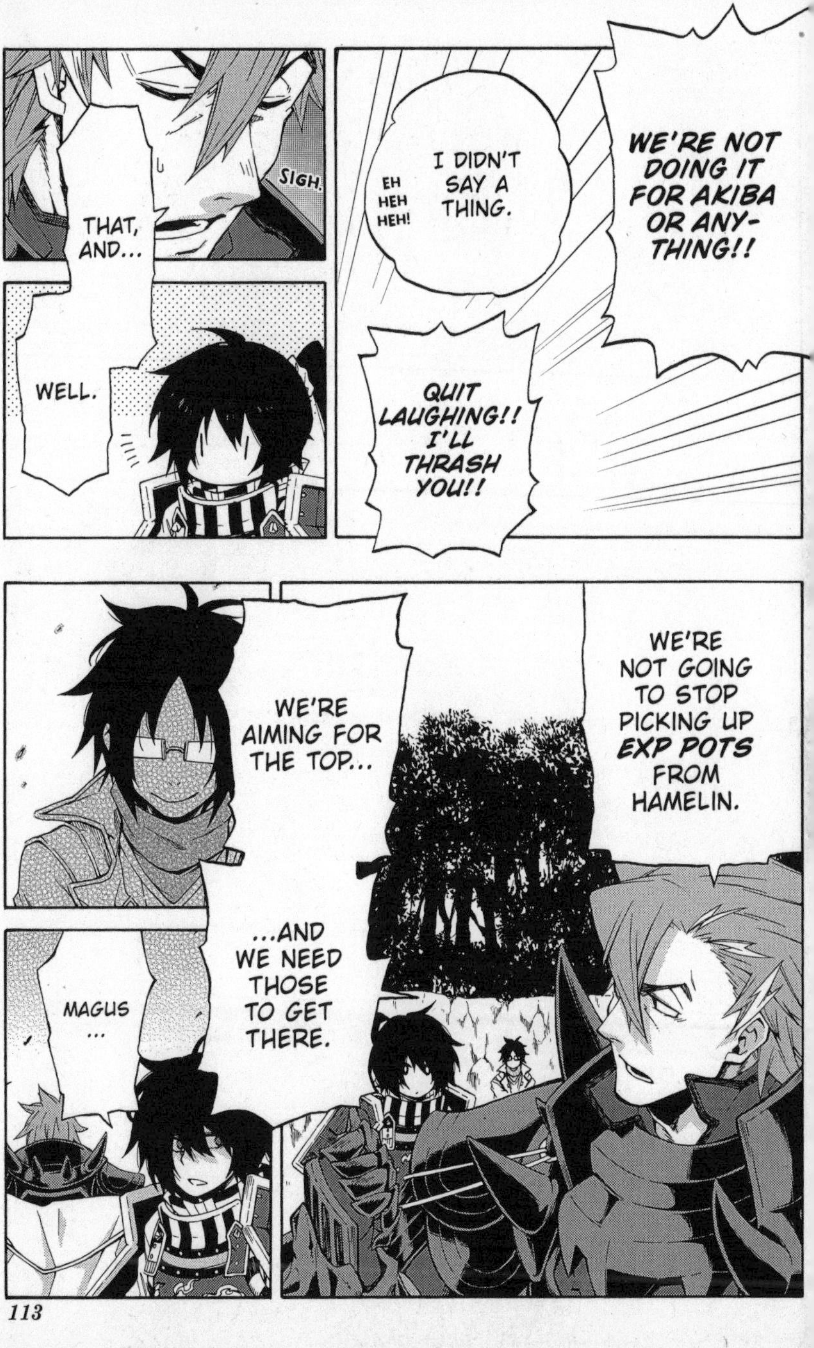
WE'RE NOT DOING IT FOR AKIBA OR ANYTHING!!
I DIDN'T SAY A THING.
EH HEH HEH!
QUIT LAUGHING!! I'LL THRASH YOU!!
SIGH.
THAT, AND...
WELL.
WE'RE NOT GOING TO STOP PICKING UP EXP POTS FROM HAMELIN.
WE'RE AIMING FOR THE TOP...
...AND WE NEED THOSE TO GET THERE.
MAGUS ...

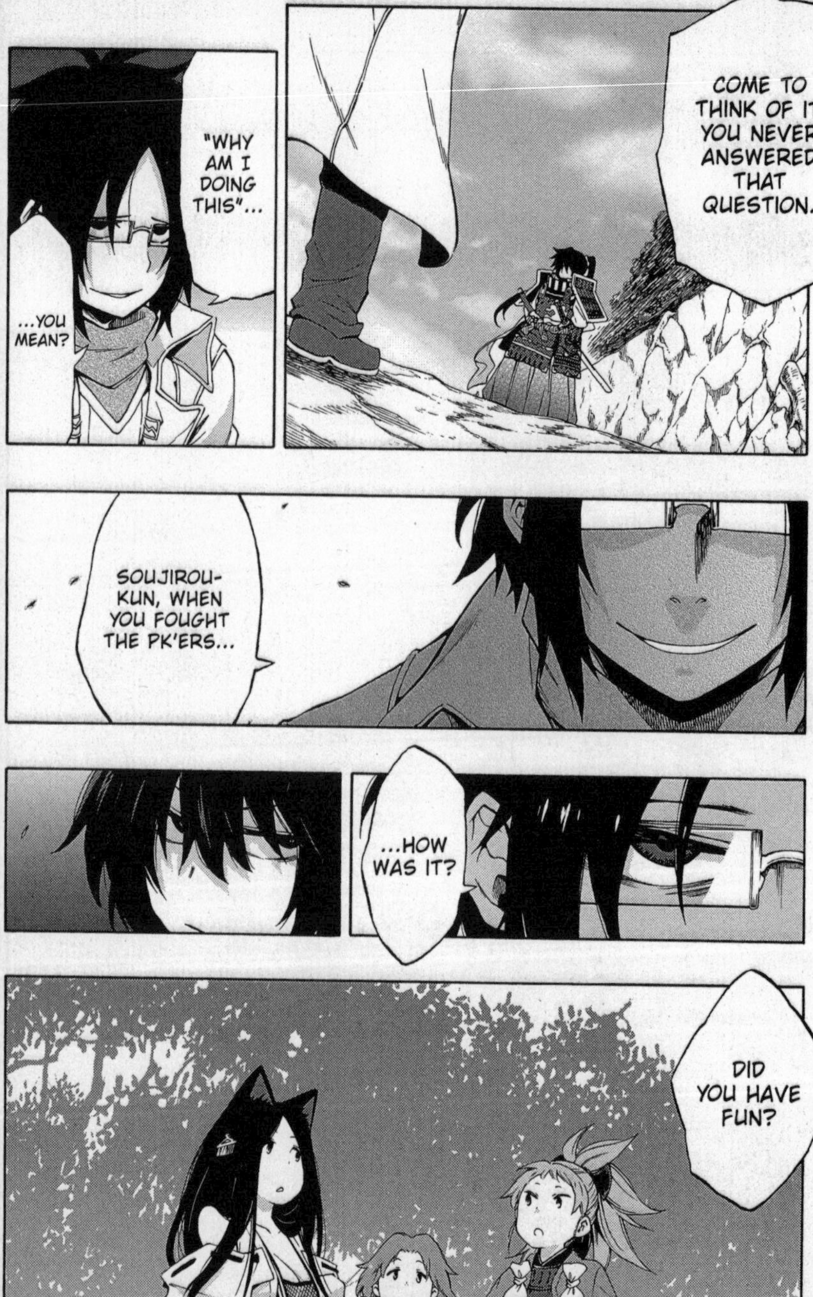
COME TO THINK OF IT, YOU NEVER ANSWERED THAT QUESTION.
"WHY AM I DOING THIS"...
...YOU MEAN?
SOUJIROU-KUN, WHEN YOU FOUGHT THE PK'ERS...
...HOW WAS IT?
DID YOU HAVE FUN?

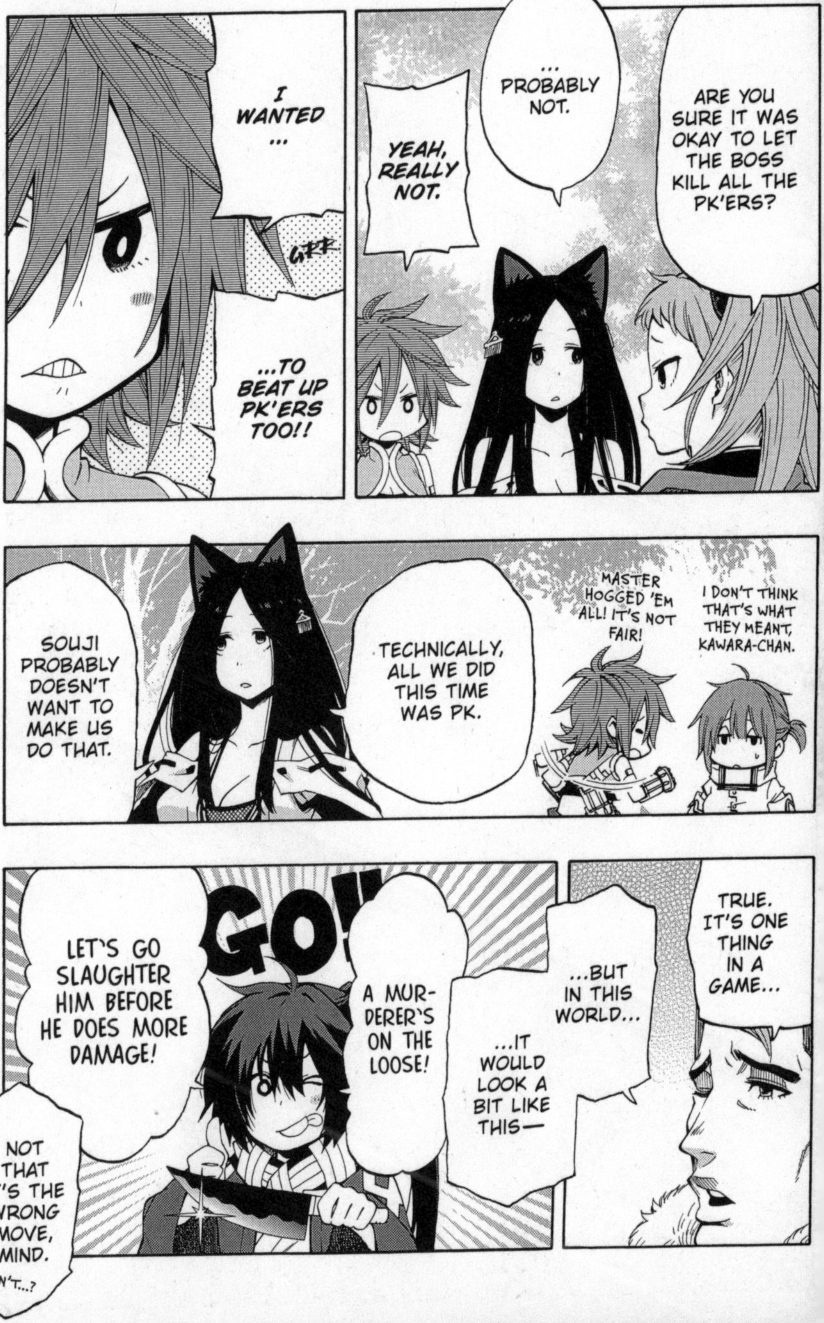
ARE YOU SURE IT WAS OKAY TO LET THE BOSS KILL ALL THE PK'ERS?
...PROBABLY NOT.
YEAH, REALLY NOT.
I WANTED ...
GRR
...TO BEAT UP PK'ERS TOO!!
MASTER HOGGED 'EM ALL! IT'S NOT FAIR!
I DON'T THINK THAT'S WHAT THEY MEANT, KAWARA-CHAN.
TECHNICALLY, ALL WE DID THIS TIME WAS PK.
SOUJI PROBABLY DOESN'T WANT TO MAKE US DO THAT.
TRUE. IT'S ONE THING IN A GAME...
...BUT IN THIS WORLD...
...IT WOULD LOOK A BIT LIKE THIS—
A MURDERER'S ON THE LOOSE!
GO!!
LET'S GO SLAUGHTER HIM BEFORE HE DOES MORE DAMAGE!
NOT THAT IT'S THE WRONG MOVE, MIND.
IT ISN'T...?

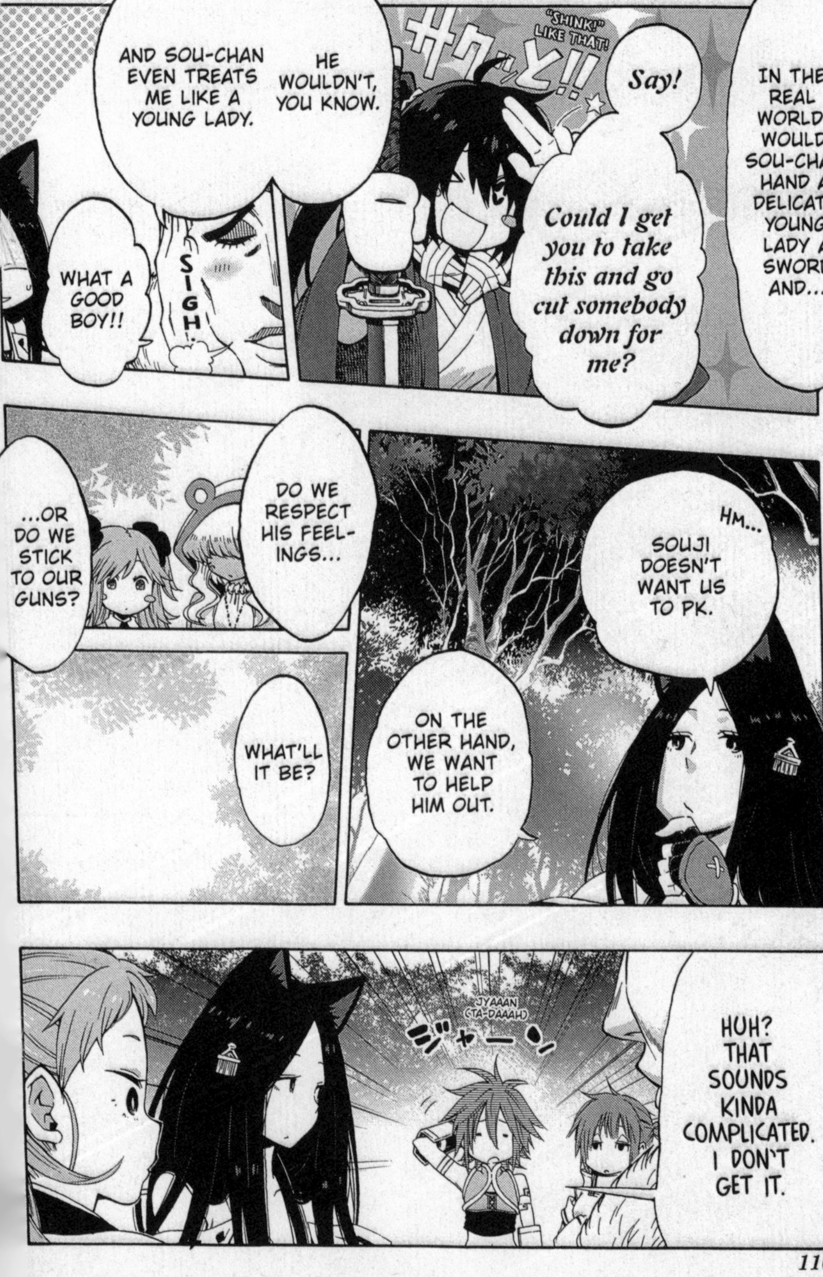
IN THE REAL WORLD, WOULD SOU-CHAN HAND A DELICATE YOUNG LADY A SWORD AND...
Say!
"SHINK!" LIKE THAT!
Could I get you to take this and go cut somebody down for me?
HE WOULDN'T, YOU KNOW.
AND SOU-CHAN EVEN TREATS ME LIKE A YOUNG LADY.
SIGH.
WHAT A GOOD BOY!!
HM...
SOUJI DOESN'T WANT US TO PK.
ON THE OTHER HAND, WE WANT TO HELP HIM OUT.
DO WE RESPECT HIS FEEL-INGS...
...OR DO WE STICK TO OUR GUNS?
WHAT'LL IT BE?
HUH? THAT SOUNDS KINDA COMPLICATED. I DON'T GET IT.
JYAAAN (TA-DAAAH)

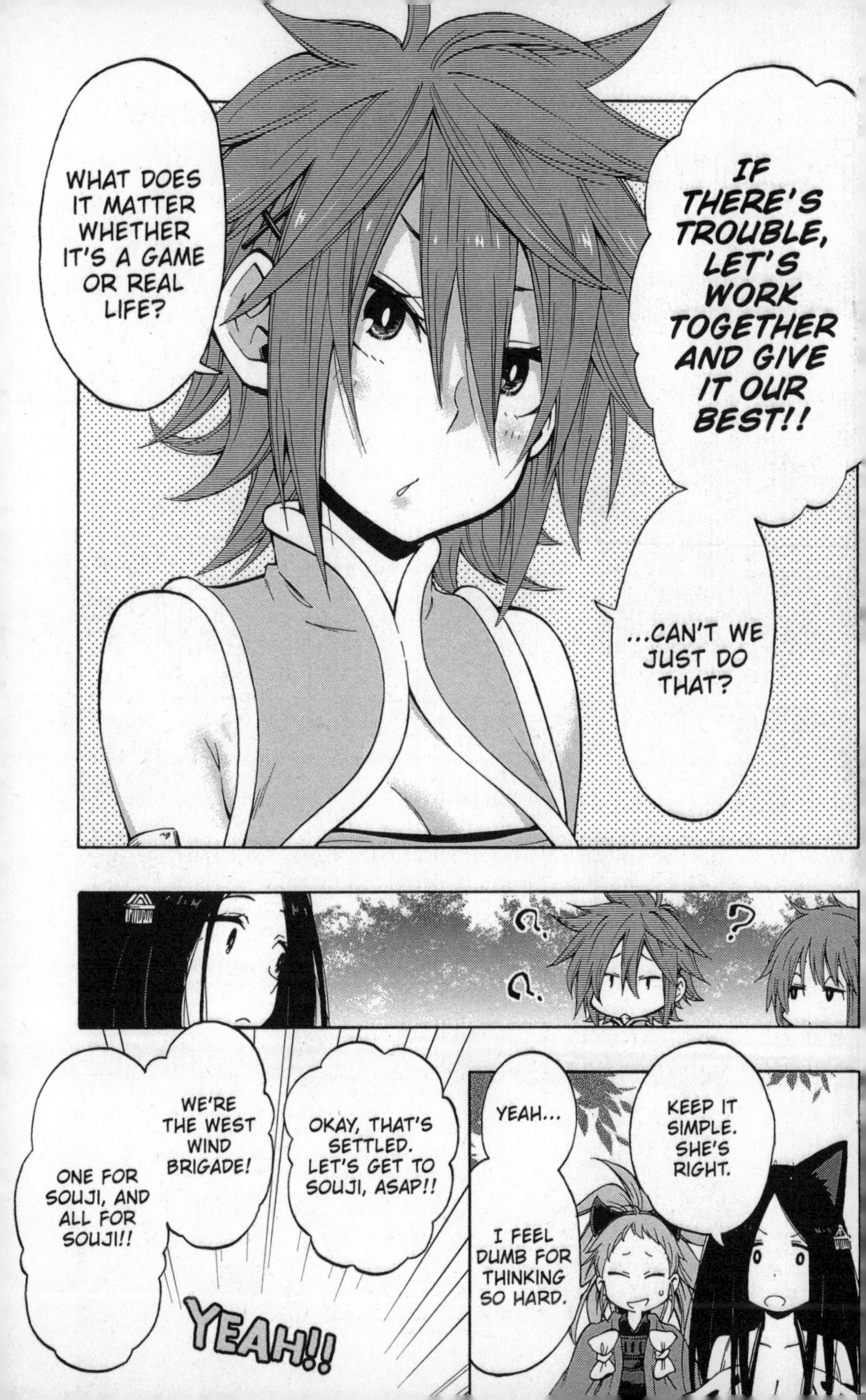
IF THERE'S TROUBLE, LET'S WORK TOGETHER AND GIVE IT OUR BEST!!
WHAT DOES IT MATTER WHETHER IT'S A GAME OR REAL LIFE?
...CAN'T WE JUST DO THAT?
KEEP IT SIMPLE. SHE'S RIGHT.
YEAH...
I FEEL DUMB FOR THINKING SO HARD.
OKAY, THAT'S SETTLED. LET'S GET TO SOUJI, ASAP!!
WE'RE THE WEST WIND BRIGADE!
ONE FOR SOUJI, AND ALL FOR SOUJI!!
YEAH!!

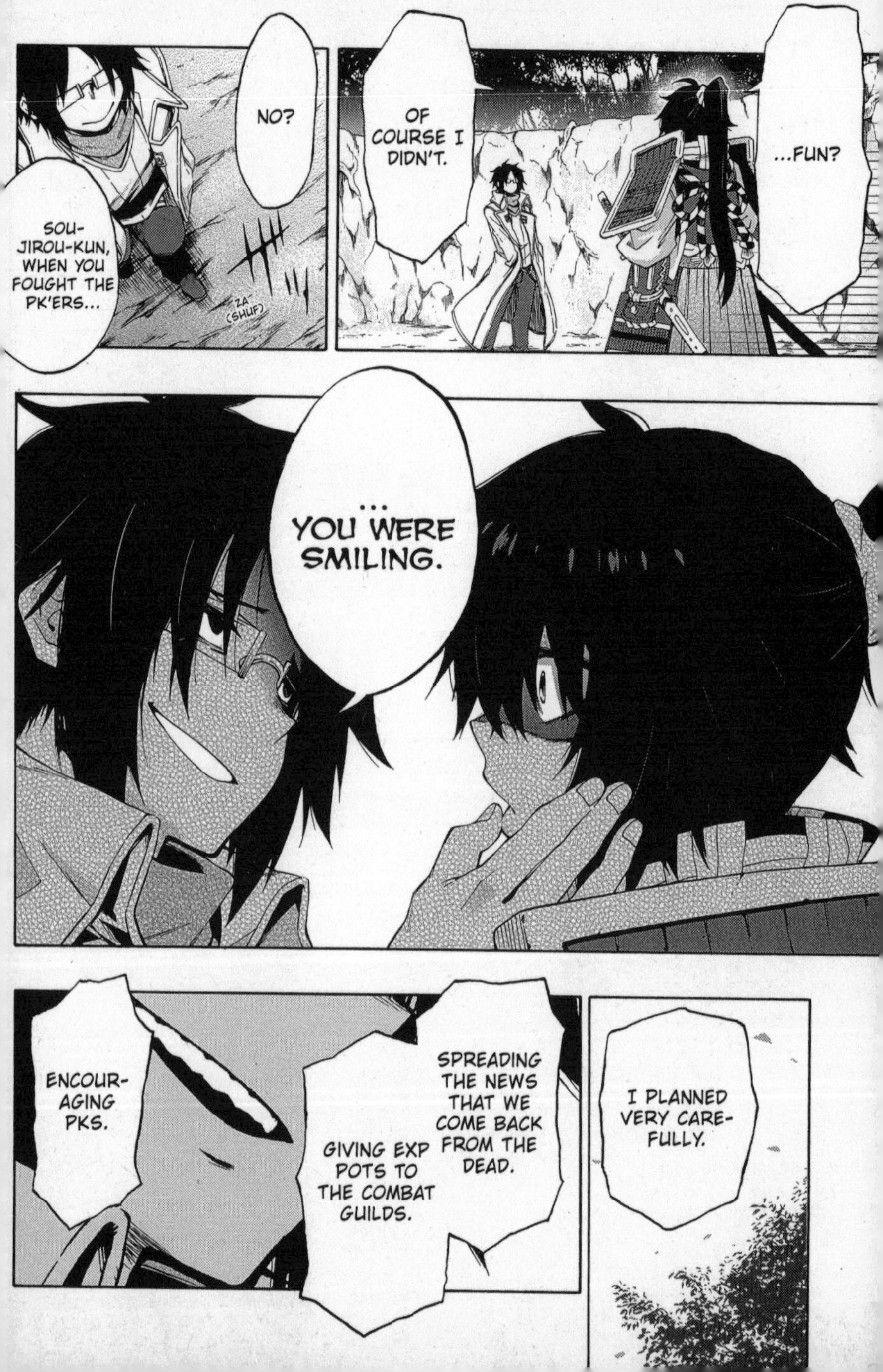
...FUN?
OF COURSE I DIDN'T.
NO?
SOU-JIROU-KUN, WHEN YOU FOUGHT THE PK'ERS...
ZA (SHUF)
... YOU WERE SMILING.
I PLANNED VERY CARE-FULLY.
SPREADING THE NEWS THAT WE COME BACK FROM THE DEAD.
ENCOUR-AGING PKS.
GIVING EXP POTS TO THE COMBAT GUILDS.

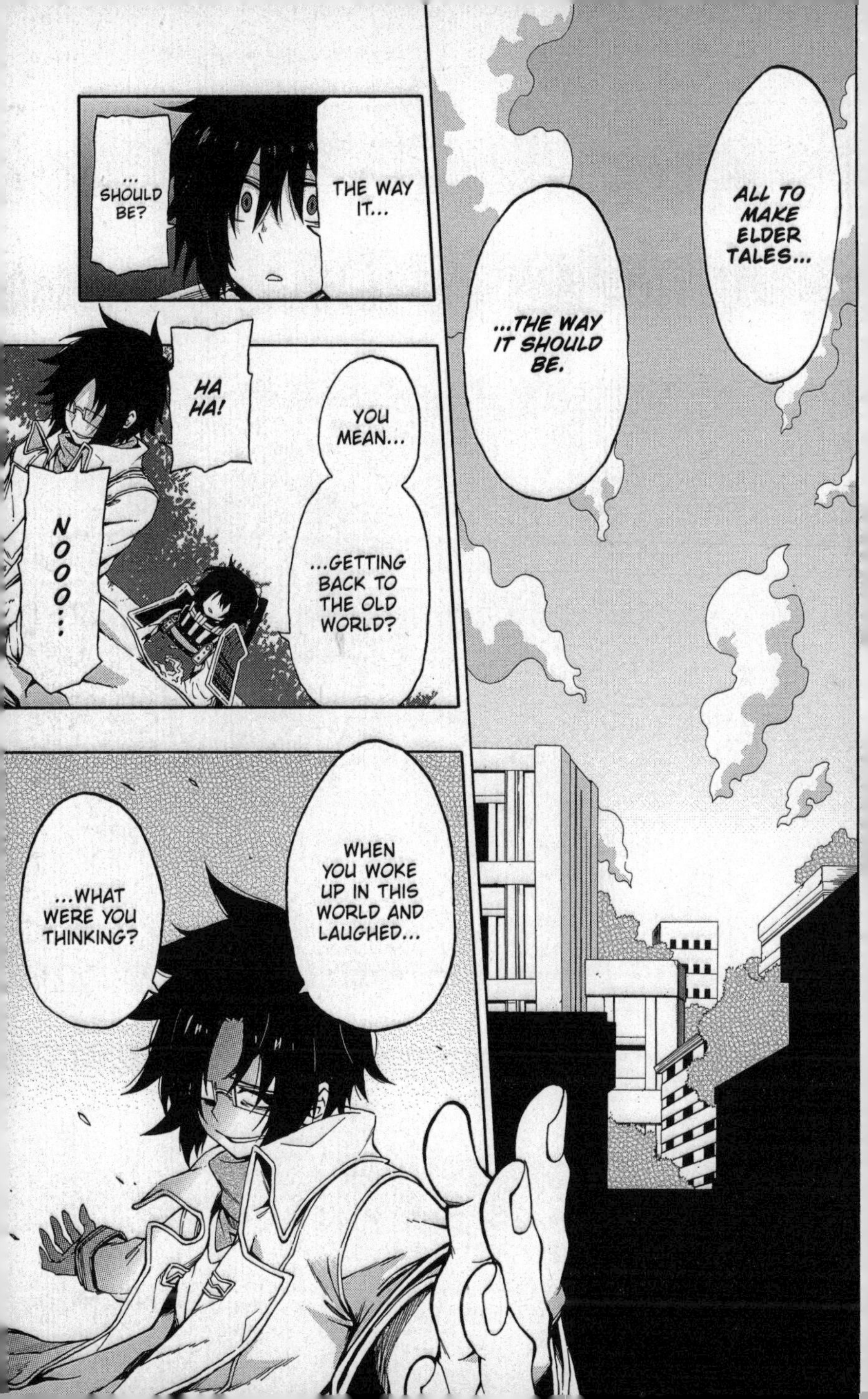
ALL TO MAKE ELDER TALES...
...THE WAY IT SHOULD BE.
THE WAY IT...
...SHOULD BE?
YOU MEAN...
...GETTING BACK TO THE OLD WORLD?
HA HA!
NOOOO...
WHEN YOU WOKE UP IN THIS WORLD AND LAUGHED...
...WHAT WERE YOU THINKING?

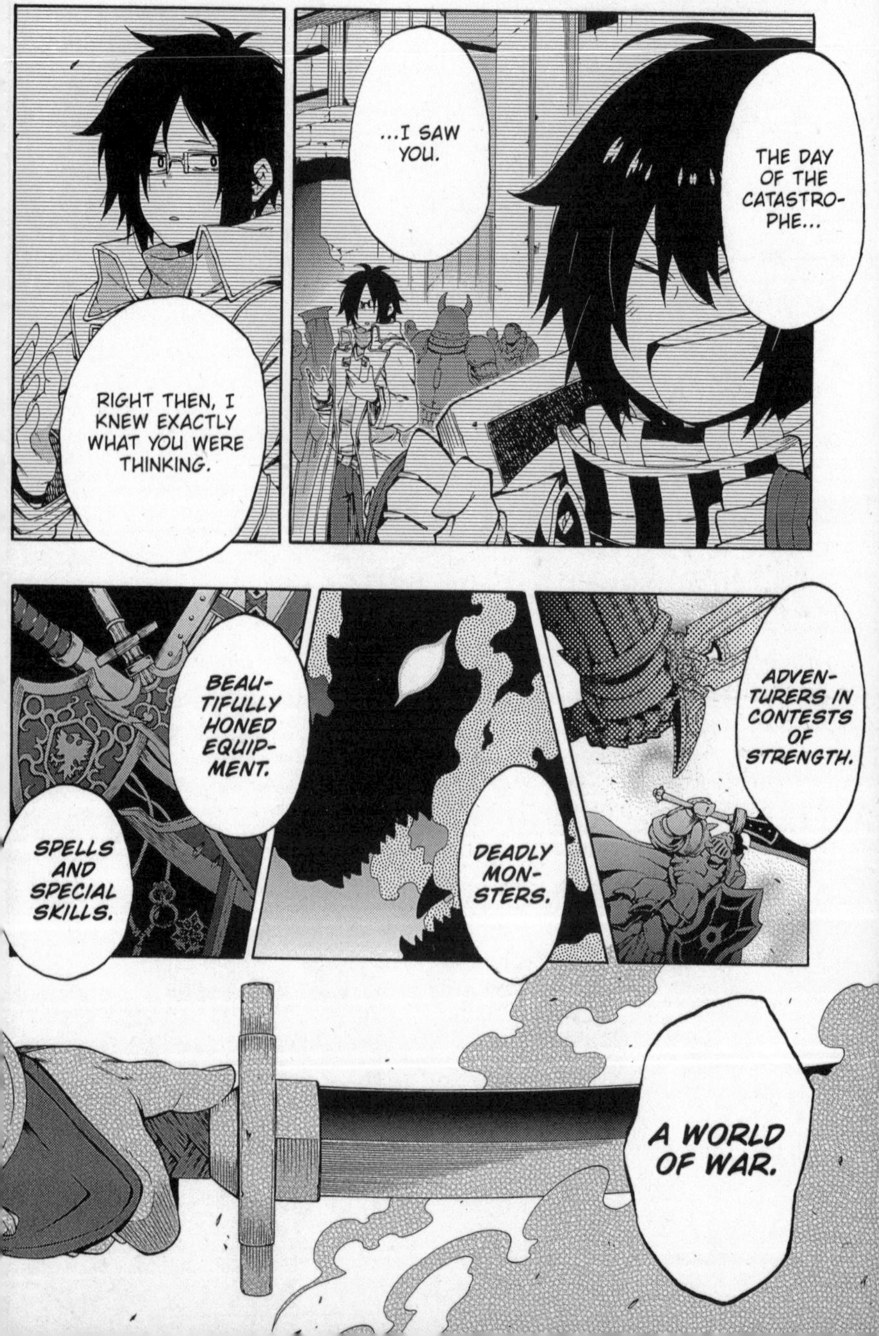
THE DAY OF THE CATASTROPHE...
...I SAW YOU.
RIGHT THEN, I KNEW EXACTLY WHAT YOU WERE THINKING.
ADVENTURERS IN CONTESTS OF STRENGTH.
DEADLY MONSTERS.
BEAUTIFULLY HONED EQUIPMENT.
SPELLS AND SPECIAL SKILLS.
A WORLD OF WAR.

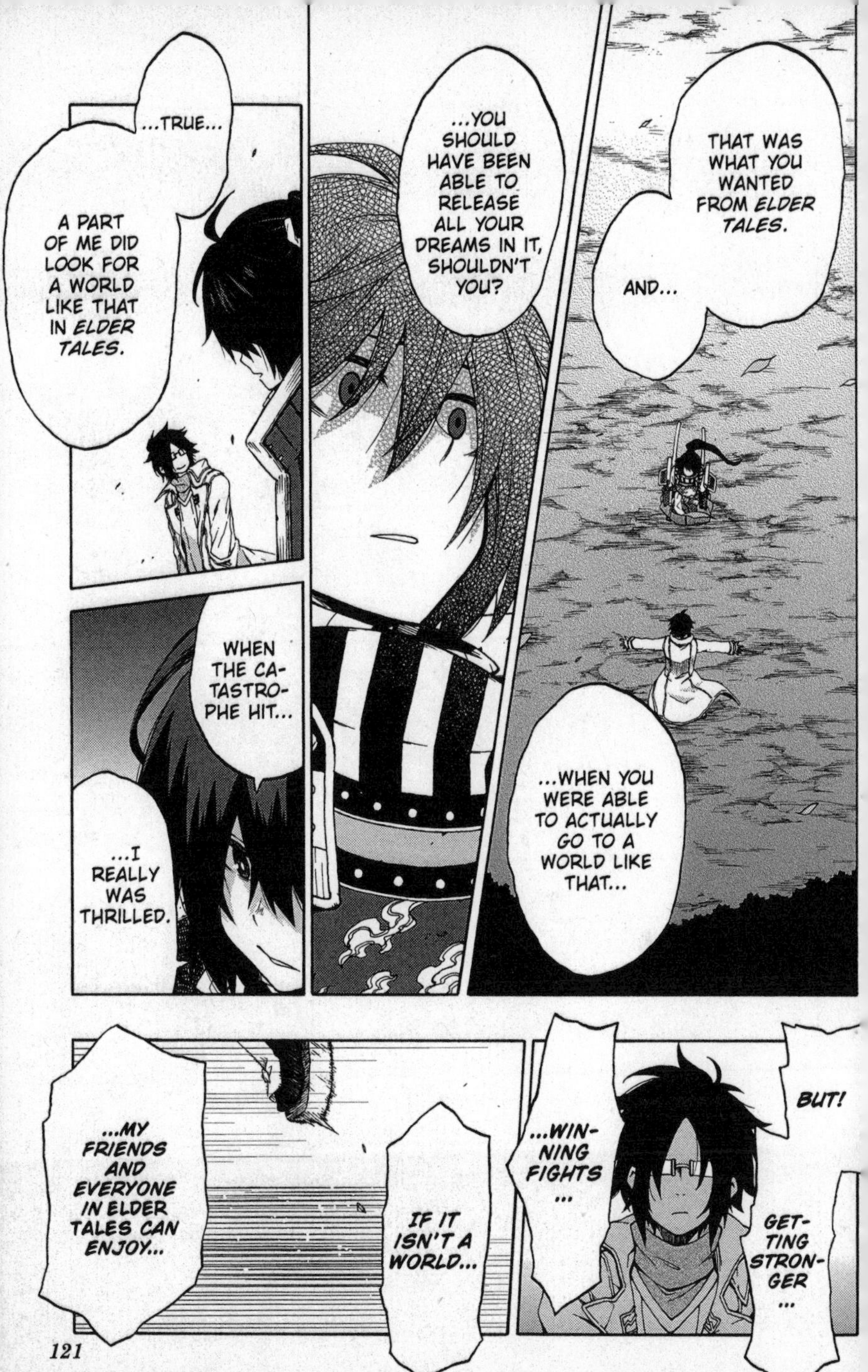
THAT WAS WHAT YOU WANTED FROM *ELDER TALES*.
AND...
...WHEN YOU WERE ABLE TO ACTUALLY GO TO A WORLD LIKE THAT...
...YOU SHOULD HAVE BEEN ABLE TO RELEASE ALL YOUR DREAMS IN IT, SHOULDN'T YOU?
...TRUE...
A PART OF ME DID LOOK FOR A WORLD LIKE THAT IN *ELDER TALES*.
WHEN THE CATASTROPHE HIT...
...I REALLY WAS THRILLED.
BUT!
GETTING STRONGER...
...WINNING FIGHTS...
IF IT ISN'T A WORLD...
...MY FRIENDS AND EVERYONE IN ELDER TALES CAN ENJOY...

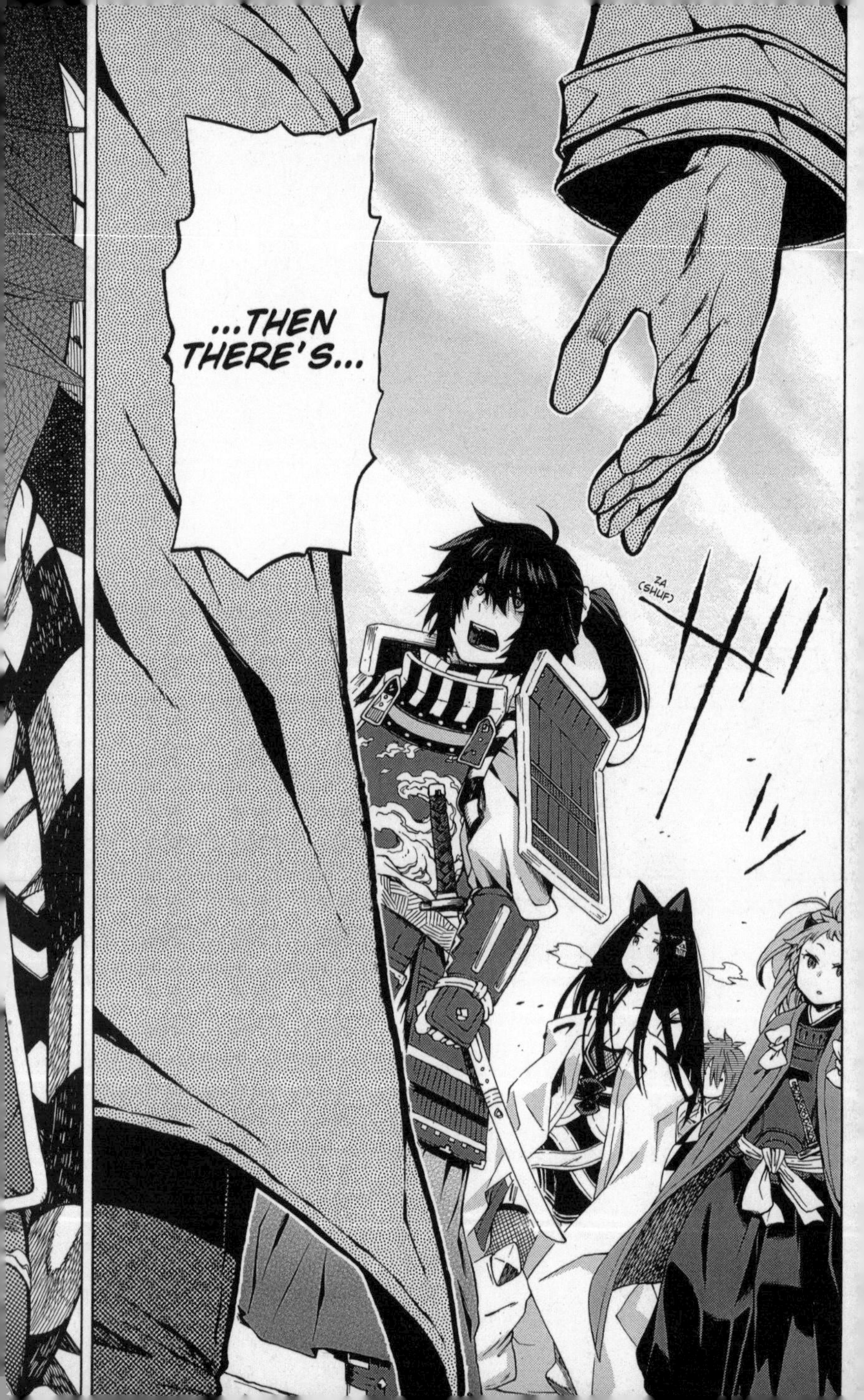
...THEN THERE'S...
ZA (SHUF)

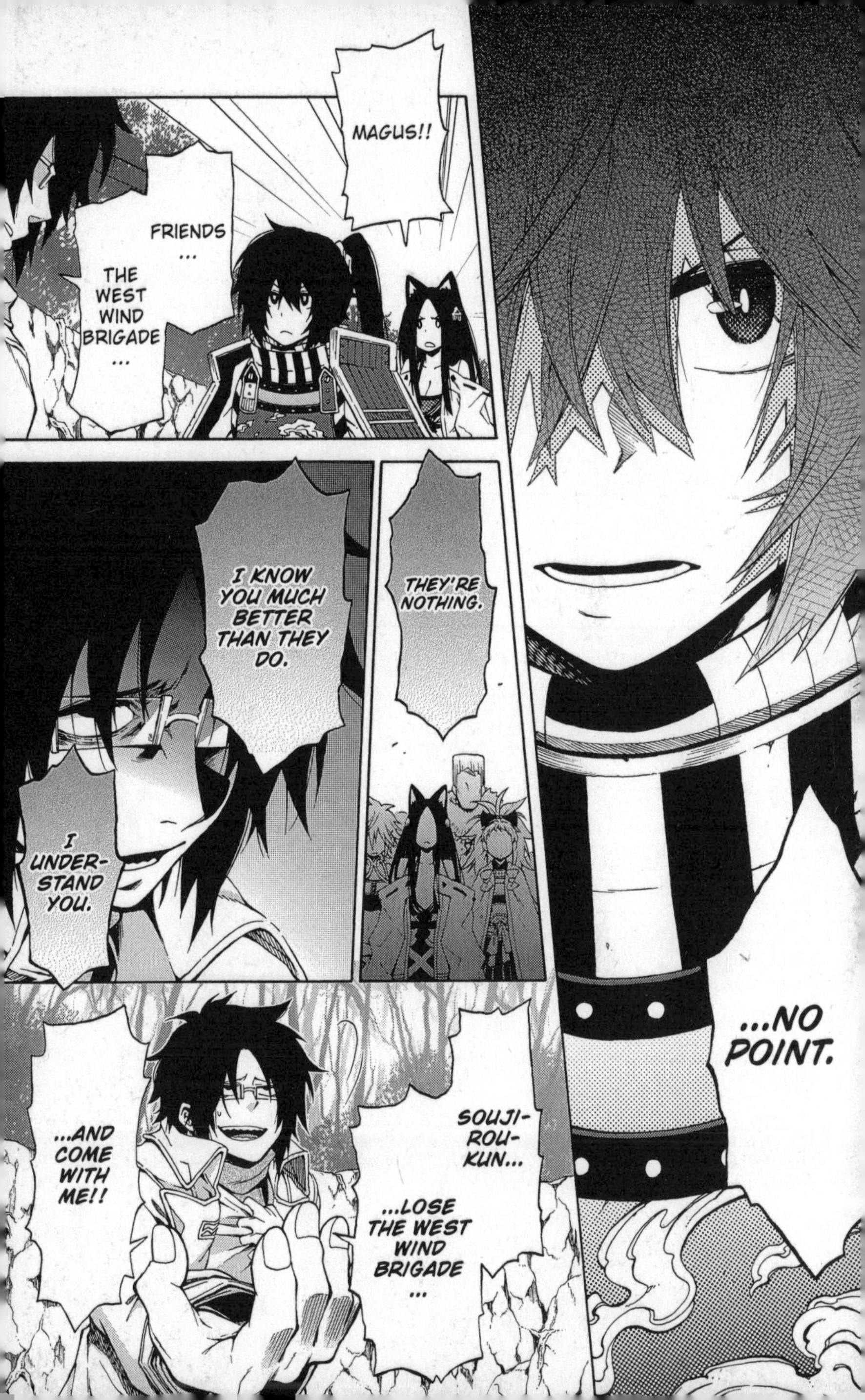
...NO POINT.
MAGUS!!
FRIENDS ...
THE WEST WIND BRIGADE ...
THEY'RE NOTHING.
I KNOW YOU MUCH BETTER THAN THEY DO.
I UNDER-STAND YOU.
SOUJI-ROU-KUN...
...LOSE THE WEST WIND BRIGADE ...
...AND COME WITH ME!!

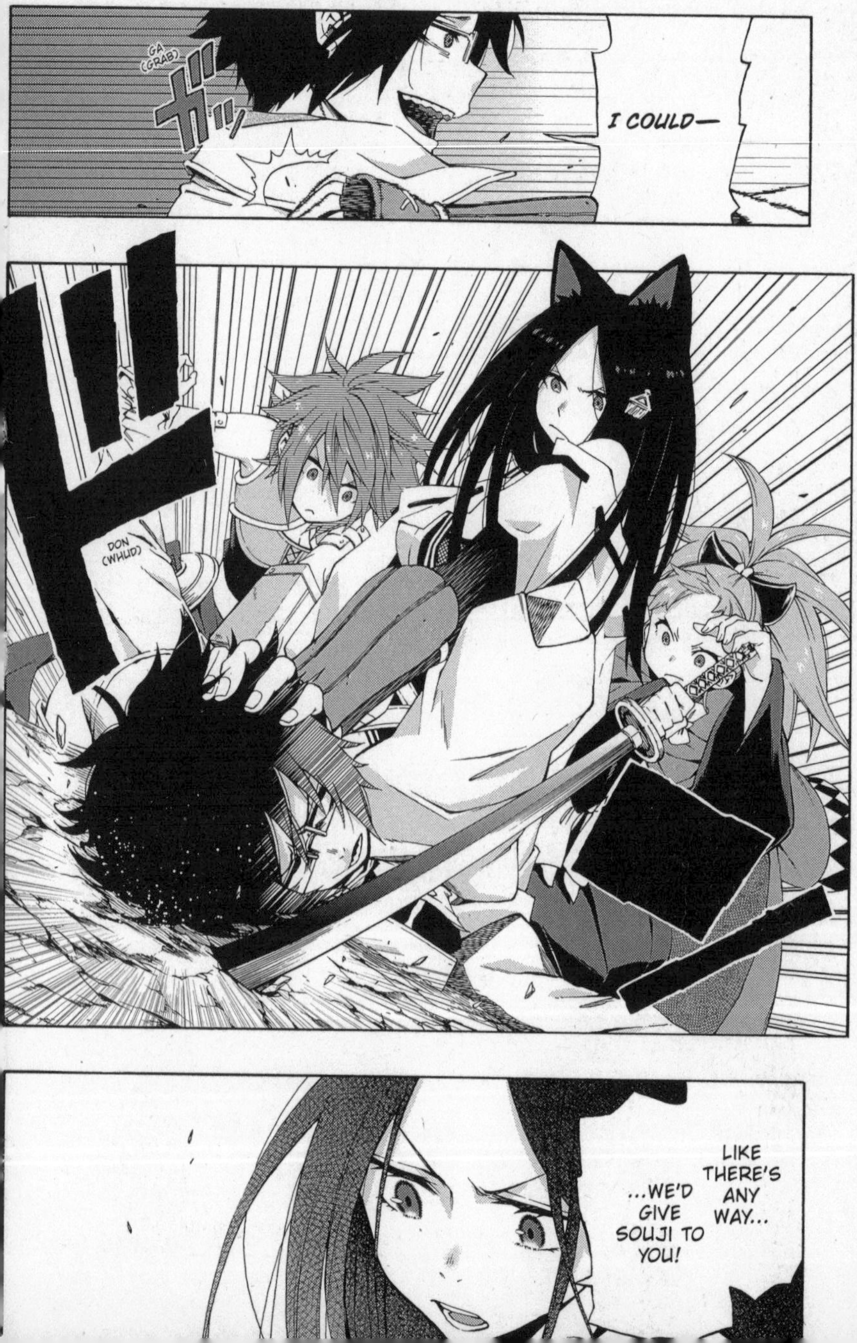

I COULD—
GA (GRAB)
DON (WHUD)
LIKE THERE'S ANY WAY...
...WE'D GIVE SOUJI TO YOU!

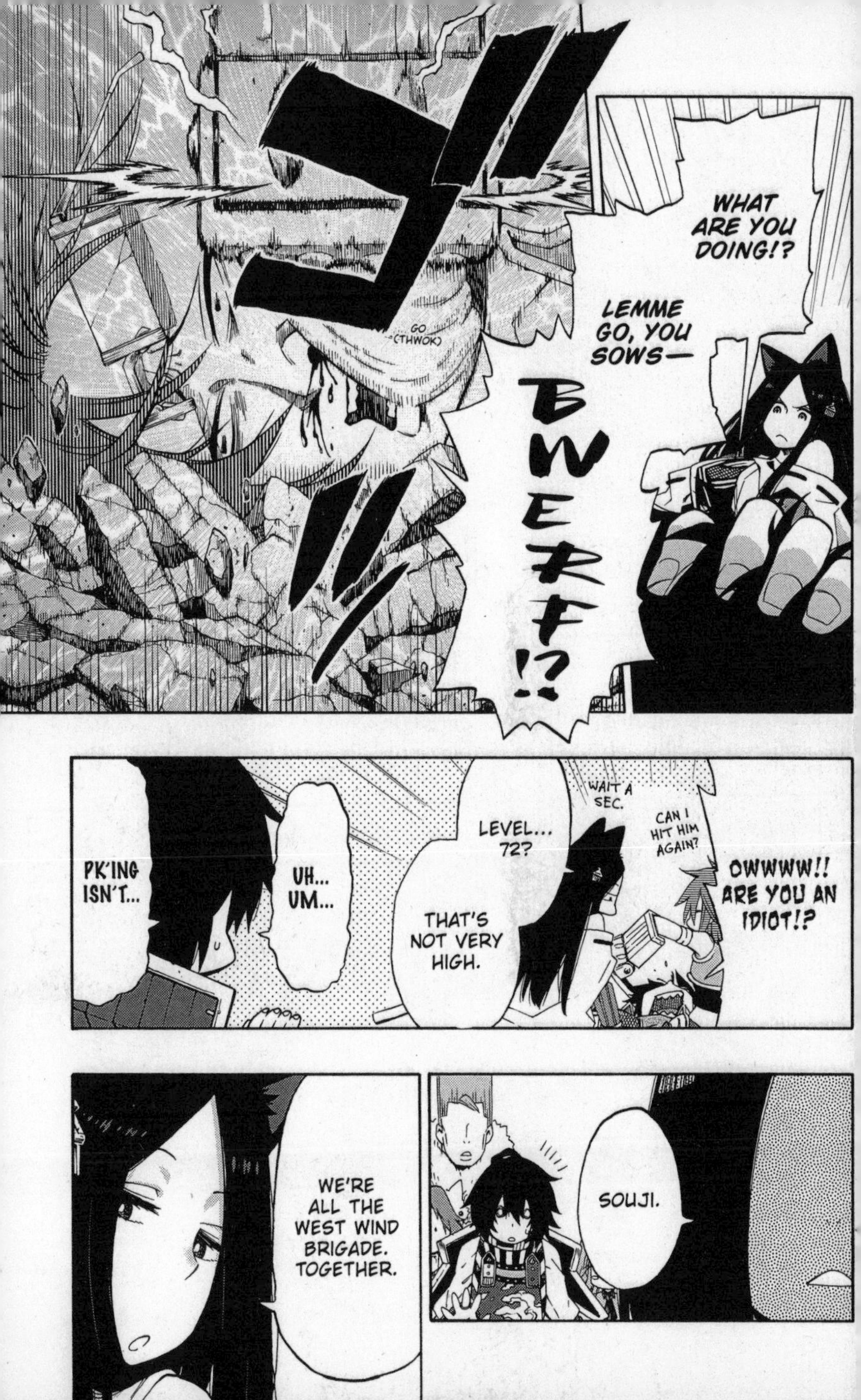
WHAT ARE YOU DOING!?
LEMME GO, YOU SOWS—
BWERF!?
GO (THWOK)
OWWWW!! ARE YOU AN IDIOT!?
CAN I HIT HIM AGAIN?
WAIT A SEC.
LEVEL... 72?
THAT'S NOT VERY HIGH.
UH... UM...
PK'ING ISN'T...
SOUJI.
WE'RE ALL THE WEST WIND BRIGADE. TOGETHER.

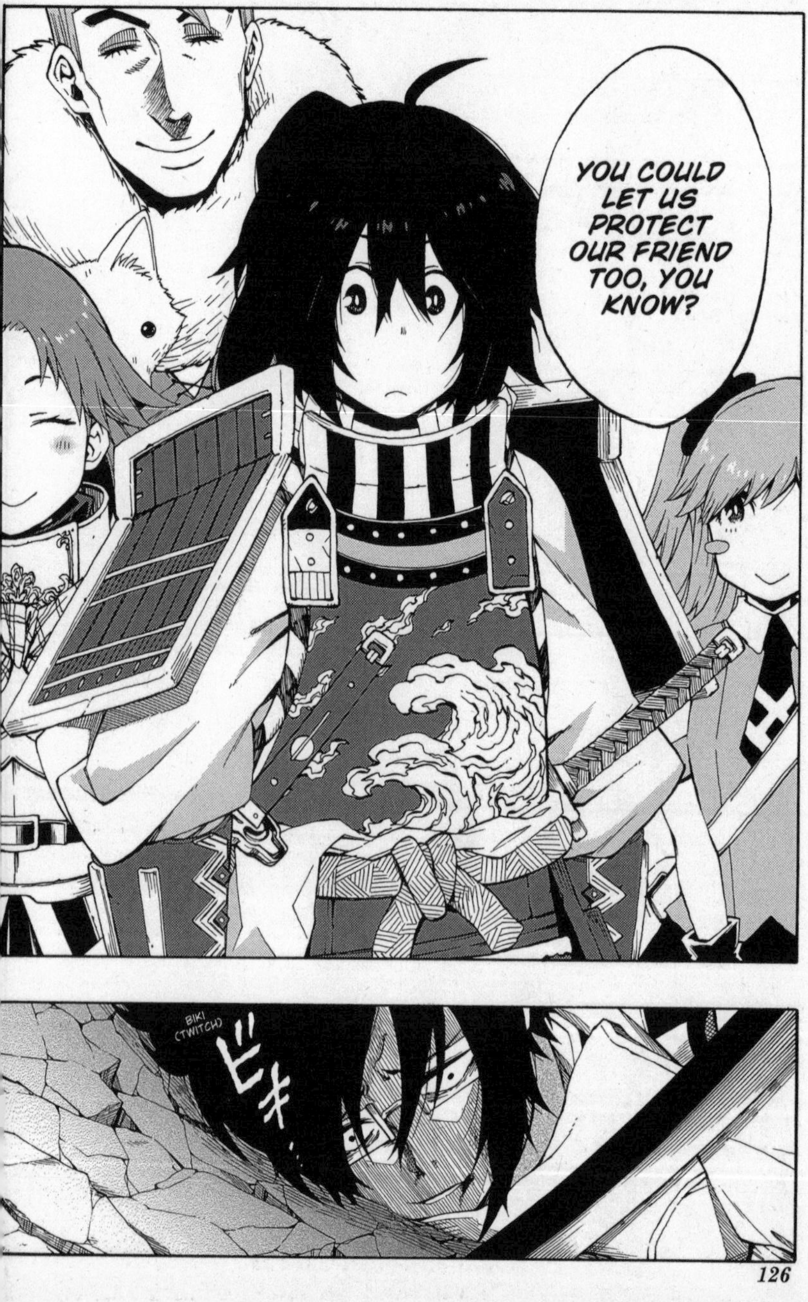
YOU COULD LET US PROTECT OUR FRIEND TOO, YOU KNOW?
BIKI (TWITCH)
ビキ

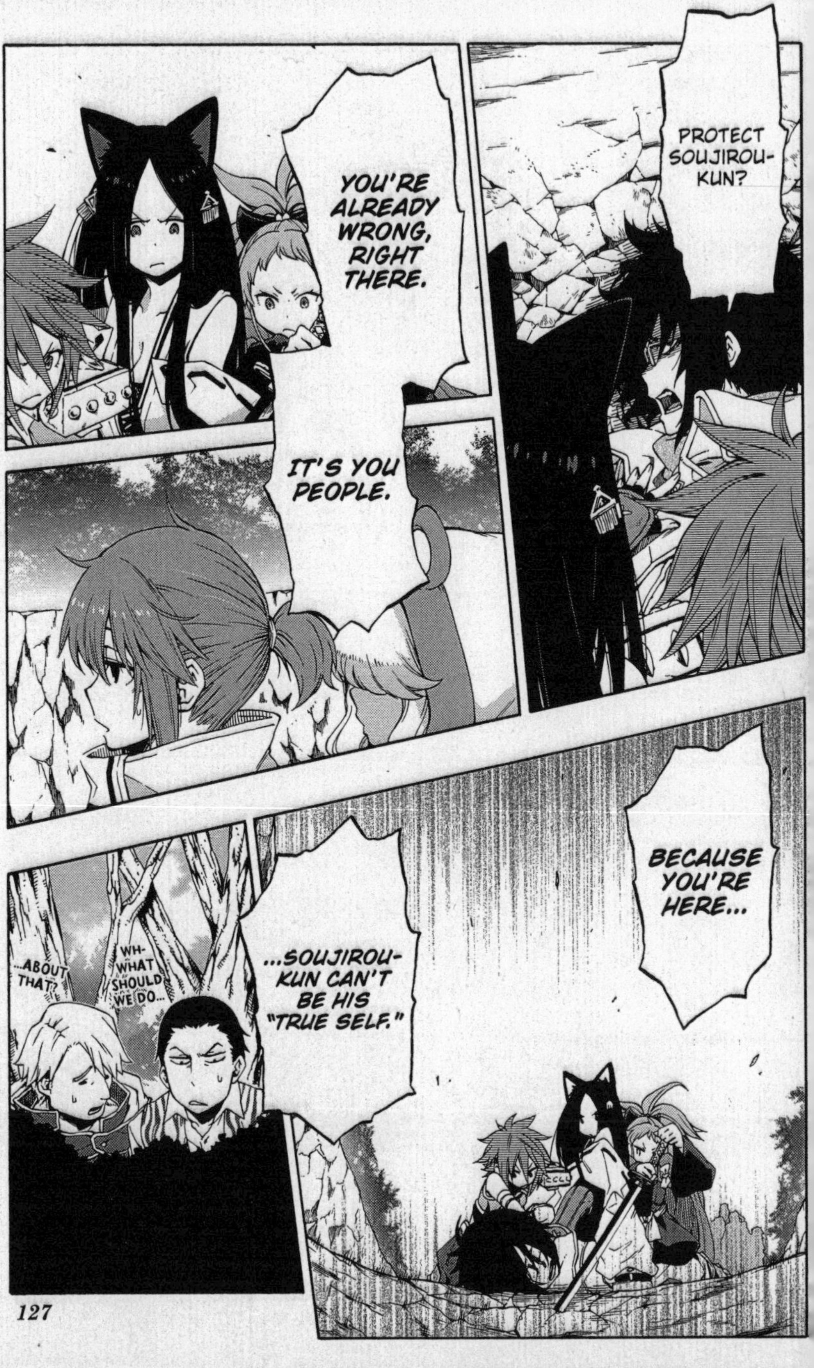
PROTECT SOUJIROU-KUN?
YOU'RE ALREADY WRONG, RIGHT THERE.
IT'S YOU PEOPLE.
BECAUSE YOU'RE HERE...
...SOUJIROU-KUN CAN'T BE HIS "TRUE SELF."
WH-WHAT SHOULD WE DO...
...ABOUT THAT?

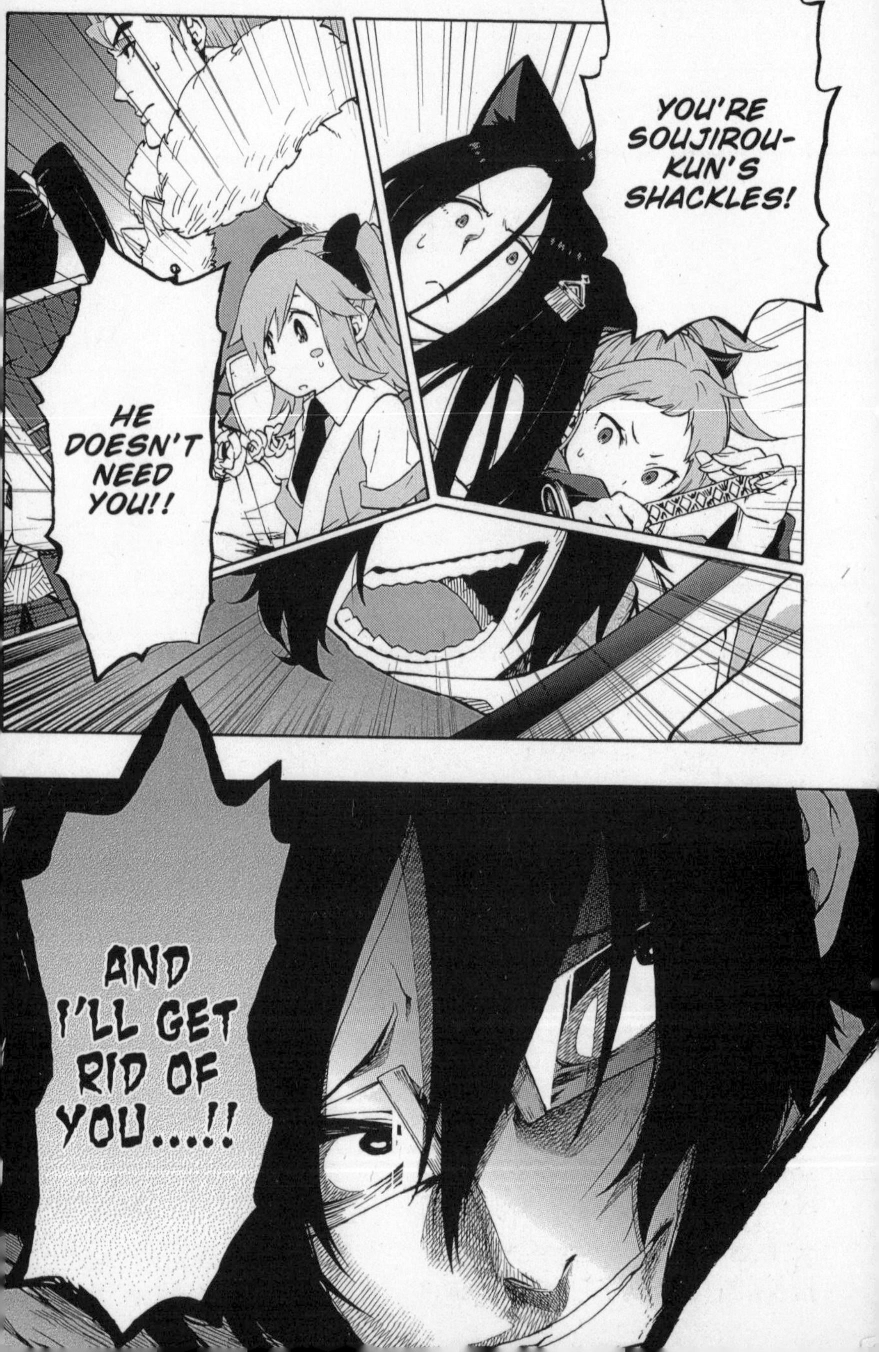
YOU'RE SOUJIROU-KUN'S SHACKLES!
HE DOESN'T NEED YOU!!
AND I'LL GET RID OF YOU...!!

LOG HORIZON
THE WEST WIND BRIGADE

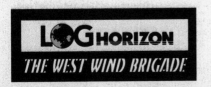

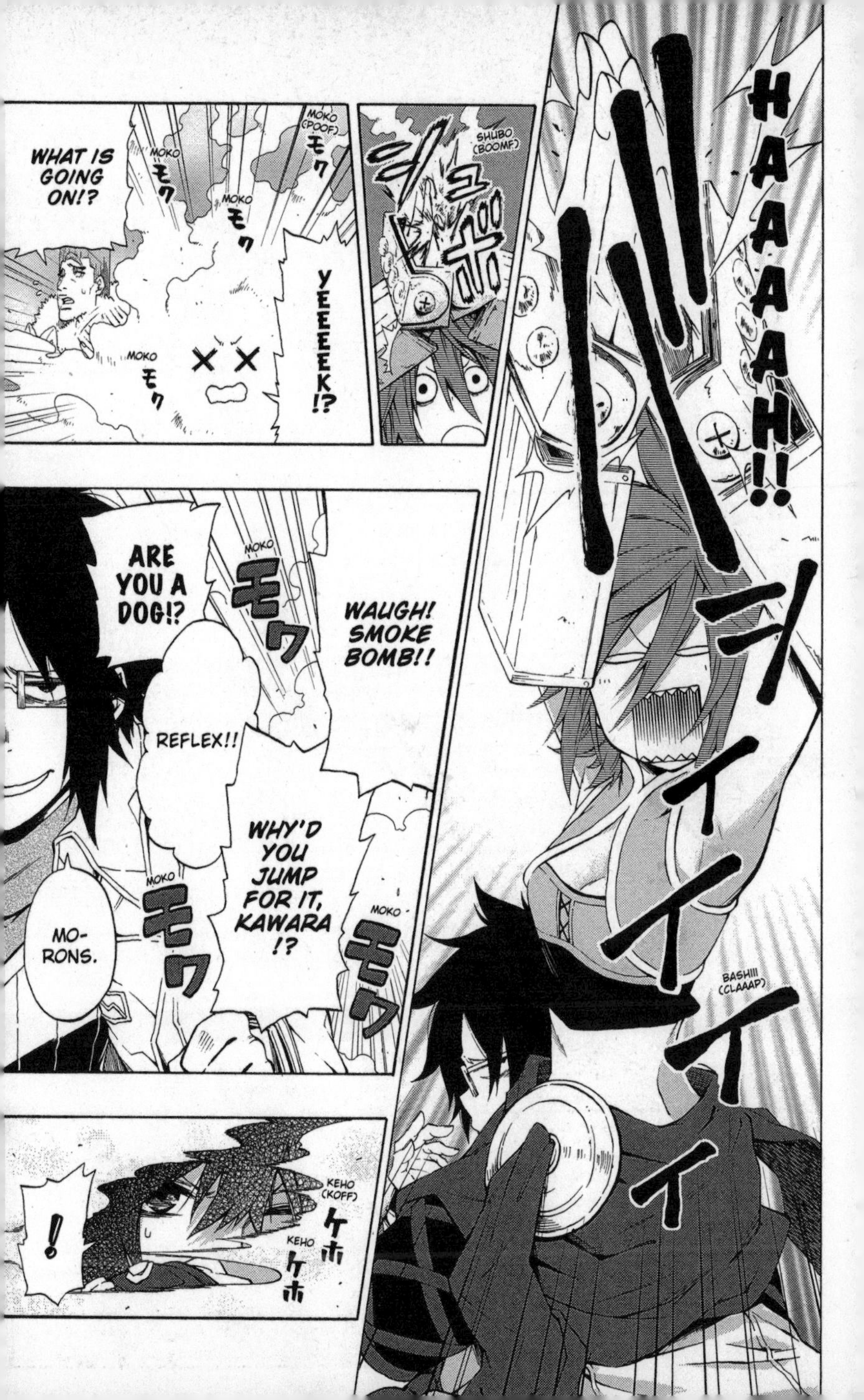
HAAAAAH!!
BASHIII (CLAAAP)
SHUBO (BOOMF)
MOKO (POOF) モク
YEEEEEK!?
MOKO モク
MOKO モク
WHAT IS GOING ON!?
MOKO モク
WAUGH! SMOKE BOMB!!
MOKO モク
ARE YOU A DOG!?
REFLEX!!
MOKO モク
WHY'D YOU JUMP FOR IT, KAWARA!?
MOKO モク
MO-RONS.
KEHO (KOFF) ケホ
KEHO ケホ
!

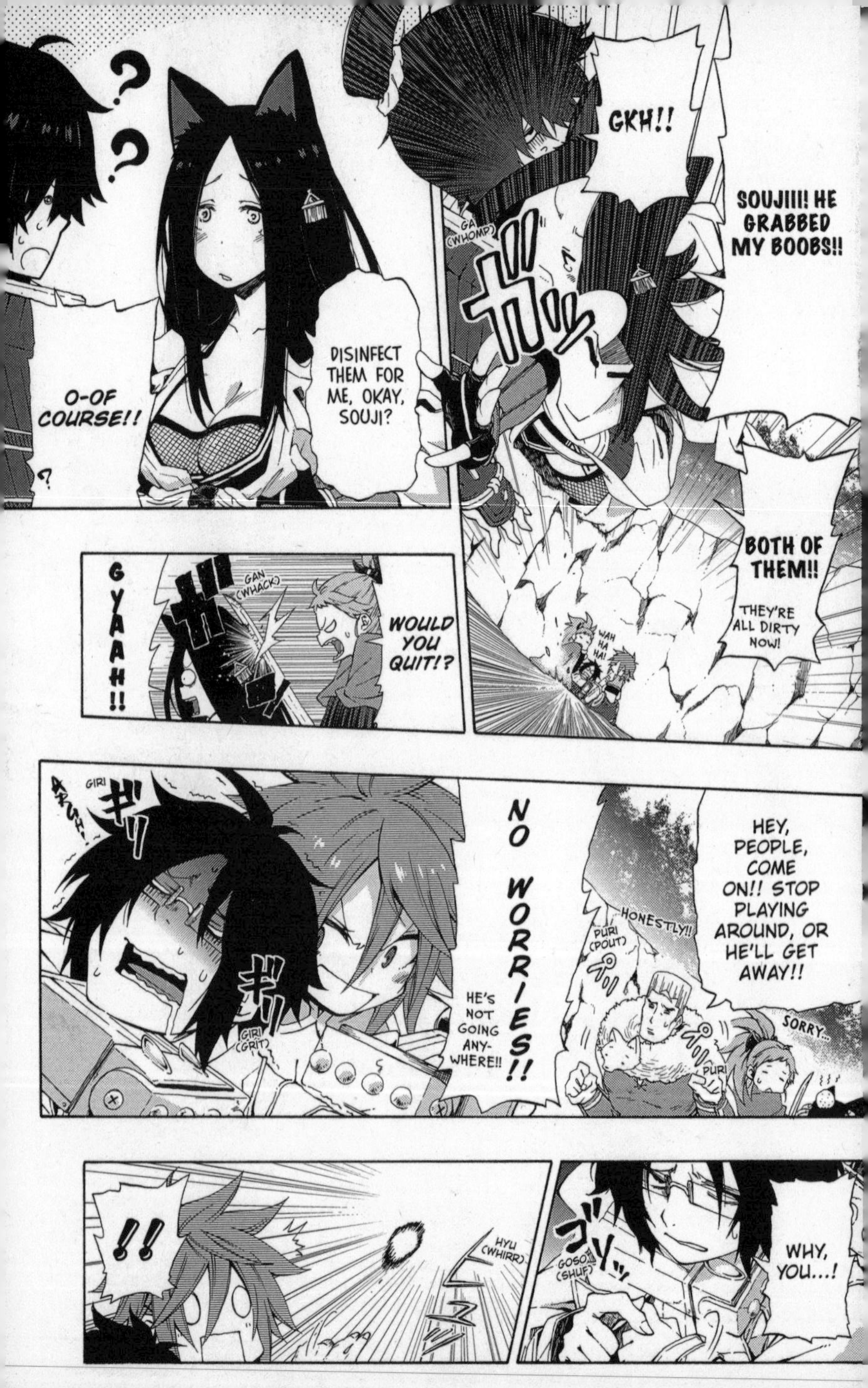
GKH!!
SOUJIII! HE GRABBED MY BOOBS!!
GA (WHOMP)
BOTH OF THEM!!
THEY'RE ALL DIRTY NOW!
WAH HA HA!
DISINFECT THEM FOR ME, OKAY, SOUJI?
O-OF COURSE!!
?
GAN (WHACK)
WOULD YOU QUIT!?
GYAAH!!
HEY, PEOPLE, COME ON!! STOP PLAYING AROUND, OR HE'LL GET AWAY!!
HONESTLY!!
PURI (POUT)
SORRY...
PURI
NO WORRIES!!
HE'S NOT GOING ANYWHERE!!
GIRI (GRIT)
GIRI
WHY, YOU...!
GOSO (SHUF)
HYU (WHIRR)
!!

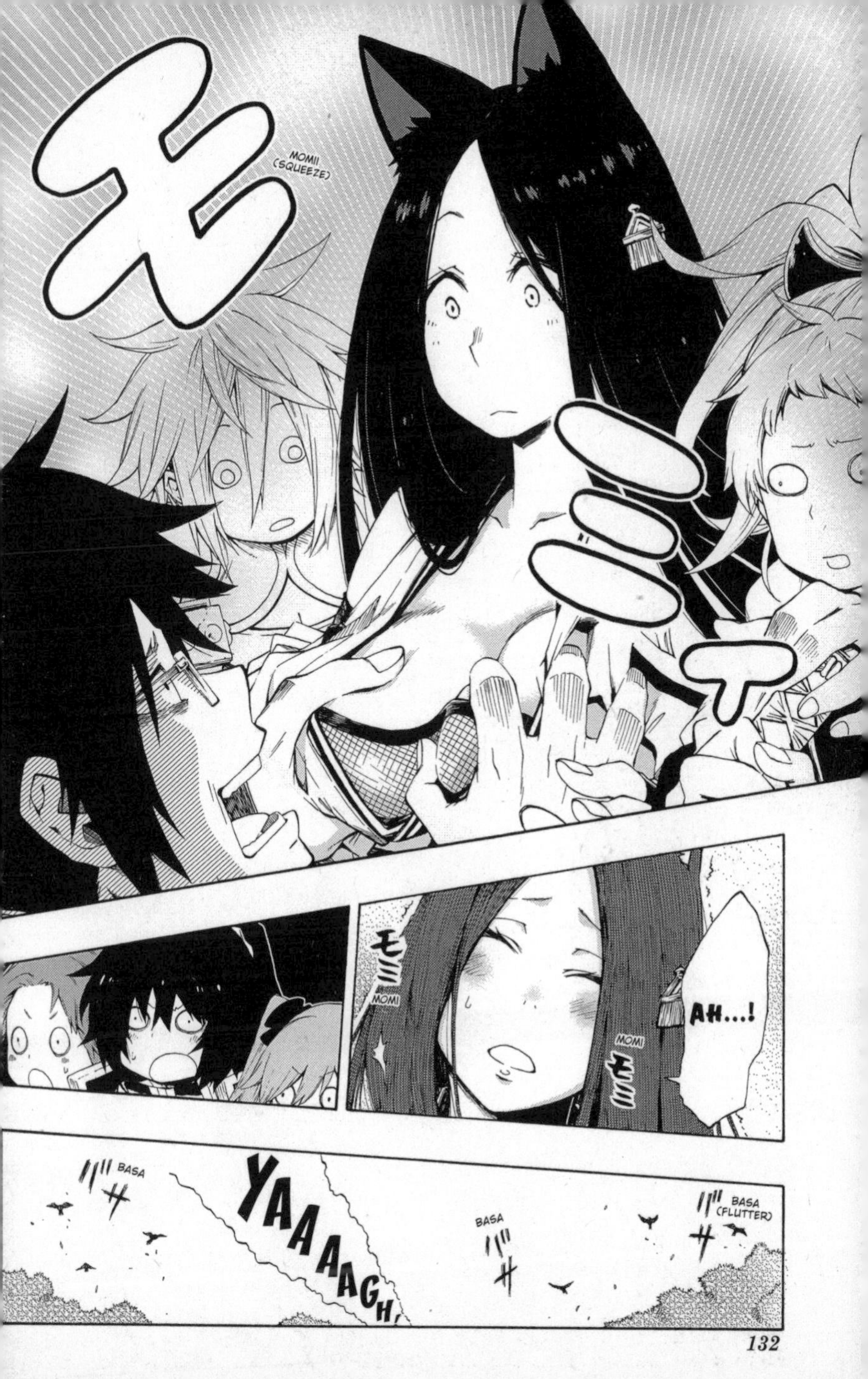

モミーッ
MOMII (SQUEEZE)
AH...!
モミ
MOMI
モミ
MOMI
BASA (FLUTTER)
BASA
YAAAAAGH,
BASA

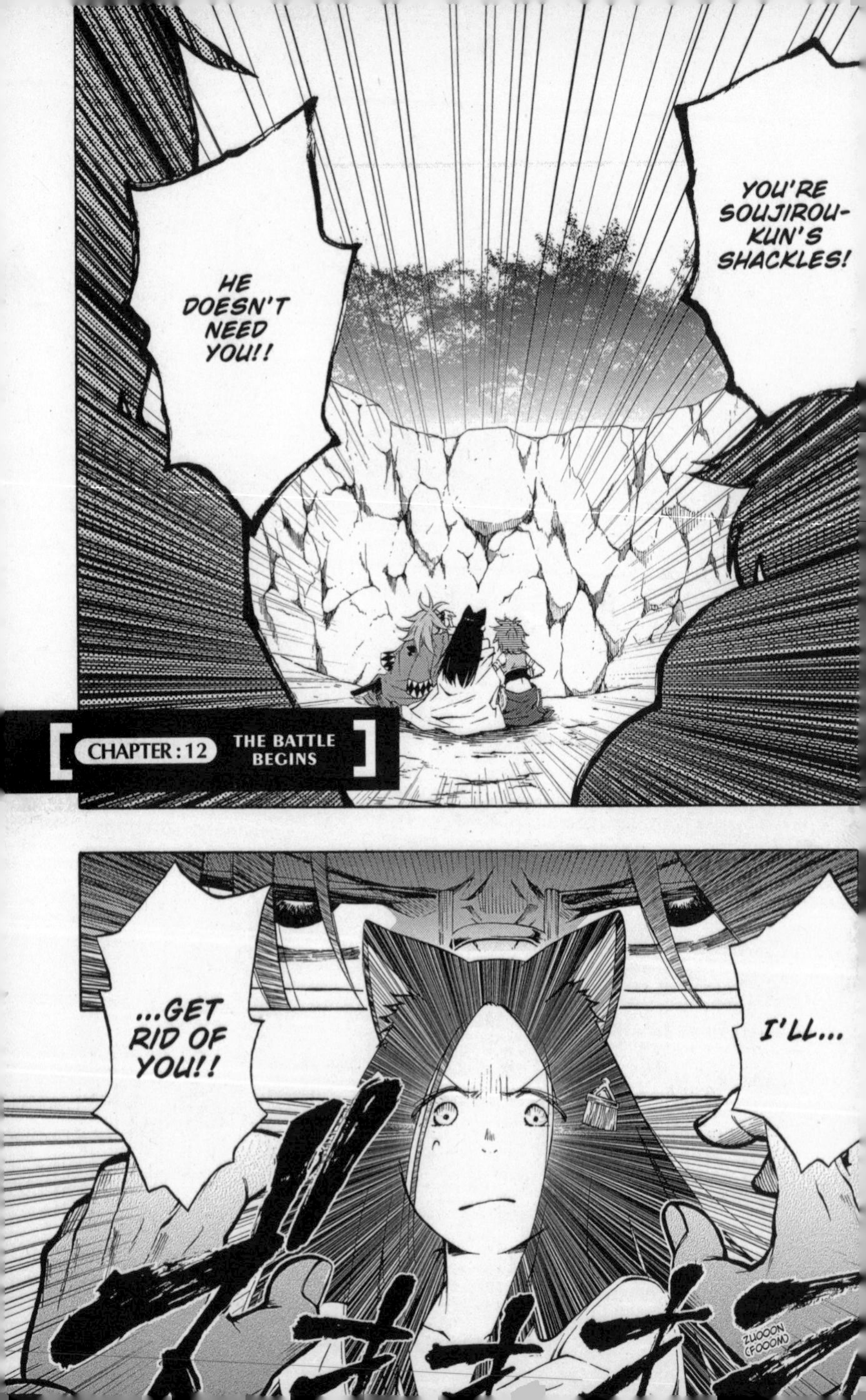
YOU'RE SOUJIROU-KUN'S SHACKLES!
HE DOESN'T NEED YOU!!
CHAPTER : 12 THE BATTLE BEGINS
I'LL...
...GET RID OF YOU!!
ZUOOON (FOOOM)

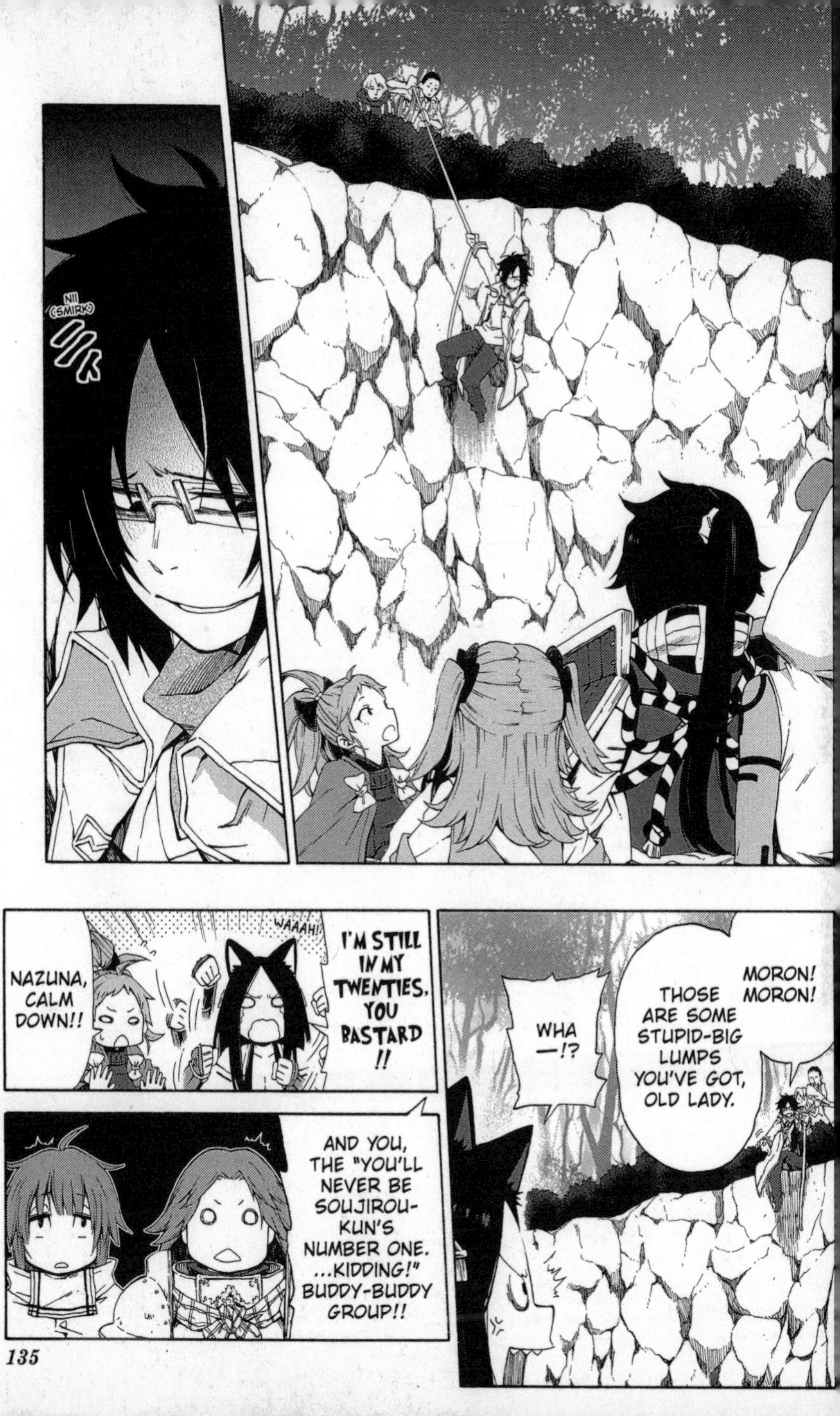
NII (SMIRK)
MORON! MORON!
THOSE ARE SOME STUPID-BIG LUMPS YOU'VE GOT, OLD LADY.
WHA—!?
I'M STILL IN MY TWENTIES, YOU BASTARD!!
WAAAH!
NAZUNA, CALM DOWN!!
AND YOU, THE "YOU'LL NEVER BE SOUJIROU-KUN'S NUMBER ONE. ...KIDDING!" BUDDY-BUDDY GROUP!!

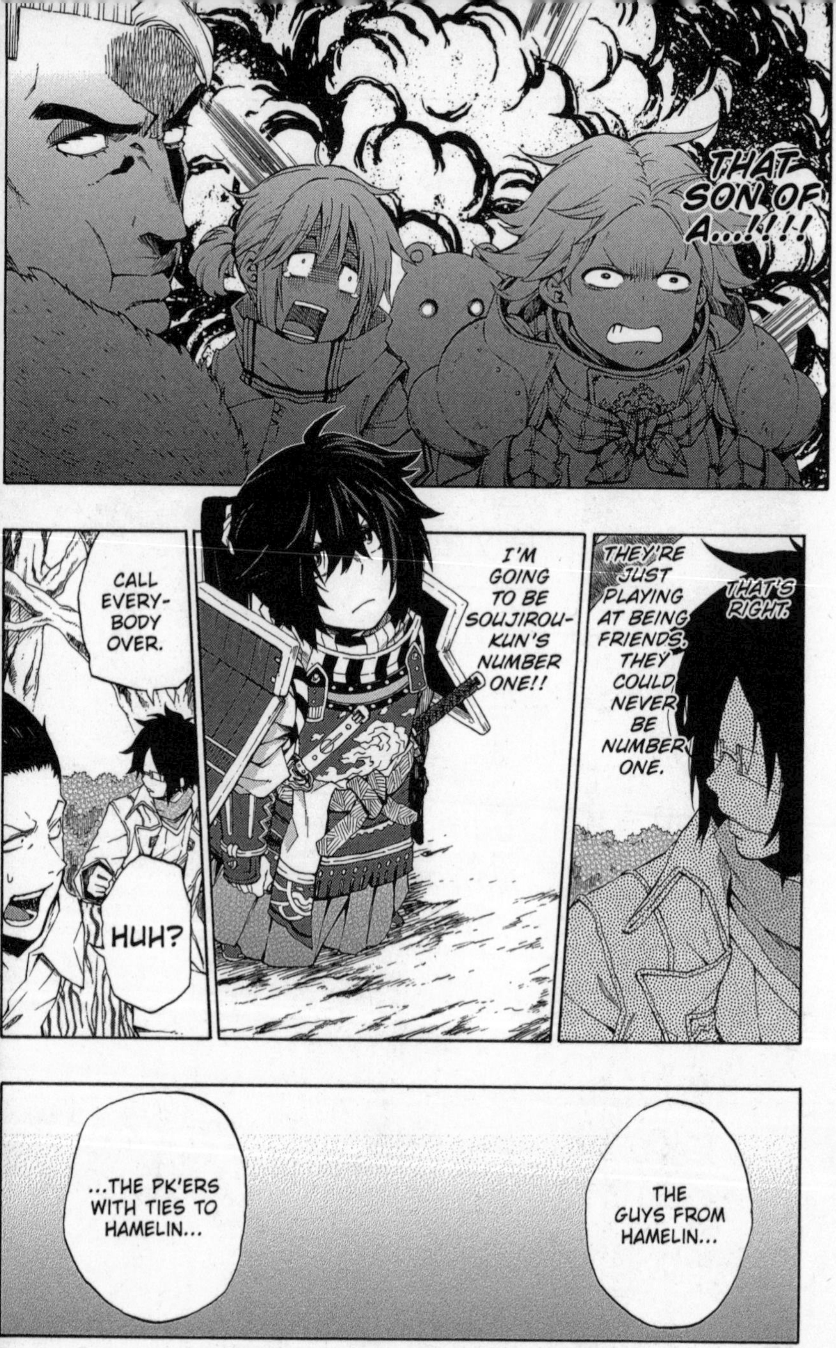
THAT SON OF A...!!!!
THAT'S RIGHT.
THEY'RE JUST PLAYING AT BEING FRIENDS. THEY COULD NEVER BE NUMBER ONE.
I'M GOING TO BE SOUJIROU-KUN'S NUMBER ONE!!
CALL EVERY-BODY OVER.
HUH?
THE GUYS FROM HAMELIN...
...THE PK'ERS WITH TIES TO HAMELIN...

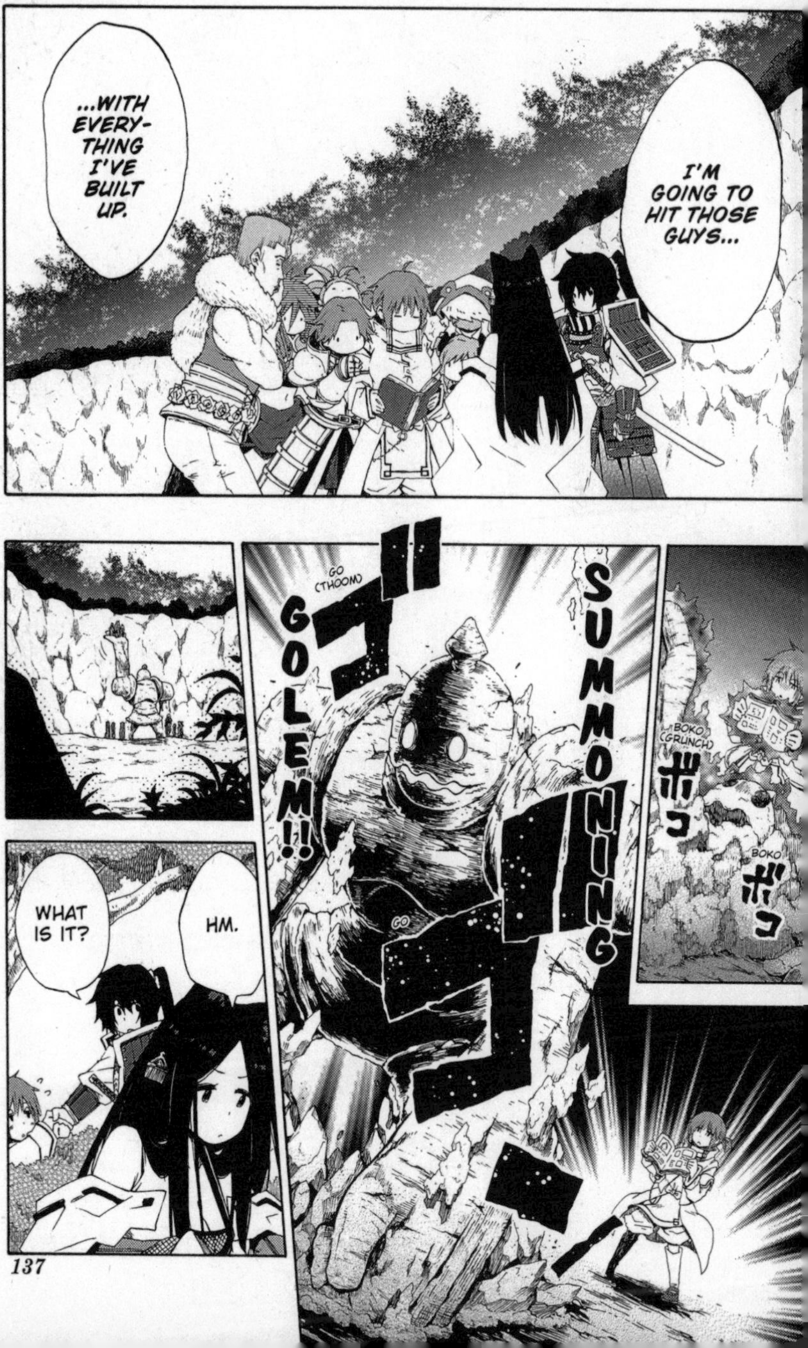
I'M GOING TO HIT THOSE GUYS...
...WITH EVERY-THING I'VE BUILT UP.
BOKO (GRUNCH)
BOKO
GO (THOOM)
SUMMONING GOLEM!!
GO
HM.
WHAT IS IT?

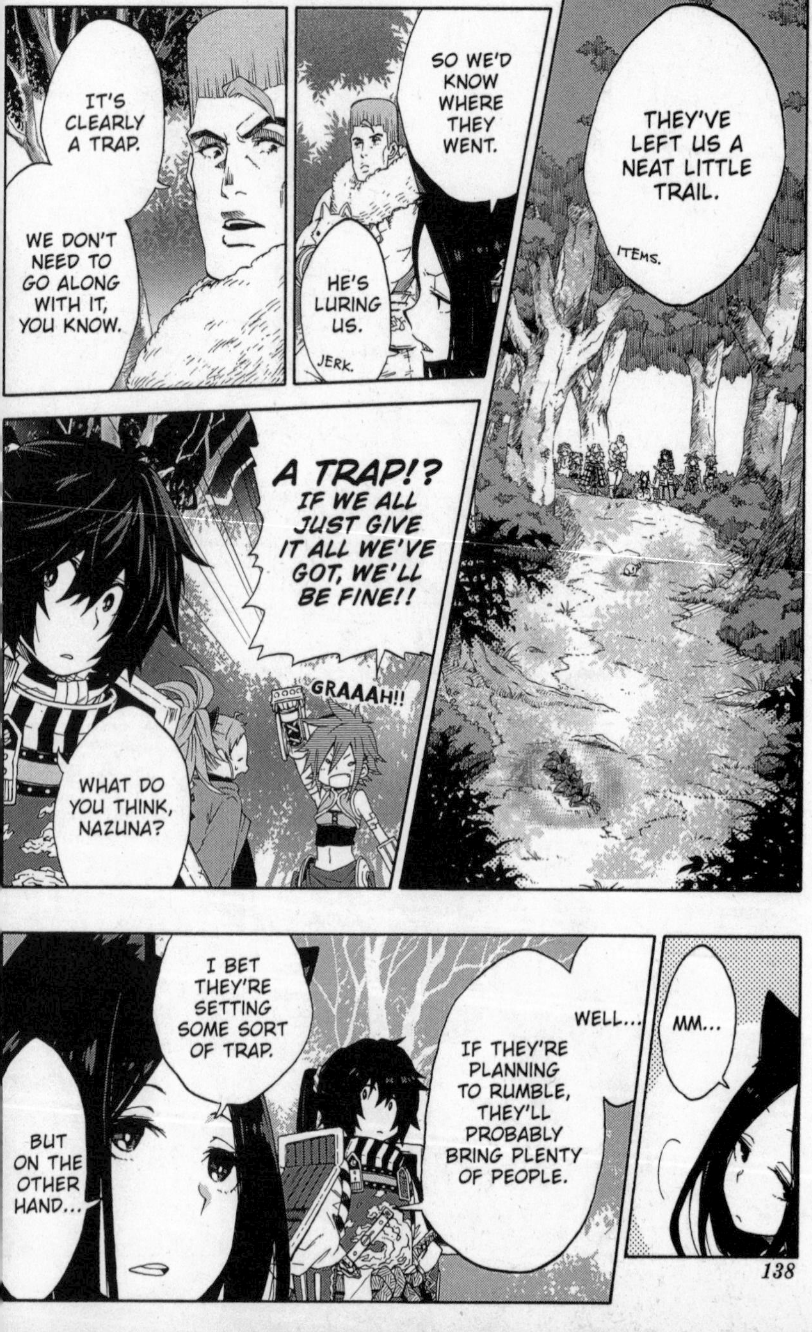
THEY'VE LEFT US A NEAT LITTLE TRAIL.
ITEMS.
SO WE'D KNOW WHERE THEY WENT.
HE'S LURING US.
JERK.
IT'S CLEARLY A TRAP.
WE DON'T NEED TO GO ALONG WITH IT, YOU KNOW.
A TRAP!? IF WE ALL JUST GIVE IT ALL WE'VE GOT, WE'LL BE FINE!!
GRAAAH!!
WHAT DO YOU THINK, NAZUNA?
MM...
WELL...
IF THEY'RE PLANNING TO RUMBLE, THEY'LL PROBABLY BRING PLENTY OF PEOPLE.
I BET THEY'RE SETTING SOME SORT OF TRAP.
BUT ON THE OTHER HAND...

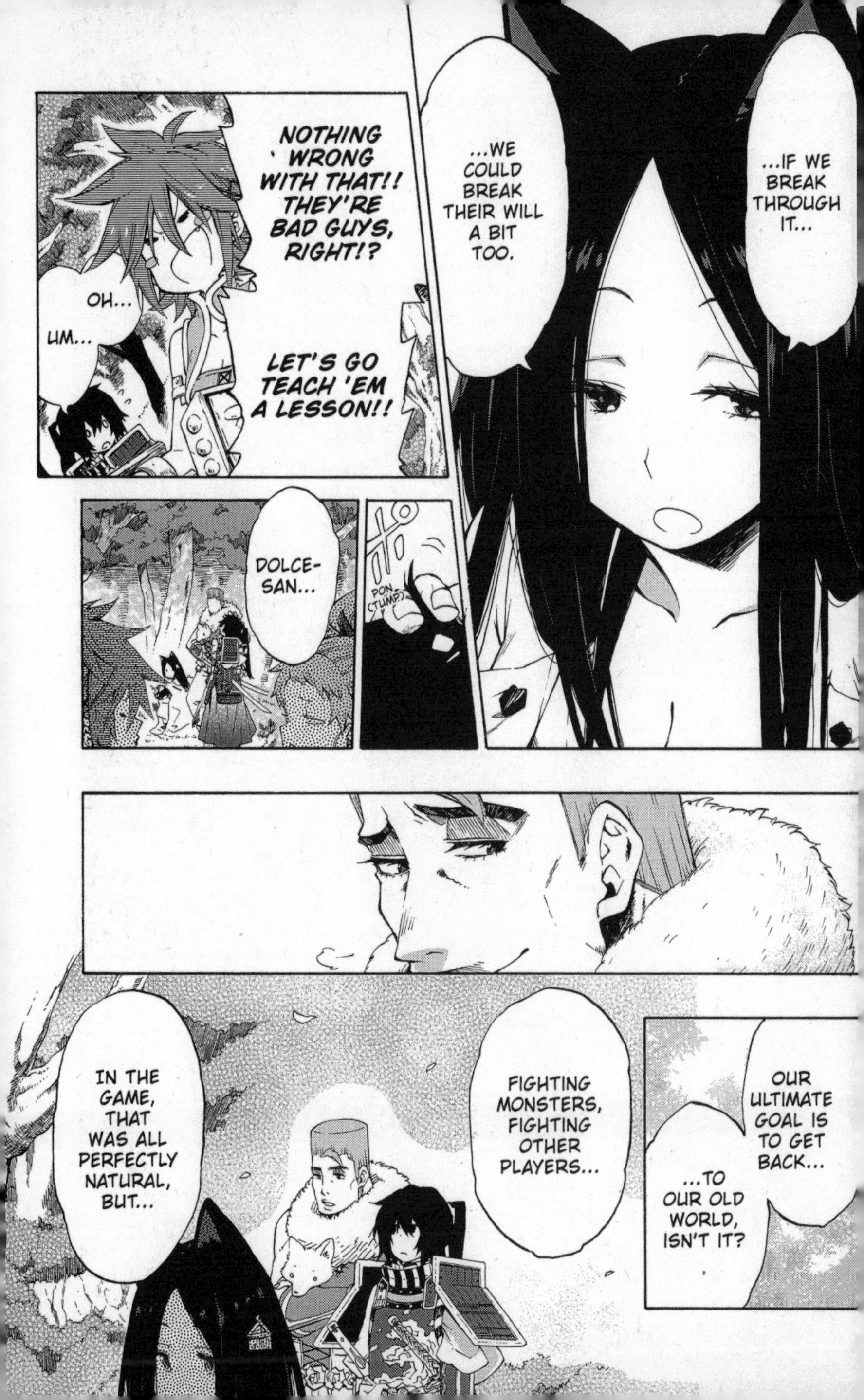
...IF WE BREAK THROUGH IT...
...WE COULD BREAK THEIR WILL A BIT TOO.
NOTHING WRONG WITH THAT!! THEY'RE BAD GUYS, RIGHT!?
LET'S GO TEACH 'EM A LESSON!!
OH... UM...
PON (TUMP)
DOLCE-SAN...
OUR ULTIMATE GOAL IS TO GET BACK...
...TO OUR OLD WORLD, ISN'T IT?
FIGHTING MONSTERS, FIGHTING OTHER PLAYERS...
IN THE GAME, THAT WAS ALL PERFECTLY NATURAL, BUT...

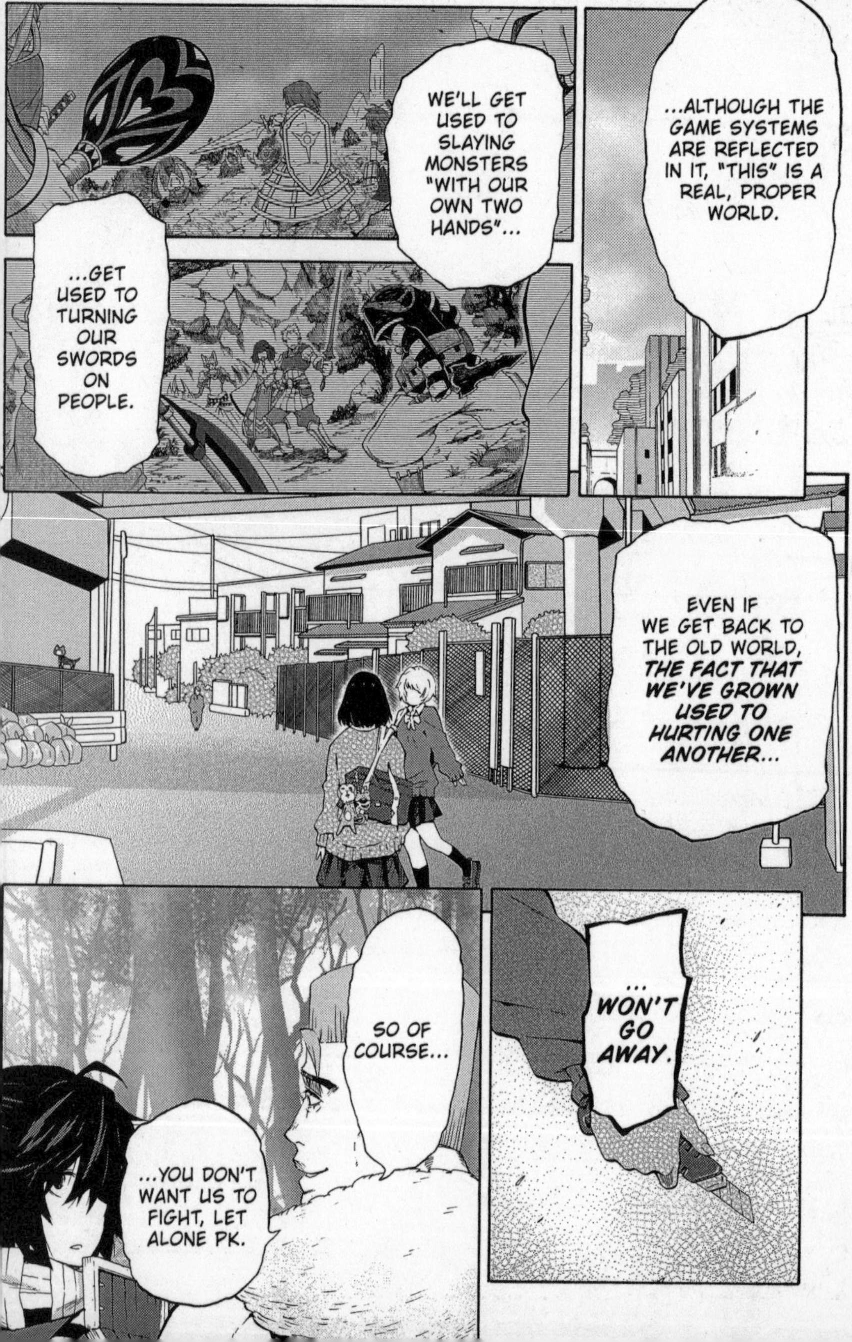
...ALTHOUGH THE GAME SYSTEMS ARE REFLECTED IN IT, "THIS" IS A REAL, PROPER WORLD.
WE'LL GET USED TO SLAYING MONSTERS "WITH OUR OWN TWO HANDS"...
...GET USED TO TURNING OUR SWORDS ON PEOPLE.
EVEN IF WE GET BACK TO THE OLD WORLD, *THE FACT THAT WE'VE GROWN USED TO HURTING ONE ANOTHER...*
...*WON'T GO AWAY.*
SO OF COURSE...
...YOU DON'T WANT US TO FIGHT, LET ALONE PK.

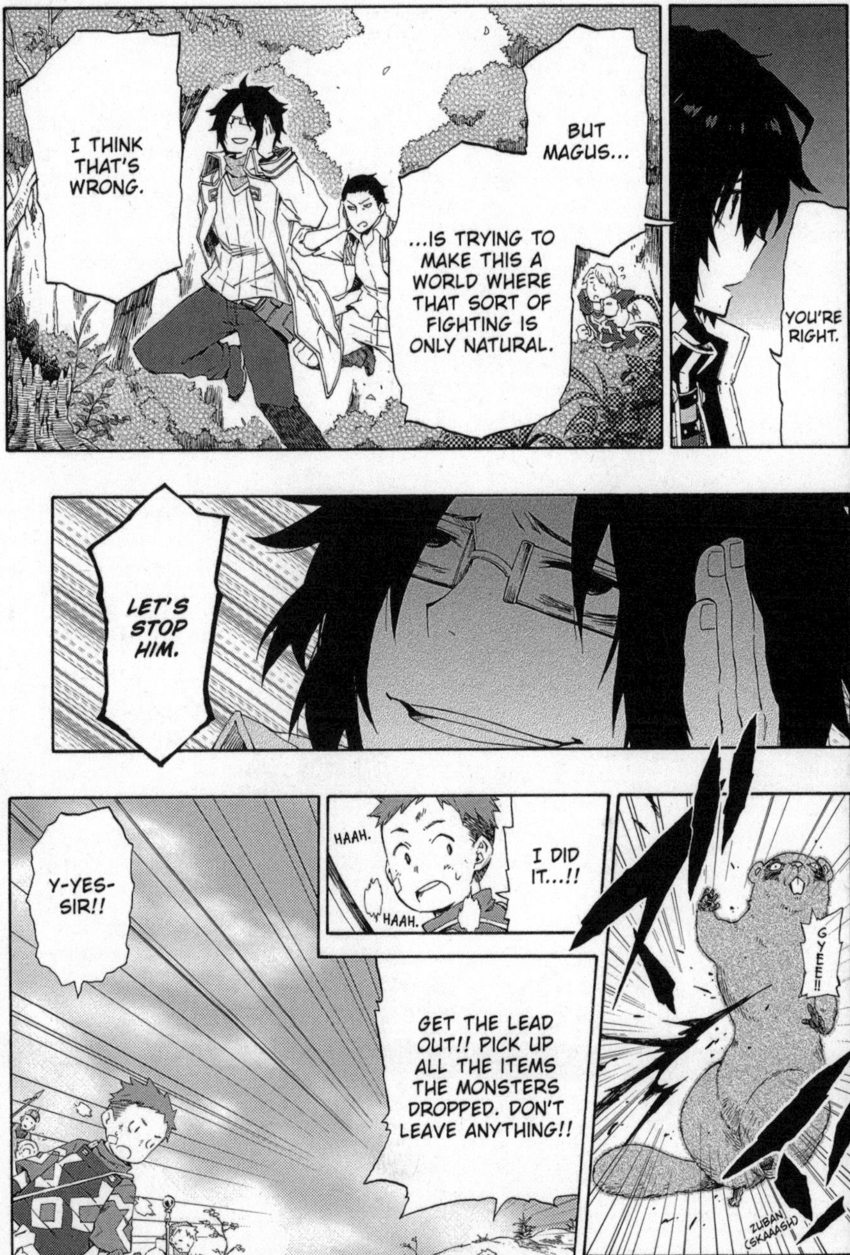
YOU'RE RIGHT.
BUT MAGUS...
...IS TRYING TO MAKE THIS A WORLD WHERE THAT SORT OF FIGHTING IS ONLY NATURAL.
I THINK THAT'S WRONG.
LET'S STOP HIM.
GYEEE!!
ZUBAN (SKAAASH)
HAAH.
I DID IT...!!
HAAH.
GET THE LEAD OUT!! PICK UP ALL THE ITEMS THE MONSTERS DROPPED. DON'T LEAVE ANYTHING!!
Y-YES-SIR!!

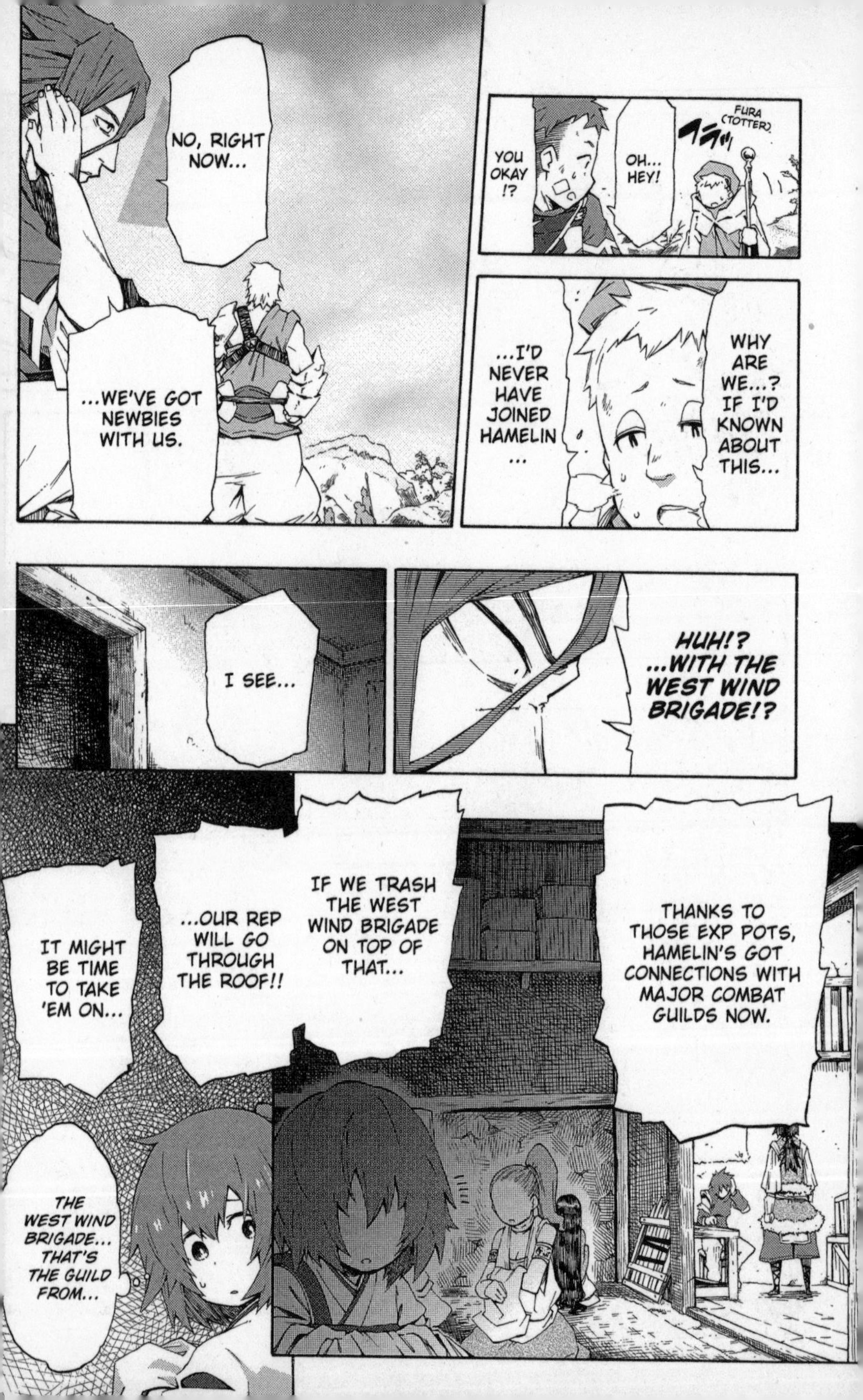
FURA (TOTTER)
OH... HEY!
YOU OKAY !?
WHY ARE WE...? IF I'D KNOWN ABOUT THIS...
...I'D NEVER HAVE JOINED HAMELIN ...
NO, RIGHT NOW...
...WE'VE GOT NEWBIES WITH US.
HUH!? ...WITH THE WEST WIND BRIGADE!?
I SEE...
THANKS TO THOSE EXP POTS, HAMELIN'S GOT CONNECTIONS WITH MAJOR COMBAT GUILDS NOW.
IF WE TRASH THE WEST WIND BRIGADE ON TOP OF THAT...
...OUR REP WILL GO THROUGH THE ROOF!!
IT MIGHT BE TIME TO TAKE 'EM ON...
THE WEST WIND BRIGADE... THAT'S THE GUILD FROM...

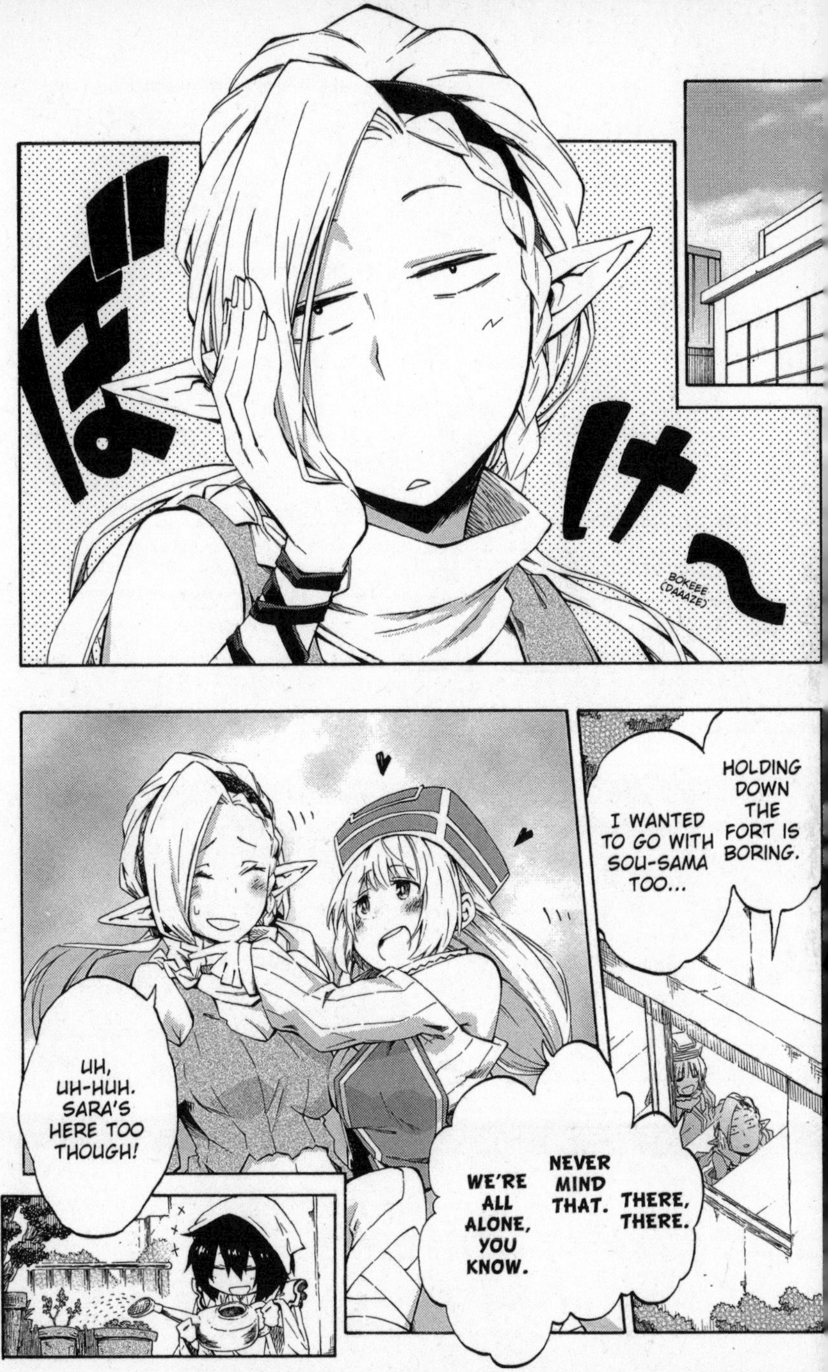
ぼけ〜
BOKEEE (DAAAZE)
HOLDING DOWN THE FORT IS BORING.
I WANTED TO GO WITH SOU-SAMA TOO...
UH, UH-HUH. SARA'S HERE TOO THOUGH!
THERE, THERE.
NEVER MIND THAT.
WE'RE ALL ALONE, YOU KNOW.

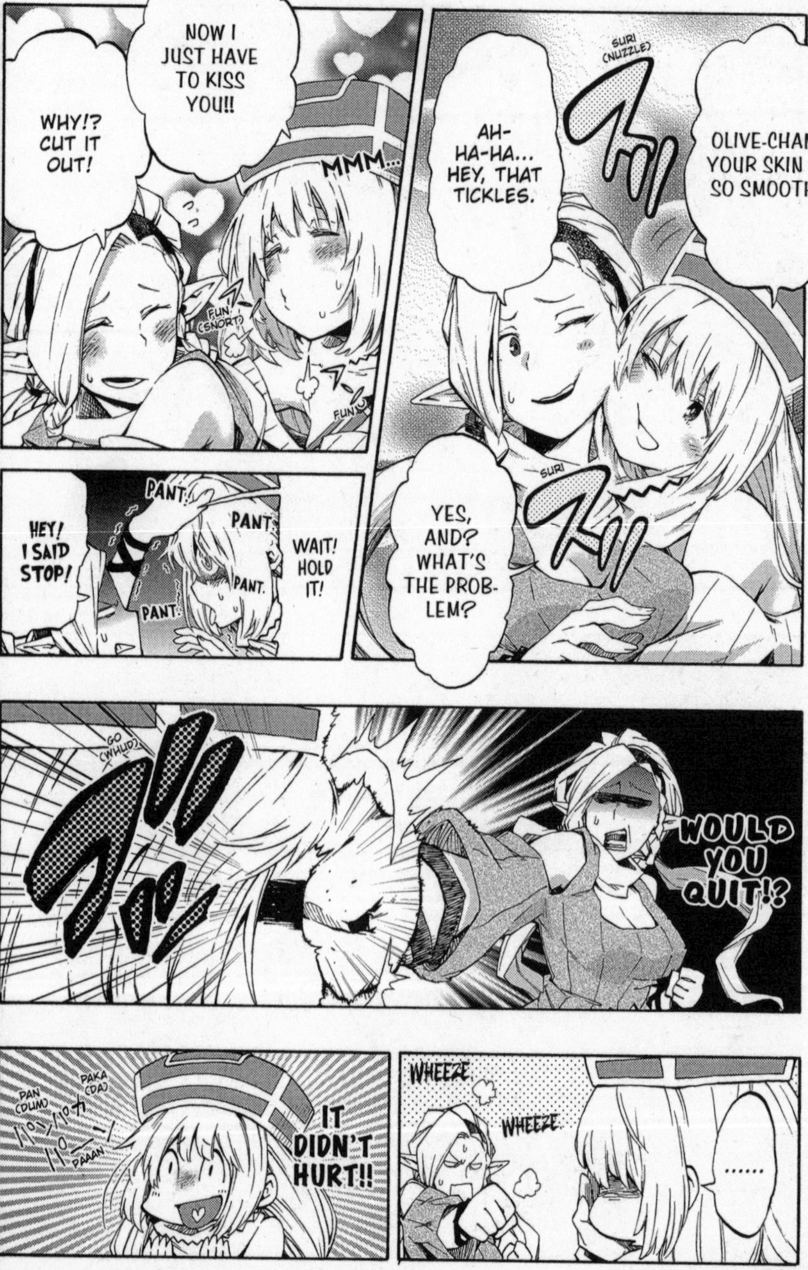
OLIVE-CHAN, YOUR SKIN IS SO SMOOTH!
SURI (NUZZLE)
AH-HA-HA... HEY, THAT TICKLES.
SURI
YES, AND? WHAT'S THE PROB-LEM?
NOW I JUST HAVE TO KISS YOU!!
MMM...
WHY!? CUT IT OUT!
FUN (SNORT)
FUN
WAIT! HOLD IT!
PANT
PANT
PANT.
PANT
HEY! I SAID STOP!
WOULD YOU QUIT!?
GO (WHUD)
WHEEZE
WHEEZE
......
IT DIDN'T HURT!!
PAKA (DA)
PAN (DUM)
PAAAN

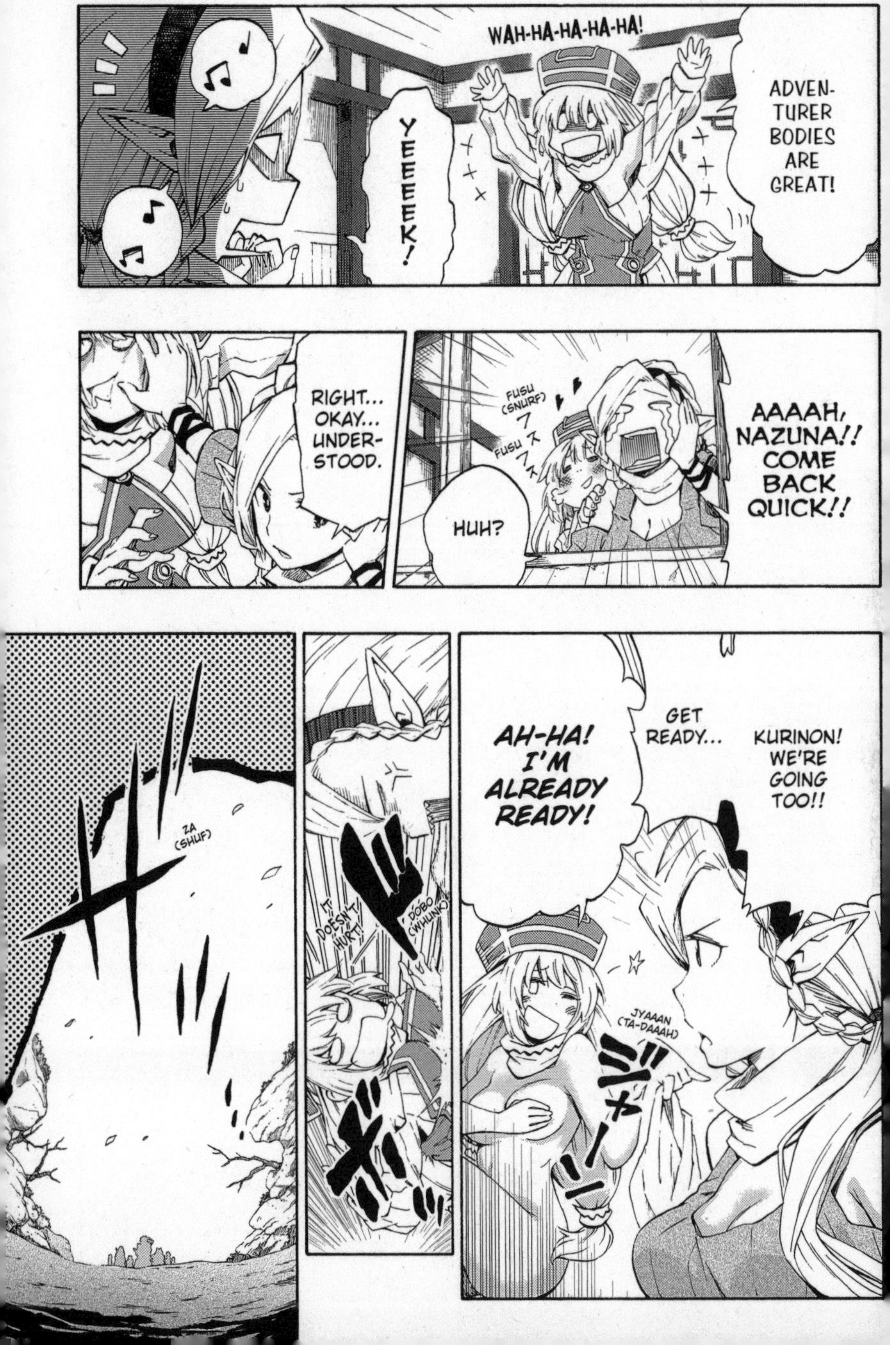
ADVENTURER BODIES ARE GREAT!
WAH-HA-HA-HA-HA!
YEEEEK!
AAAAH, NAZUNA!! COME BACK QUICK!!
FUSU (SNURF)
FUSU
HUH?
RIGHT... OKAY... UNDERSTOOD.
KURINON! WE'RE GOING TOO!!
GET READY...
AH-HA! I'M ALREADY READY!
JYAAAN (TA-DAAAH)
DOBO (WHUNK)
IT DOESN'T HURT!
ZA (SHUF)

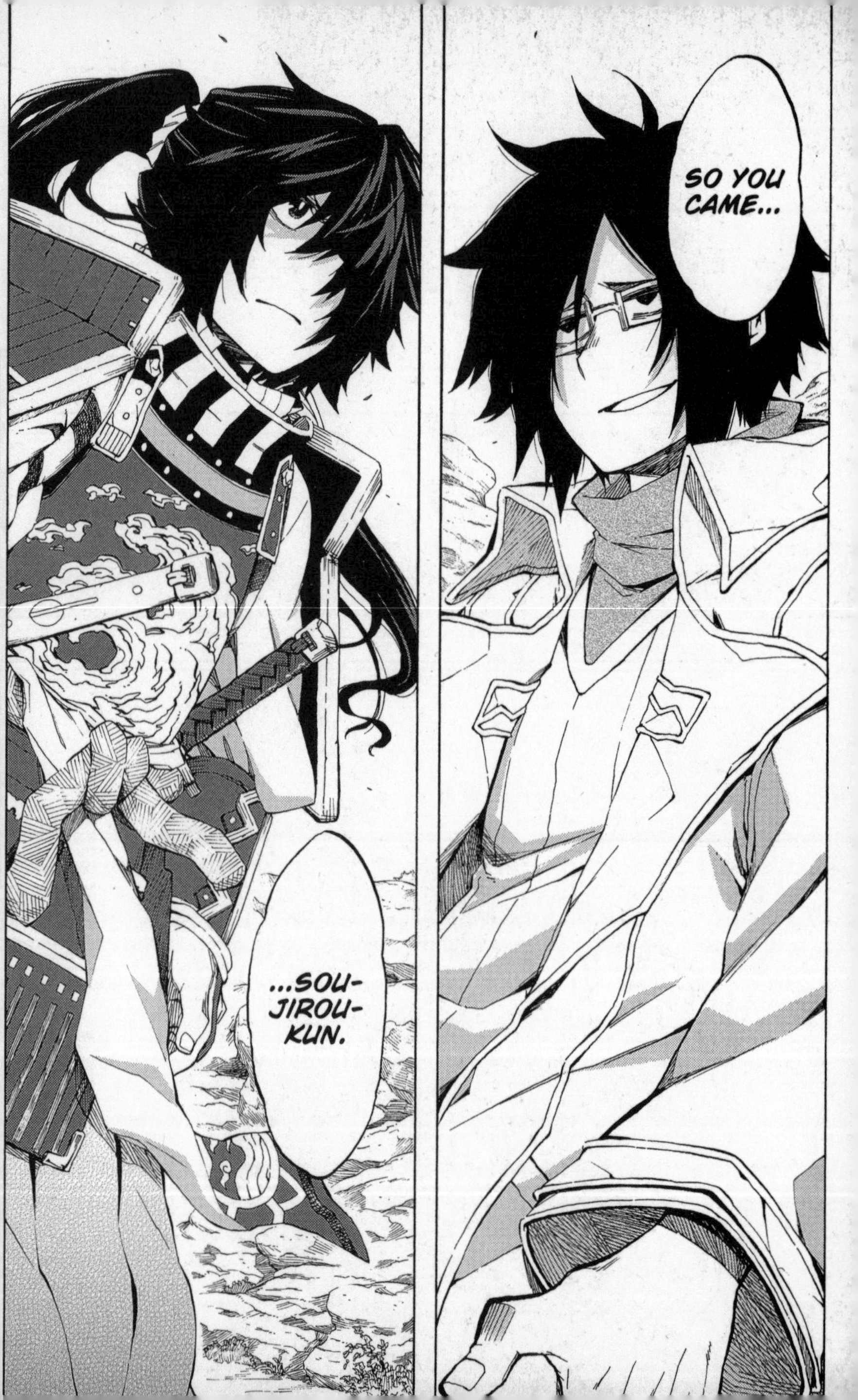
SO YOU CAME...
...SOU-JIROU-KUN.

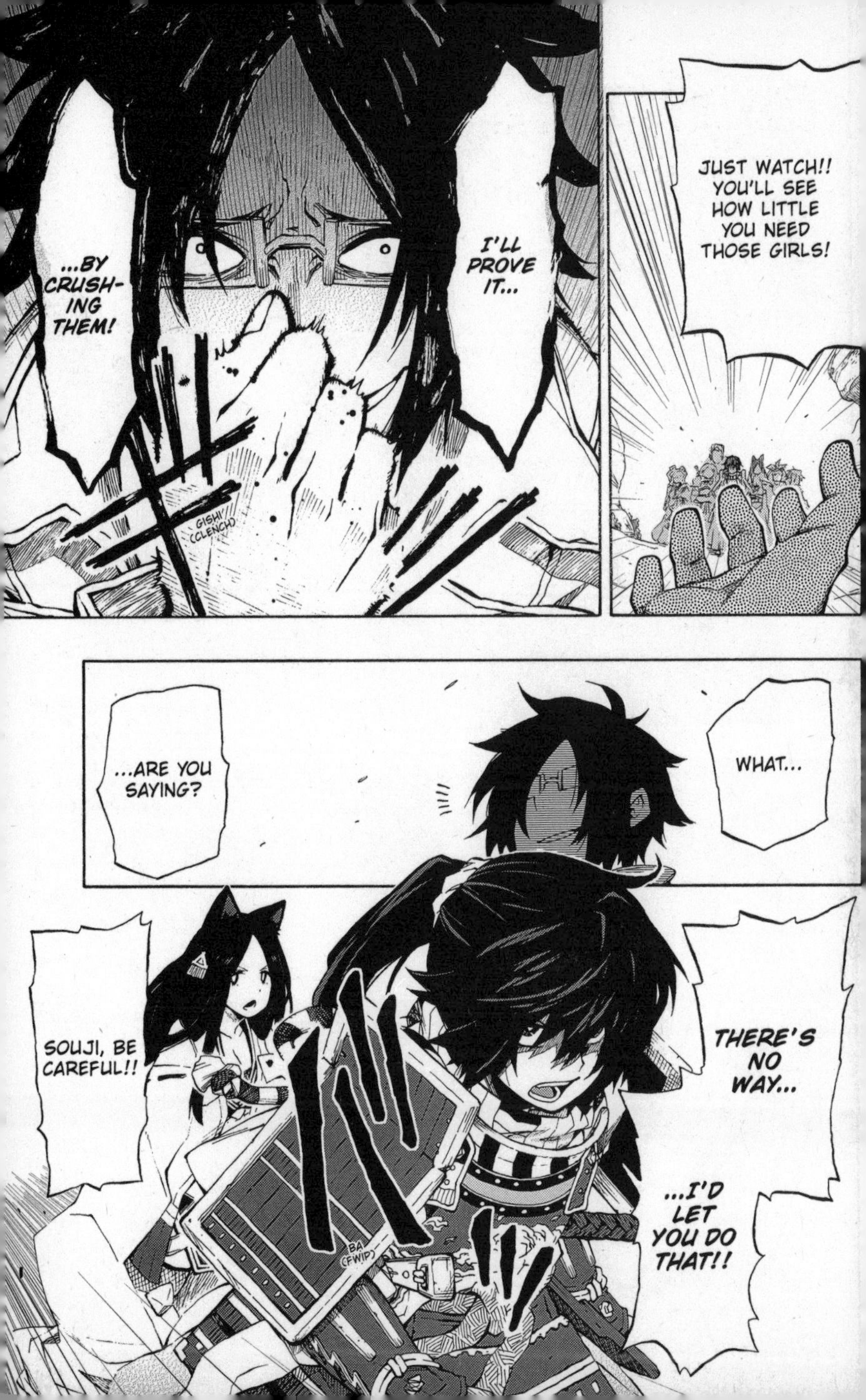
JUST WATCH!! YOU'LL SEE HOW LITTLE YOU NEED THOSE GIRLS!
I'LL PROVE IT...
...BY CRUSHING-ING THEM!
GISHI (CLENCH)
WHAT...
...ARE YOU SAYING?
THERE'S NO WAY...
...I'D LET YOU DO THAT!!
BA (FWIP)
SOUJI, BE CAREFUL!!

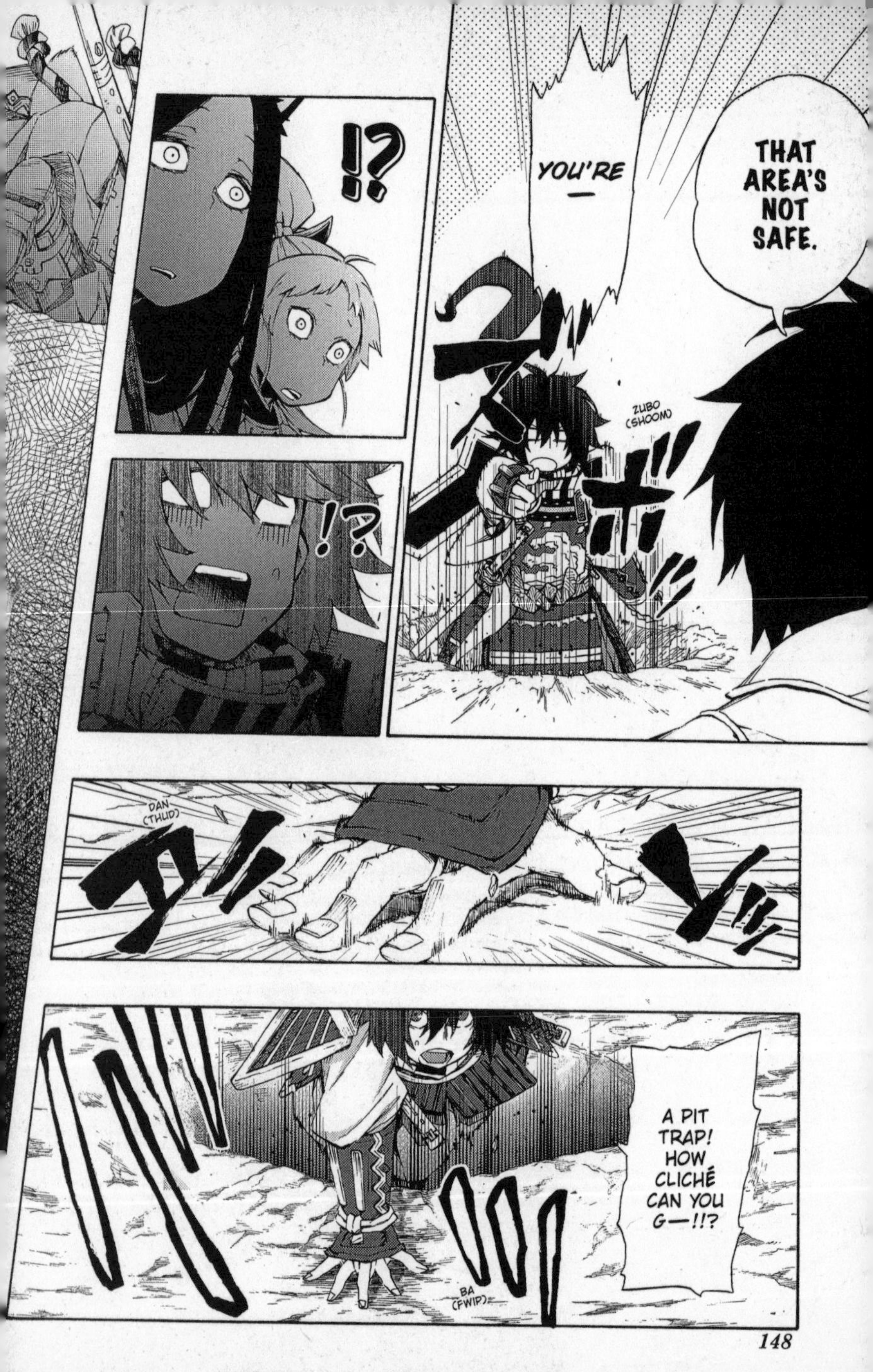
THAT AREA'S NOT SAFE.
YOU'RE —
ZUBO (SHOOM)
!?
!?
DAN (THUD)
A PIT TRAP! HOW CLICHÉ CAN YOU G—!!?
BA (FWIP)

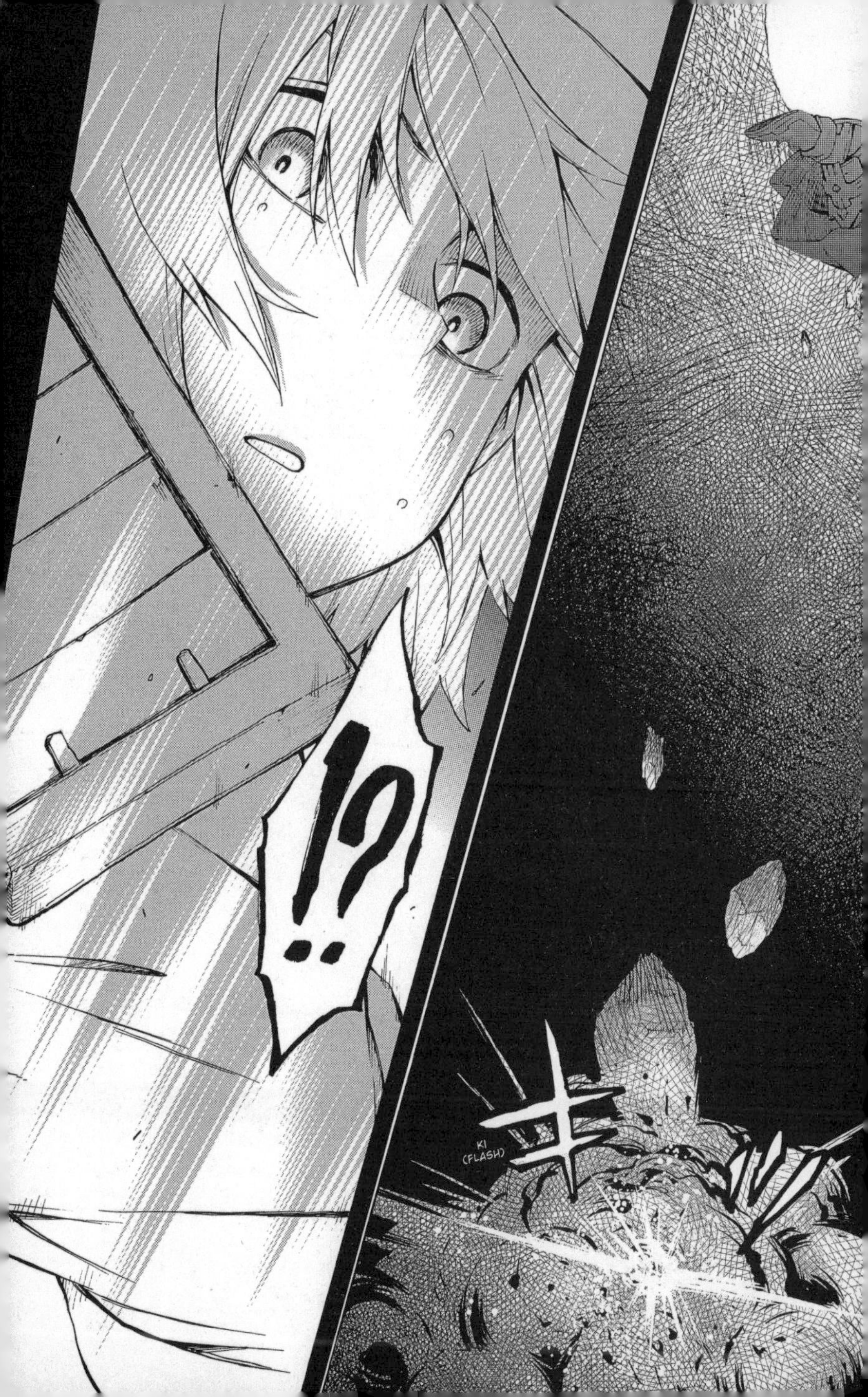
!?
KI
(FLASH)

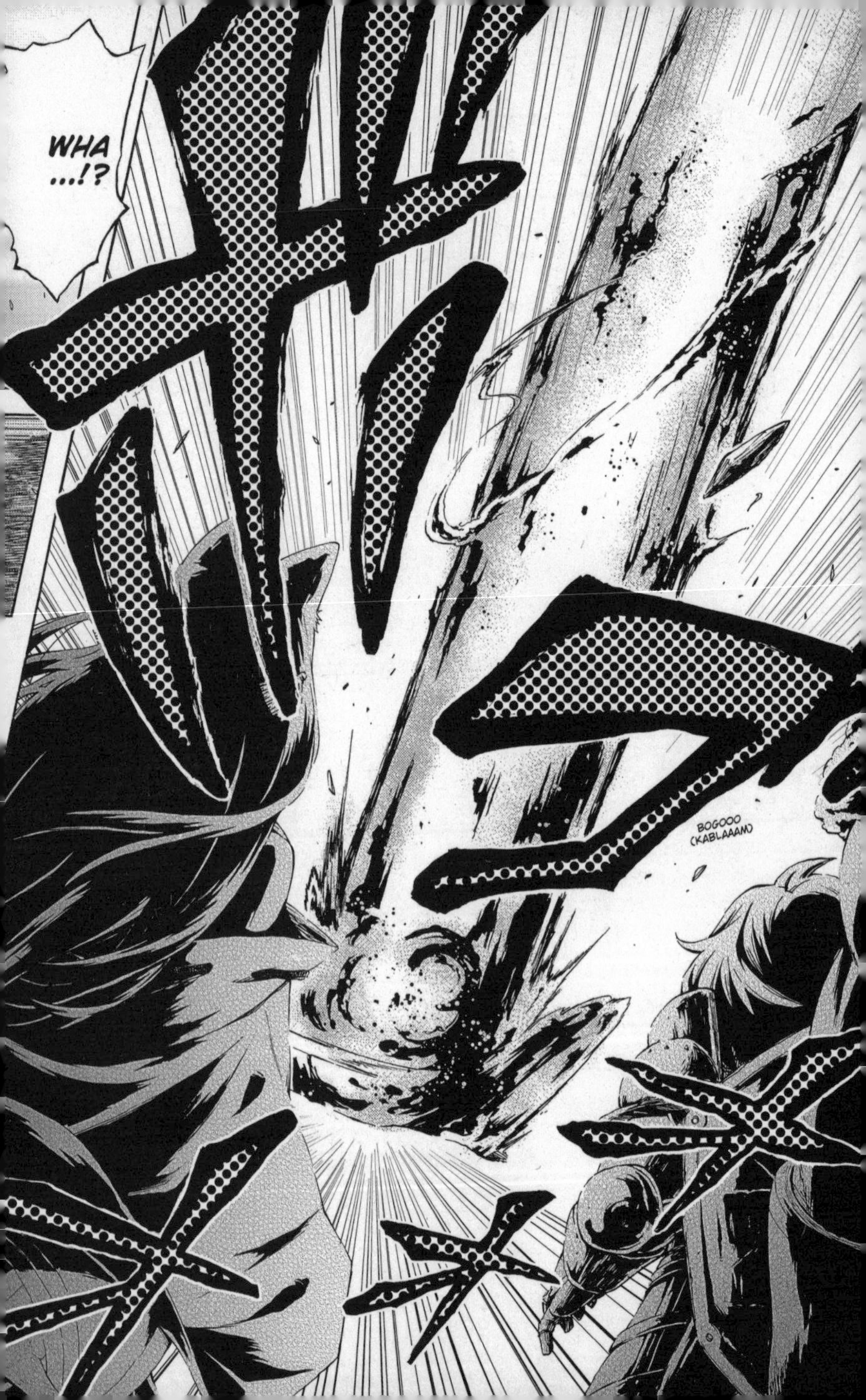
WHA ...!?
BOGOOO (KABLAAAM)

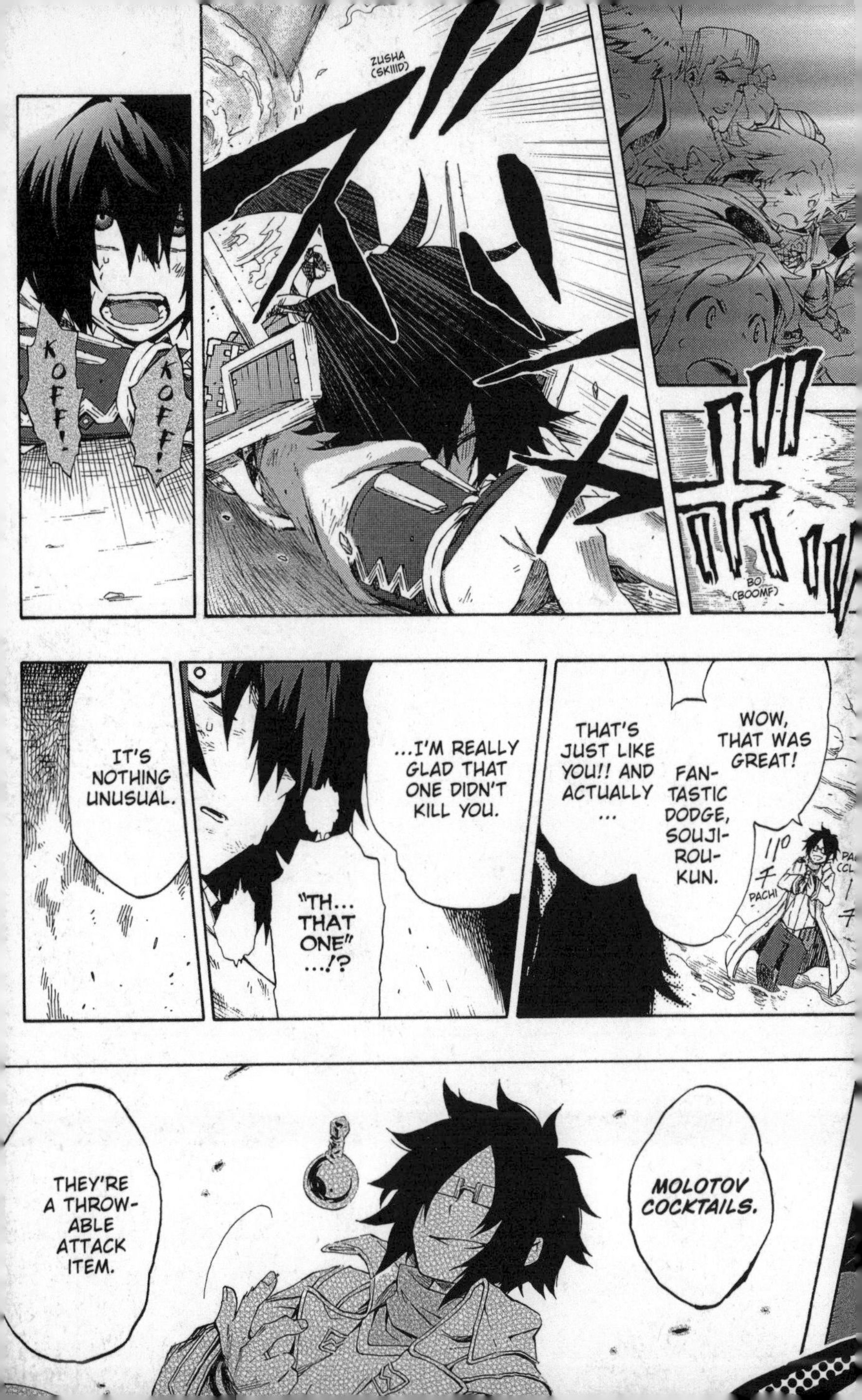
BO (BOOMF)
ZUSHA (SKIIID)
KOFF! KOFF!
WOW, THAT WAS GREAT!
FANTASTIC DODGE, SOUJIROU-KUN.
PACHI
THAT'S JUST LIKE YOU!! AND ACTUALLY ...
...I'M REALLY GLAD THAT ONE DIDN'T KILL YOU.
"TH... THAT ONE" ...!?
IT'S NOTHING UNUSUAL.
MOLOTOV COCKTAILS.
THEY'RE A THROWABLE ATTACK ITEM.

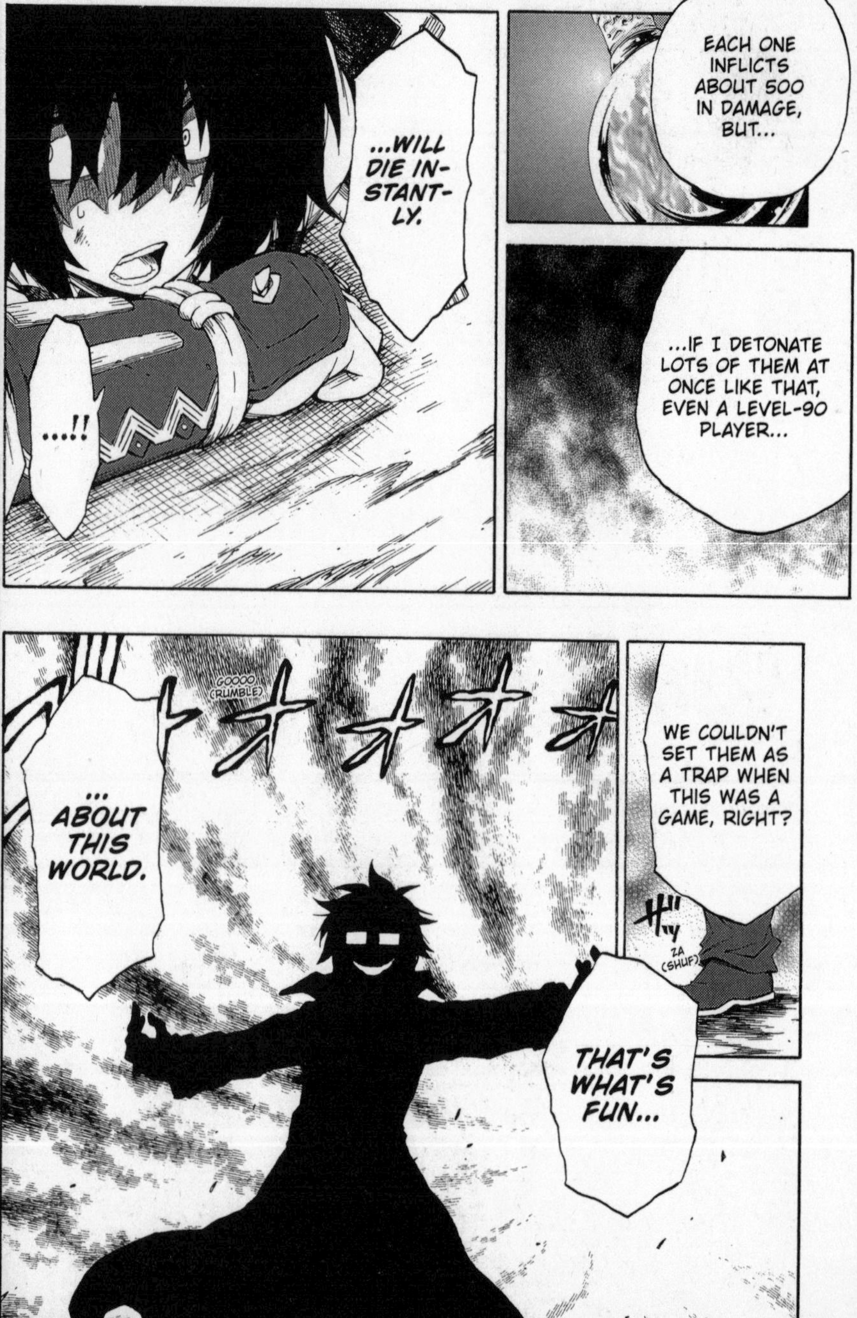

EACH ONE INFLICTS ABOUT 500 IN DAMAGE, BUT...
...IF I DETONATE LOTS OF THEM AT ONCE LIKE THAT, EVEN A LEVEL-90 PLAYER...
...WILL DIE IN-STANT-LY.
...!!
WE COULDN'T SET THEM AS A TRAP WHEN THIS WAS A GAME, RIGHT?
ZA (SHUF)
GOOOO (RUMBLE)
THAT'S WHAT'S FUN...
... ABOUT THIS WORLD.

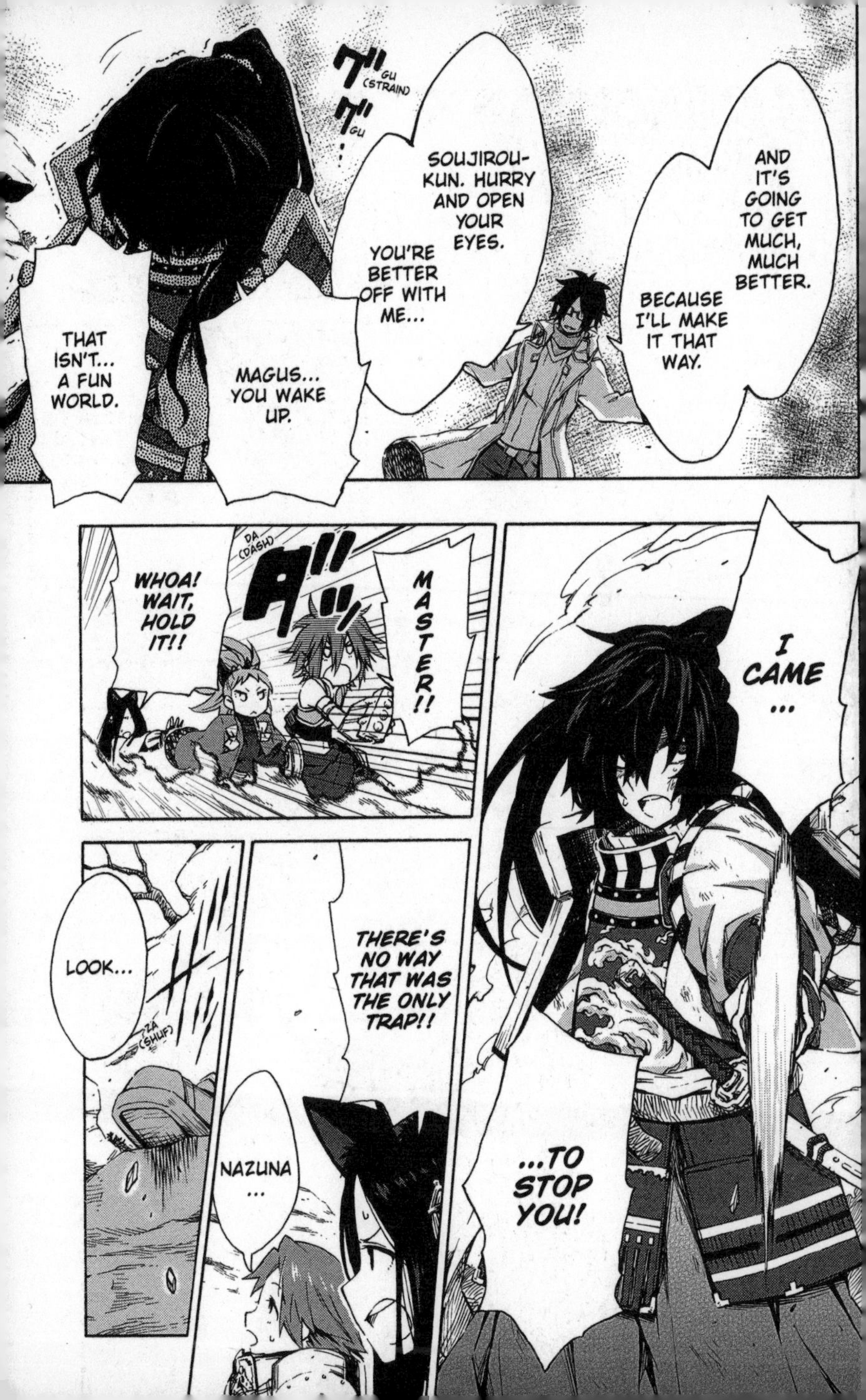
AND IT'S GOING TO GET MUCH, MUCH BETTER.
BECAUSE I'LL MAKE IT THAT WAY.
SOUJIROU-KUN. HURRY AND OPEN YOUR EYES.
YOU'RE BETTER OFF WITH ME...
GU (STRAIN)
GU
MAGUS... YOU WAKE UP.
THAT ISN'T... A FUN WORLD.
I CAME...
...TO STOP YOU!
MASTER!!
DA (DASH)
WHOA! WAIT, HOLD IT!!
THERE'S NO WAY THAT WAS THE ONLY TRAP!!
NAZUNA...
LOOK...
ZA (SHUF)

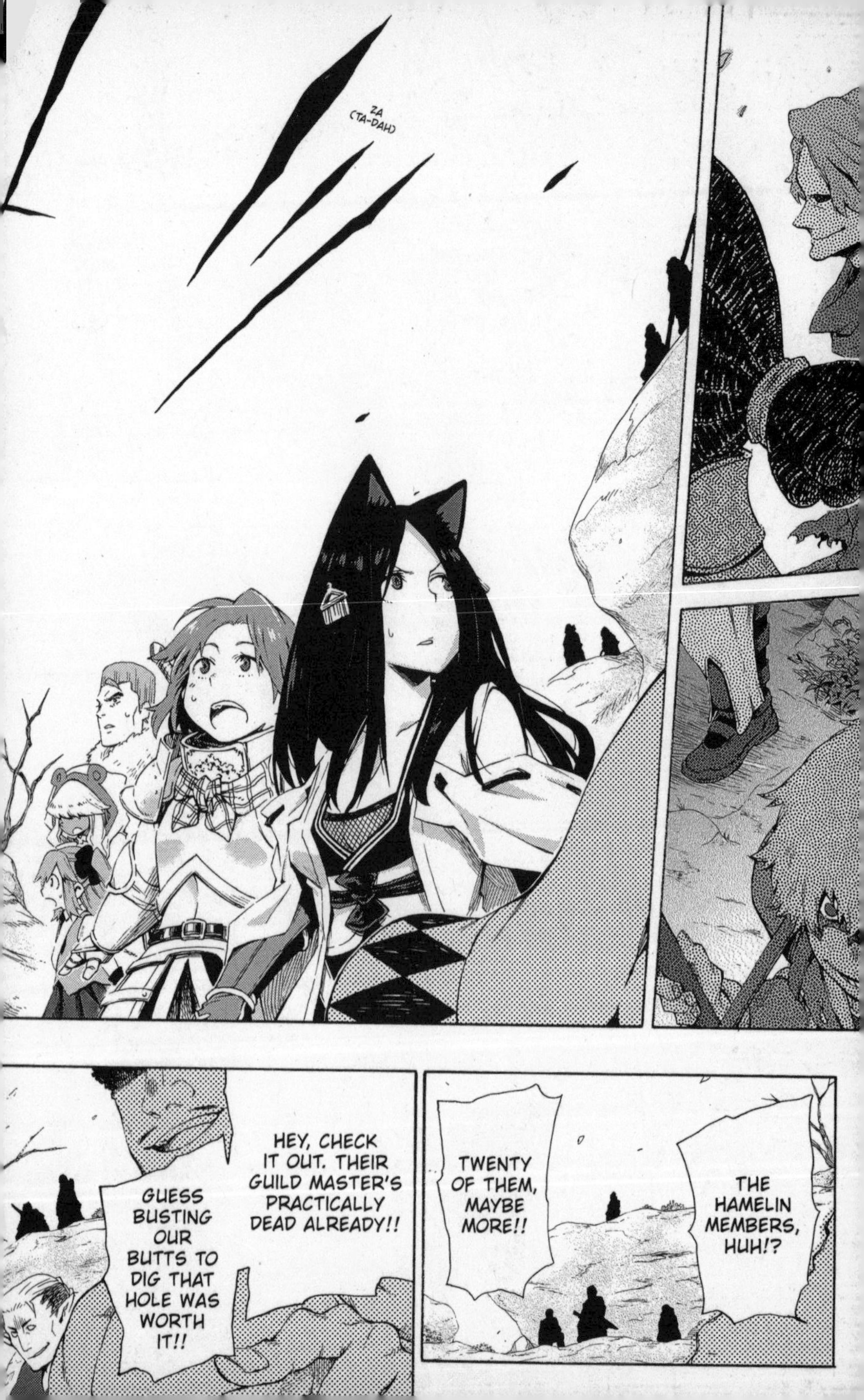
ZA (TA-DAH)
THE HAMELIN MEMBERS, HUH!?
TWENTY OF THEM, MAYBE MORE!!
HEY, CHECK IT OUT. THEIR GUILD MASTER'S PRACTICALLY DEAD ALREADY!!
GUESS BUSTING OUR BUTTS TO DIG THAT HOLE WAS WORTH IT!!

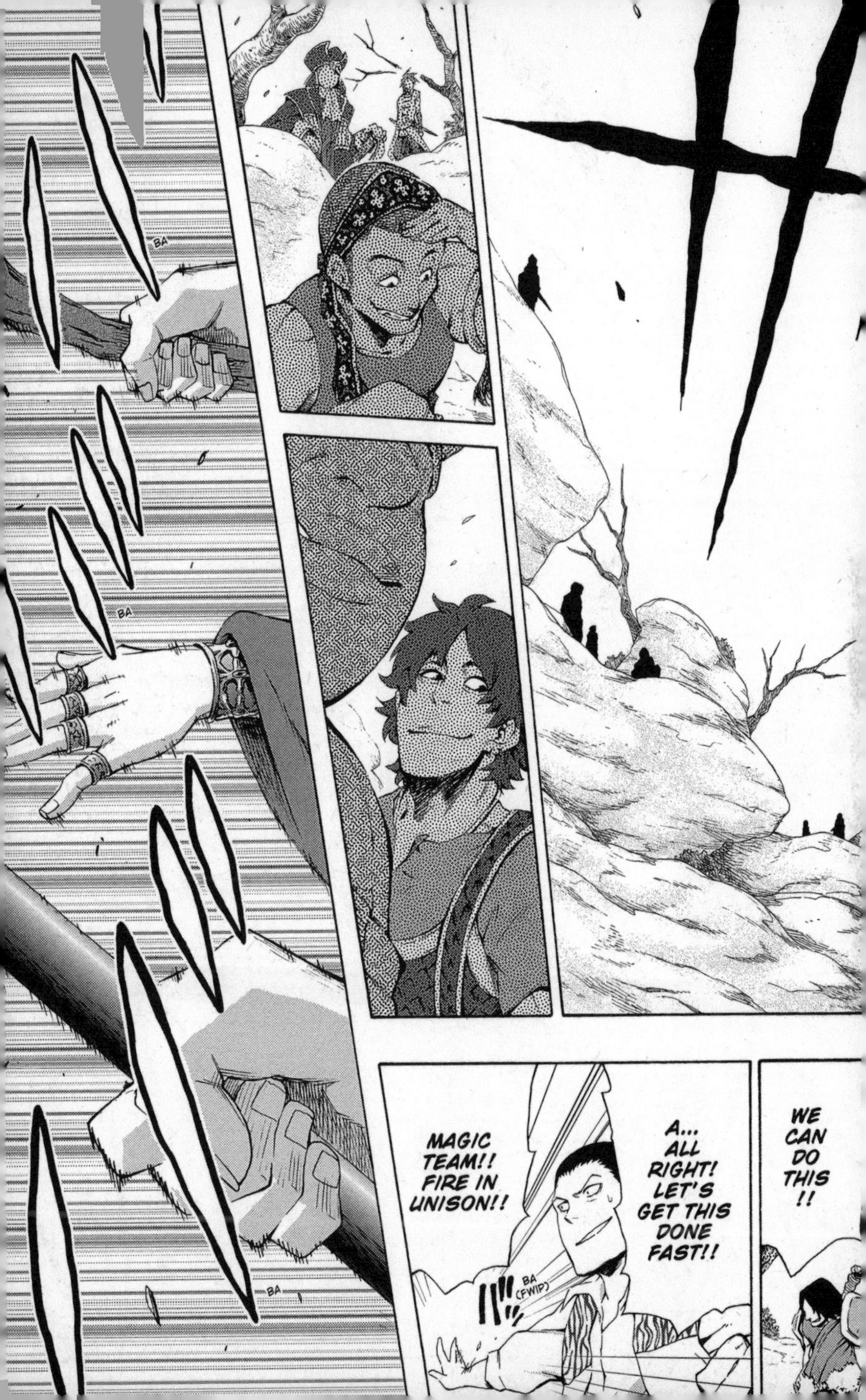
BA
BA
BA
WE CAN DO THIS!!
A... ALL RIGHT! LET'S GET THIS DONE FAST!!
MAGIC TEAM!! FIRE IN UNISON!!
BA (FWIP)

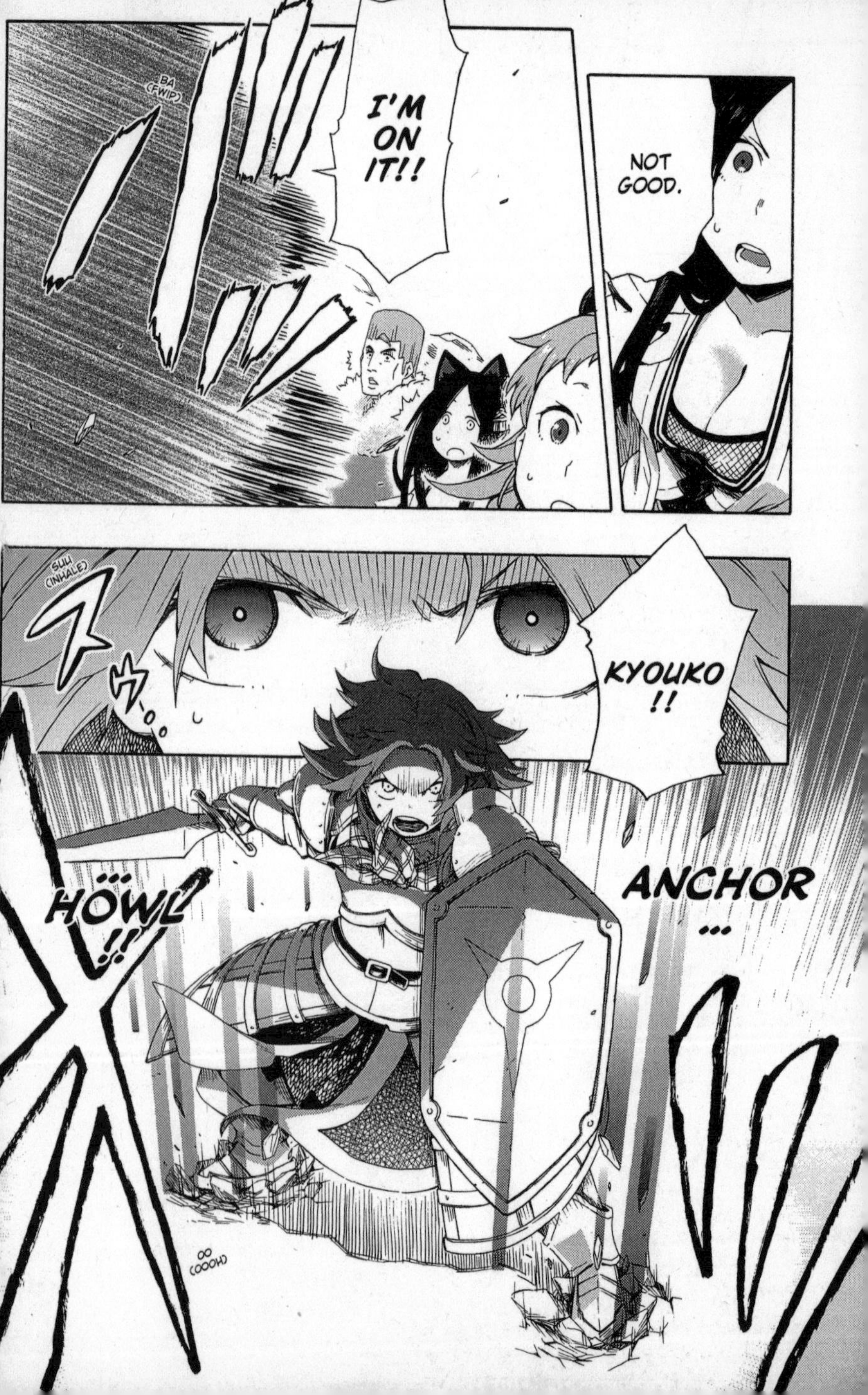
NOT GOOD.
I'M ON IT!!
BA (FWIP)
KYOUKO!!
SUU (INHALE)
ANCHOR...
...HOWL!!
OO (OOOH)

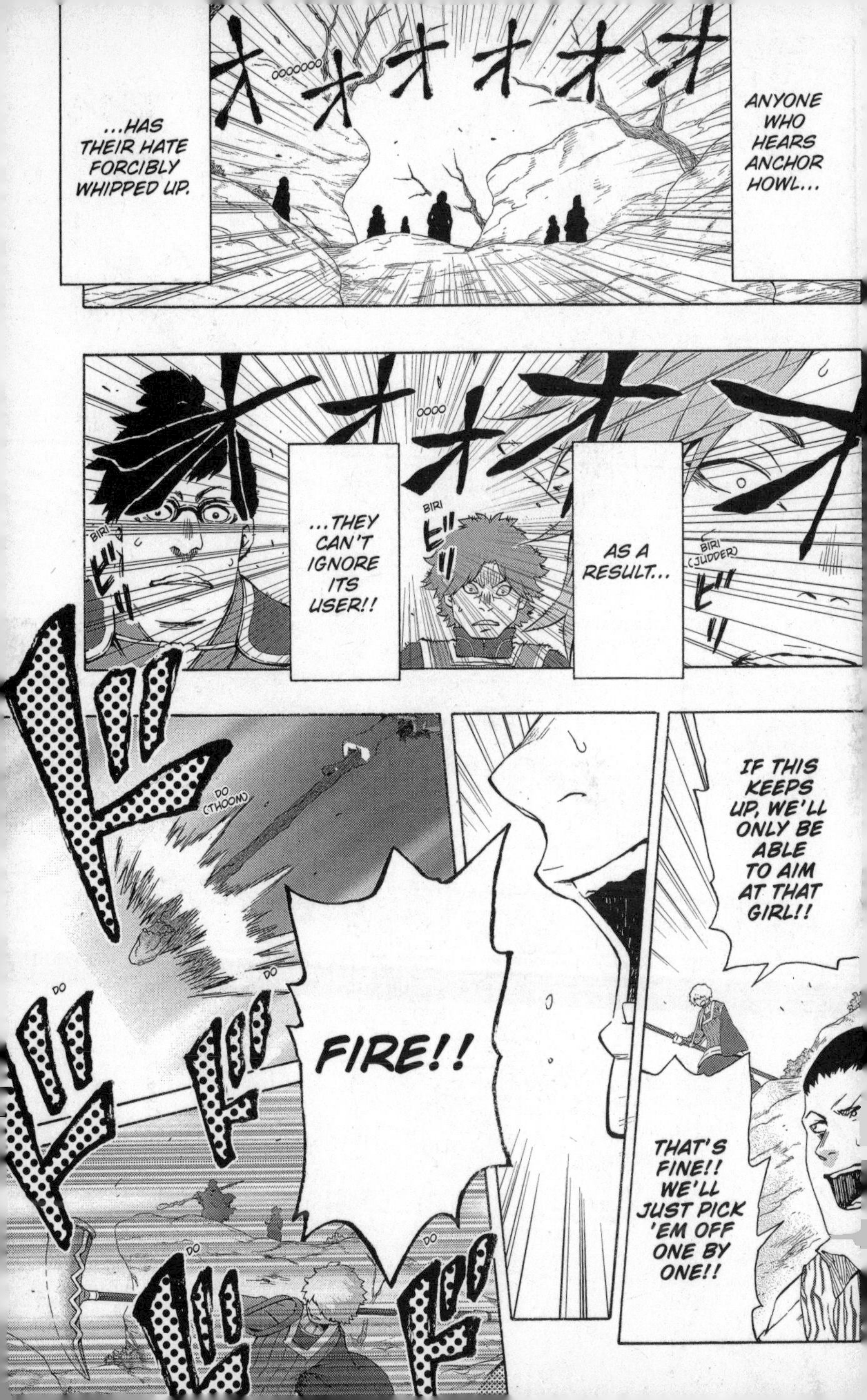
OOOOOOO
ANYONE WHO HEARS ANCHOR HOWL...
...HAS THEIR HATE FORCIBLY WHIPPED UP.
BIRI (JUDDER)
AS A RESULT...
BIRI
...THEY CAN'T IGNORE ITS USER!!
OOOO
BIRI
IF THIS KEEPS UP, WE'LL ONLY BE ABLE TO AIM AT THAT GIRL!!
THAT'S FINE!! WE'LL JUST PICK 'EM OFF ONE BY ONE!!
FIRE!!
DO (THOOM)
DO
DO
DO
DO

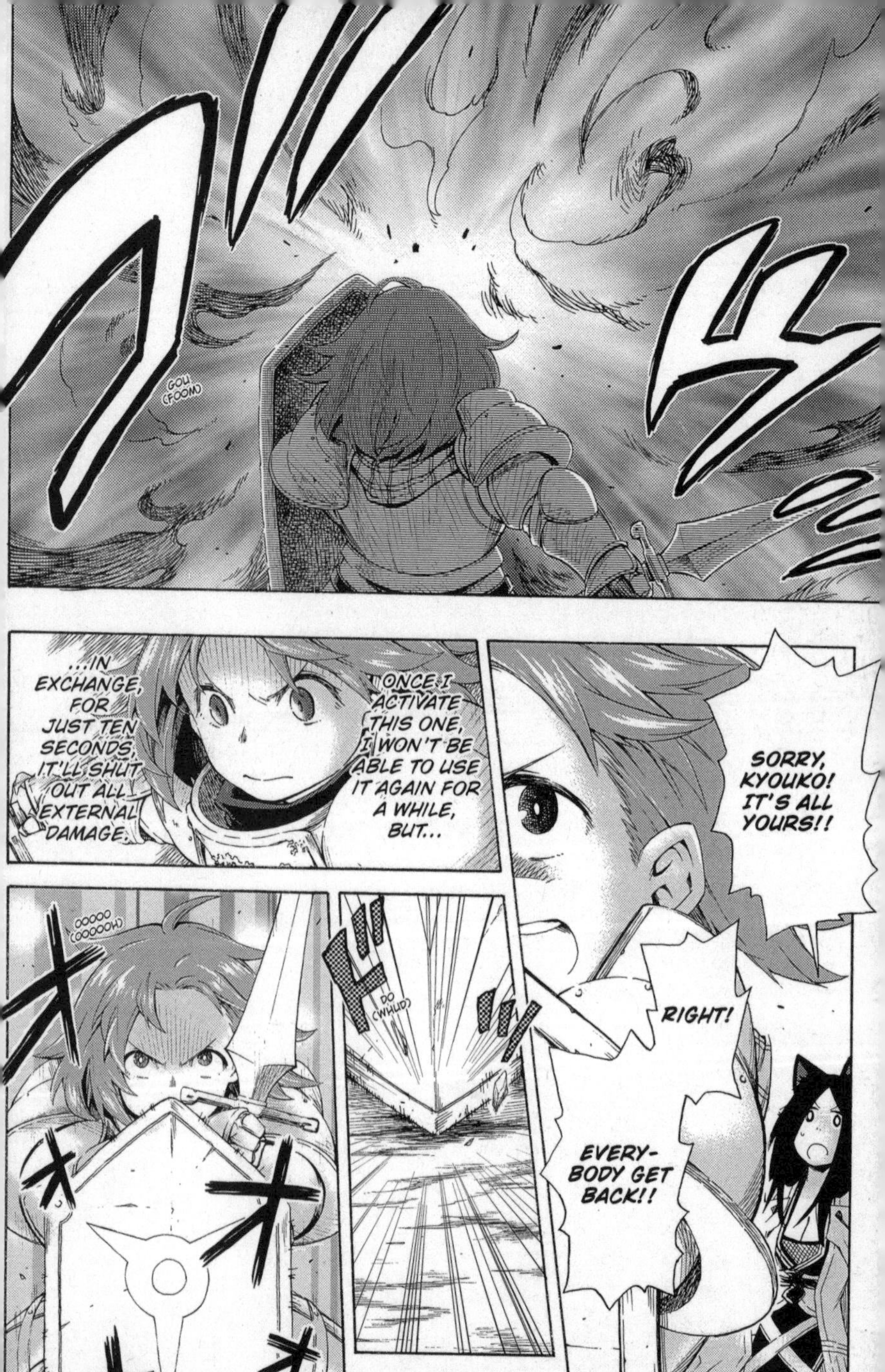
GOU (FOOM)
SORRY, KYOUKO! IT'S ALL YOURS!!
RIGHT!
EVERY-BODY GET BACK!!
ONCE I ACTIVATE THIS ONE, I WON'T BE ABLE TO USE IT AGAIN FOR A WHILE, BUT...
...IN EXCHANGE, FOR JUST TEN SECONDS, IT'LL SHUT OUT ALL EXTERNAL DAMAGE.
DO (WHUD)
OOOOO (OOOOOOH)

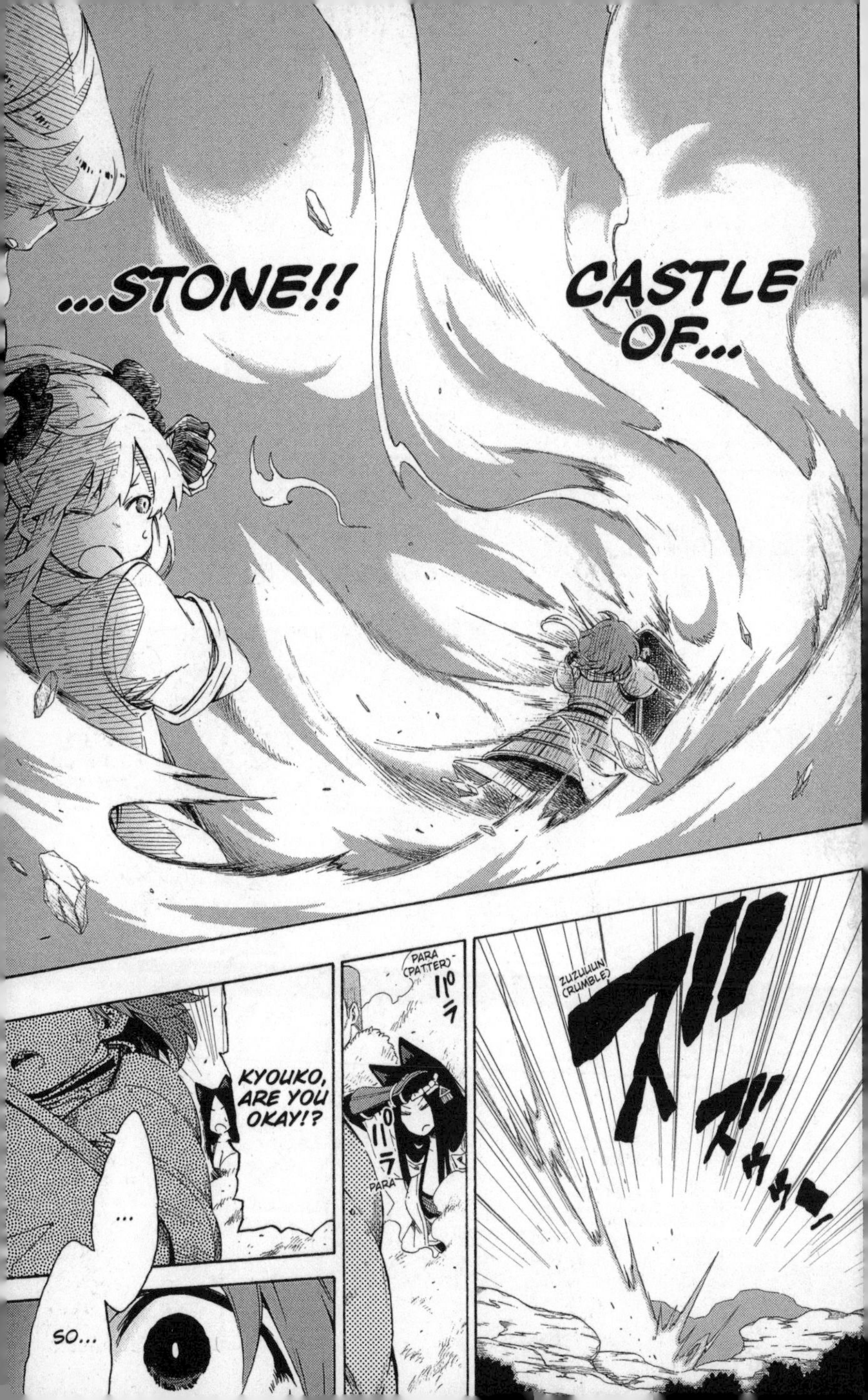
CASTLE OF...
...STONE!!
ZUZUUUN (RUMBLE)
PARA (PATTER)
PARA
KYOUKO, ARE YOU OKAY!?
...
SO...

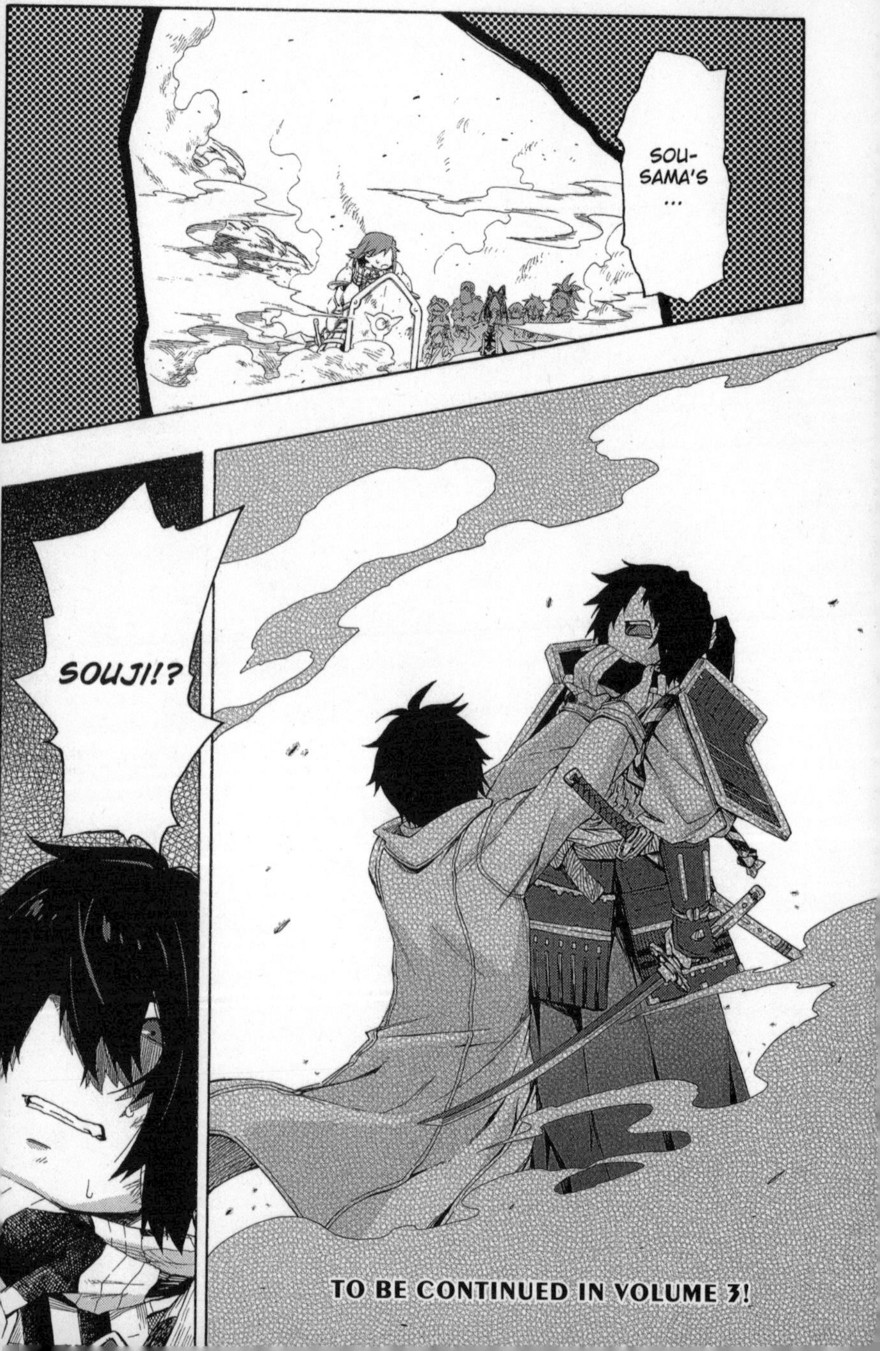
SOU-SAMA'S ...
SOUJI!?
TO BE CONTINUED IN VOLUME 3!

LOG HORIZON

THE WEST WIND BRIGADE

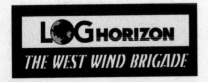

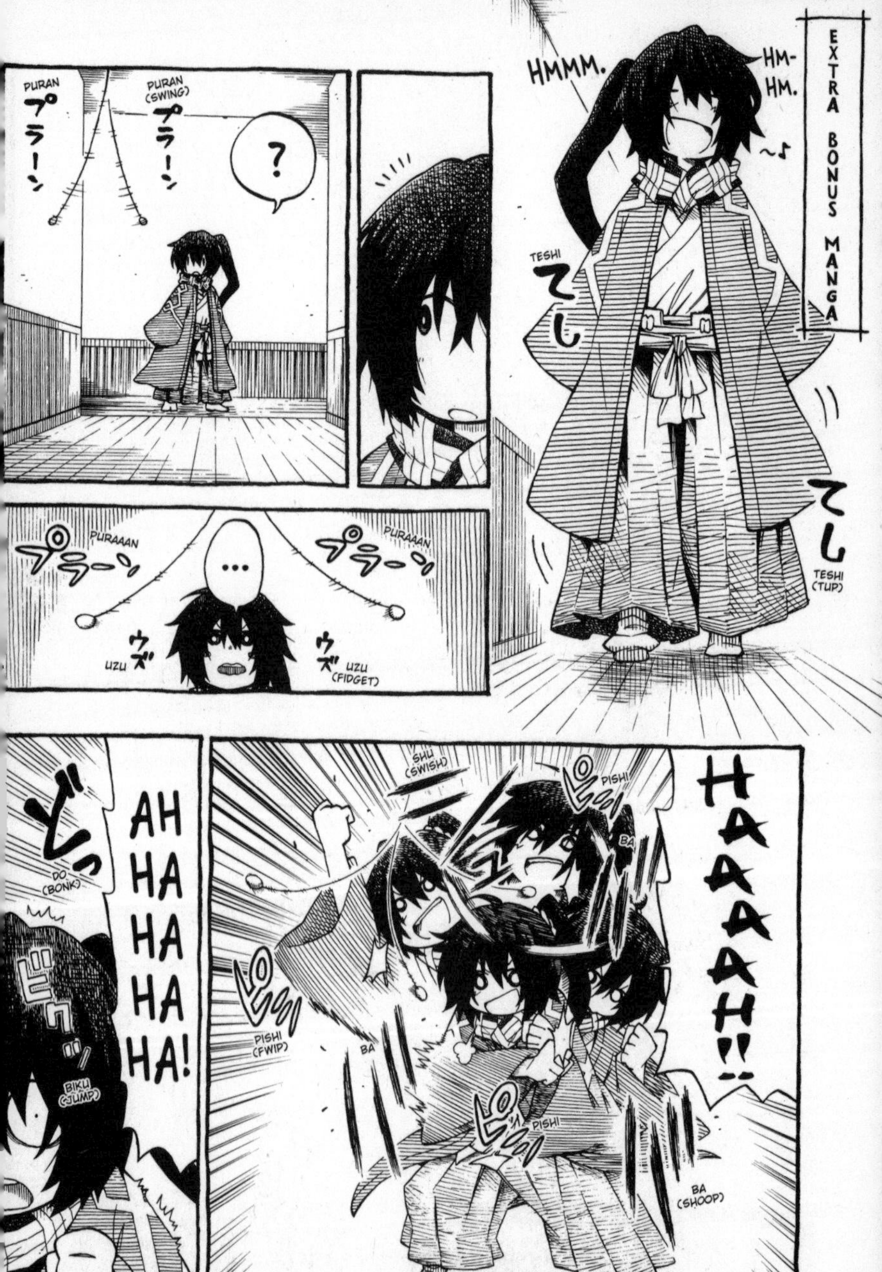
EXTRA BONUS MANGA
HMMM.
HM-HM.
~♪
TESHI
てし
てし
TESHI (TUP)
PURAN (SWING)
プラーン
PURAN
プラーン
?
PURAAAN
PURAAAN
...
UZU (FIDGET)
UZU
HAAAAAH!!
SHU (SWISH)
PISHI
BA
PISHI (FWIP)
BA
PISHI
BA (SHOOP)
AH HA HA HA HA HA!
DO (BONK)
BIKU (JUMP)

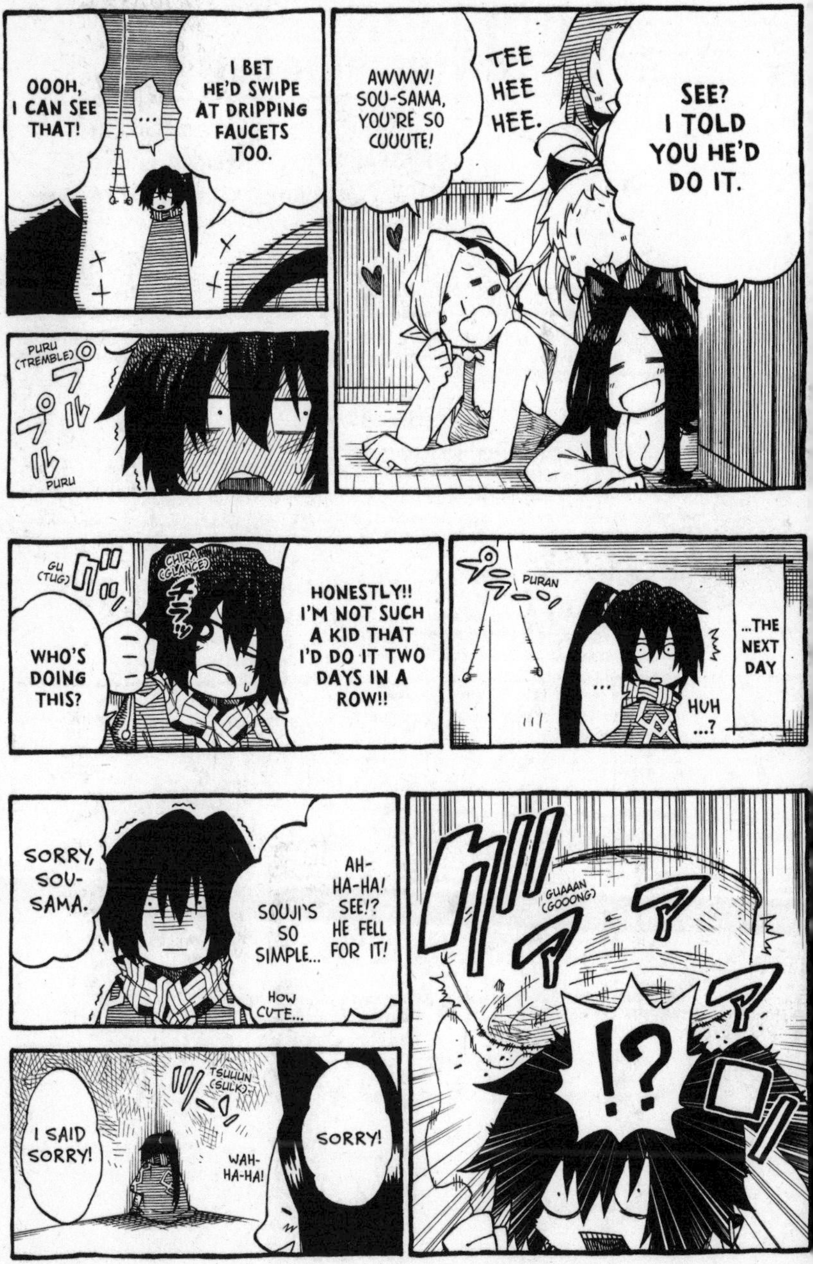
SEE? I TOLD YOU HE'D DO IT.
TEE HEE HEE.
AWWW! SOU-SAMA, YOU'RE SO CUUUTE!
I BET HE'D SWIPE AT DRIPPING FAUCETS TOO.
...
OOOH, I CAN SEE THAT!
PURU (TREMBLE)
PURU
...THE NEXT DAY
PURAN
HUH ...?
...
HONESTLY!! I'M NOT SUCH A KID THAT I'D DO IT TWO DAYS IN A ROW!!
CHIRA (GLANCE)
GU (TUG)
WHO'S DOING THIS?
GUAAAN (GOOONG)
!?
AH-HA-HA! SEE!? HE FELL FOR IT!
SOUJI'S SO SIMPLE...
HOW CUTE...
SORRY, SOU-SAMA.
SORRY!
WAH-HA-HA!
TSUUUN (SULK)
I SAID SORRY!

# LOG HORIZON
## THE WEST WIND BRIGADE ❷

ART: KOYUKI
ORIGINAL STORY: MAMARE TOUNO
CHARACTER DESIGN: KAZUHIRO HARA

Translation: Taylor Engel
Lettering: Brndn Blakeslee

LOG HORIZON NISHIKAZE NO RYODAN volume 2
© KOYUKI 2013
© TOUNO MAMARE, KAZUHIRO HARA 2013
Edited by FUJIMISHOBO
First published in Japan in 2013 by KADOKAWA CORPORATION, Tokyo.
English translation rights arranged with KADOKAWA CORPORATION, Tokyo, through Tuttle-Mori Agency, Inc., Tokyo.

Translation © 2016 by Hachette Book Group, Inc.

Yen Press
Hachette Book Group
1290 Avenue of the Americas
New York, NY 10104

www.HachetteBookGroup.com
www.YenPress.com

Yen Press is an imprint of Hachette Book Group, Inc. The Yen Press name and logo are trademarks of Hachette Book Group, Inc.

The publisher is not responsible for websites (or their content) that are not owned by the publisher.

First Yen Press Edition: April 2016

Library of Congress Control Number: 2015960118

ISBN: 978-0-316-30904-2

10 9 8 7 6 5 4 3 2 1

BVG

Printed in the United States of America